RELIGIOUS PLURALISM
AND
TRUTH

SUNY Series in Religious Studies

Harold Coward, Editor

Religious Pluralism and Truth

Essays on Cross-Cultural Philosophy of Religion

EDITED BY

THOMAS DEAN

STATE UNIVERSITY OF NEW YORK PRESS

Published by
State University of New York Press, Albany

© 1995 State University of New York

All rights reserved

Printed in the United States of America

No part of this book may be used or reproduced
in any manner whatsoever without written permission
except in the case of brief quotations embodied in
critical articles and reviews.

For information, address State University of New York
Press, State University Plaza, Albany, N.Y., 12246

Production by Diane Ganeles
Marketing by Theresa Abad Swierzowski

Library of Congress Cataloging-in-Publication Data

Religious pluralism and truth : essays on cross-cultural philosophy
    of religion / edited by Thomas Dean.
        p. cm.
    Includes index.
    ISBN 0-7914-2123-6 (hard : acid-free). — ISBN 0-7914-2124-4
(pbk. : acid free)
    1. Religious pluralism. 2. Religion—Philosophy. 3. Religions—
Relations.
BL85.R389 1995
291.1′72—dc20   93-40598
                                                                  CIP

10 9 8 7 6 5 4 3 2 1

To

Margaret and Frank

Contents

Preface   ix

Introduction: Cross-Cultural Philosophy of Religion   1
    Thomas Dean

Part I. Religious Pluralism and Cross-Cultural Truth

1. The Philosophy of Worldviews, or the Philosophy of Religion Transformed   17
    Ninian Smart

2. Philosophical Pluralism and the Plurality of Religions   33
    Raimundo Panikkar

3. Religious Pluralism and the Future of Religions   45
    Harold Coward

Part II. Criteria of Cross-Cultural Truth in Religion

4. Truth, Criteria and Dialogue Between Religions   67
    Ninian Smart

5. Doctrinal Schemes, Metaphysics and Propositional Truth   73
    William J. Wainwright

6. Religious Pluralism and Cross-Cultural Criteria of Religious Truth   87
    Mary Ann Stenger

Part III. Models of Cross-Cultural Truth in Religion

7. The Logic of Oppositions of Religious Doctrines — 111
   William A. Christian, Sr.

8. The Doctrines of a Religious Community about Other Religions — 117
   Joseph A. DiNoia

9. The Logic of Interreligious Dialogue — 133
   Norbert M. Samuelson

10. Gadamer's Hermeneutics as a Model for Cross-Cultural Understanding and Truth in Religion — 151
    Mary Ann Stenger

Part IV. Hermeneutics of Cross-Cultural Truth in Religion

11. Rethinking the Doctrine of Double-Truth: Ambiguity, Relativity and Universality — 171
    Conrad Hyers

12. Mystical Experience as a Bridge for Cross-Cultural Philosophy of Religion: A Critique — 189
    John Y. Fenton

13. Structures of Ultimate Transformation and the Hermeneutics of Cross-Cultural Philosophy of Religion — 205
    Frederick J. Streng

14. The Hermeneutics of Comparative Ontology and Comparative Theology — 225
    Ashok K. Gangadean

Notes — 247

Contributors — 263

Index — 267

Preface

The essays in this volume were originally presented to the Working Group in Cross-Cultural Philosophy of Religion sponsored by the American Academy of Religion (A.A.R.) in annual sessions over a period of years from the late 1970s into the 1980s. They are the efforts of philosophers of religion working in tandem with and in response to colleagues in other areas of religious studies. The thinkers represented include pioneers in cross-cultural philosophy of religion as well as younger, newer voices building on their work. Coming from such disparate areas as philosophy, phenomenology and history of religions, Asian and Western, together they worked to give definition to and provide examples of a new, cross-cultural approach to philosophy of religion. The present collection is the outcome of their deliberations and may thus serve as an introduction to this emerging discipline.

Although a cross-cultural approach to philosophy of religion is still a rather novel enterprise, it is one whose importance for traditional philosophy of religion as well as for the larger field of religious studies is beginning to be recognized. Above all, the question of truth in the context of religious pluralism is coming to be seen as a, if not the, central issue confronting scholars across the discipline. According to the Hart report on religious studies in American higher education (*Journal of the American Academy of Religion*, 59, 4 [Winter 1991]), in response to the question what trends and issues will or should shape religious studies and theological studies in the foreseeable future, *pluralism* was one of the most frequently mentioned issues. In particular, "in the pluralistic study of multiple religious traditions . . . there is the problem in such a kind of study as to how *truth-claims* are to be handled (with due regard to *whether* such claims are made, to whom they are claimed to extend and, if made, their very *nature*" (p. 767). The report concludes that all subfields in religious studies will require "a greater sophistication in philosophy of religion, especially under the aegis of now emerging 'comparative philosophy' " (p. 776).

If the Hart report is an accurate indicator of where religion scholars think the field is or should be heading, then a volume of essays on cross-cultural philosophy of religion with a focus on religious pluralism and truth may be useful not only as an introduction to a new approach to philosophy of religion but also as a contribution to religious studies as a whole.

Such a volume would not have been possible without the support of a number of individuals and institutions. First, I would like to thank the contributors themselves for having agreed to present papers to the original sessions of our working group and for having cooperated in their subsequent publication. I would also like to thank the other members of the working group whose papers could not be included here but whose contributions were, and continue to be, essential to the success of this new enterprise. Next, I owe thanks to Professor C. Peter Slater, who, as chair of the A.A.R. section in Philosophy of Religion, permitted the first sessions of cross-cultural philosophy of religion to take place within that section and who subsequently supported the formation of the A.A.R. Working Group in Cross-Cultural Philosophy of Religion as a separate entity. I am indebted to the Department of Religion and the College of Arts and Sciences of Temple University for providing travel funds and other support expenses that made my work as chair of the working group possible. I am especially grateful to Dr. John C. Raines, chair of the Department of Religion, and Dr. William Sharp, dean of our branch campus in Tokyo, who between them enabled me to teach and live in Japan during the past five years and thereby increase my own cross-cultural understanding. Thanks to its generosity, Temple University Japan also freed me from other responsibilities during the summer in which I was engaged in the final editing of this work.

I am obliged to the following publishers for permission to reprint edited versions of the essays indicated: Orbis Books of Maryknoll, New York, for permission to reprint Harold Coward's essay, "Religious Pluralism and the Future of Religions," which formed chapter 6 of his book *Pluralism: Challenge to World Religions* (Orbis, 1985); Basil Blackwell Ltd. of Oxford, England, for permission to reprint Mary Ann Stenger's essay, "Religious Pluralism and Cross-Cultural Criteria of Religious Truth," which appeared as "The Problem of Cross-Cultural Criteria of Religious Truths" in *Modern Theology*, vol. 3, no. 4 (July 1987), pp. 315–332; Cambridge University Press,

North American Branch, for permission to reprint Joseph A. DiNoia's essay, "The Doctrines of a Religious Community about Other Religions," which appeared in *Religious Studies*, vol. 19 (1982–83), pp. 297–307; University Press of America of Lanham, Maryland, for permission to reprint Norbert M. Samuelson's essay, "The Logic of Interreligious Dialogue," which appeared in Norbert M. Samuelson, ed., *Studies in Jewish Philosophy: Collected Essays of the Academy for Jewish Philosophy, 1980–1985* (University Press of America, 1987), pp. 235–266; and Scholar's Press of Atlanta, Georgia, for permission to reprint John Y. Fenton's essay, "Mystical Experience as a Bridge for Cross-Cultural Philosophy of Religion: A Critique," which appeared in *Journal of the American Academy of Religion*, vol. 49, no. 1 (July 1981), pp. 51–76.

No acknowledgments would be complete without an expression of deepest thanks to William Eastman and the editorial board and staff at SUNY Press who have made the publication of this volume possible—Diane Ganeles, production editor; David Hopkins, copyeditor; and Terry Abad Swierzowski, marketing manager. They have been gracious from start to finish.

Finally, I should like to thank my wife, Seiko Yoshinaga, who in the midst of her own busy career as teacher, translator, and author, provided that love and support which makes all our efforts, academic and other, finally worthwhile.

Thomas Dean
Temple University Japan
Tokyo, January 1994

Introduction:
Cross-Cultural Philosophy of Religion

Thomas Dean

Cross-cultural philosophy of religion has recently emerged as a new field in both philosophy and religion. It offers fresh ways of thinking about and doing philosophy of religion and constructive religious thought. The essays in this volume illustrate these new ways of thinking by addressing such foundational topics as the definition and justification of cross-cultural philosophy of religion, criteria of truth across religions and cultures, models for doing cross-cultural philosophy of religion, and the hermeneutics of Asian-Western interaction in philosophy of religion.

I

Cross-cultural philosophy of religion has recently emerged as a new field in both philosophy and religion. Its story begins with the planting of a pioneer seed in the 1950s, cultivation in the 1960s, a blossoming forth in the 1970s, and the mature fruit of the 1980s. It is the story of a number of thinkers from different disciplines who have come together to define and develop a new field of research: philosophy of religion done in a cross-cultural perspective.

In 1958 the philosopher and historian of religion Ninian Smart published a pathbreaking work in philosophy of religion, *Reasons and Faiths*. Drawing on both Western and Asian traditions, his book was a call for philosophy of religion to work in close collaboration with the history of religions. It was a pioneering example of how philosophy of religion could and should be done in the emerging pluralistic or global civilization of the late twentieth century. For a more than a decade, however, this book was to stand alone in philosophy of religion.

Meanwhile, in the 1960s, with the publication of Wilfred Cantwell Smith's equally groundbreaking study, *The Meaning and End of Religion* (1962), and Frederick Streng's important book, *Emptiness: A Study in Religious Meaning* (1967), there came the first answering works showing what the history and phenomenology of religions could contribute to a cross-cultural philosophy of religion. In rejecting a view of the world's religions as conceptually closed systems in favor of a view of humanity's religious life as a dynamic historical continuum, Smith opened the way for a new formulation of the problem of understanding across cultures and religions. Streng showed how structural analysis could further mediate between the particularity of religious traditions and the philosopher's quest for universal categories and criteria of cross-cultural understanding and truth.

The results of this early call and subsequent support for collaborative work between philosophers and scholars of religion began to be seen in the first extended efforts at cross-cultural philosophy of religion that appeared in the 1970s, beginning with William Christian's analysis of the logic of *Oppositions of Religious Doctrines* (1972) and the contributions of philosophers and historians of religion to the volume edited by John Hick, *Truth and Dialogue in World Religions: Conflicting Truth-Claims* (1974). This was continued in the work of Raimundo Panikkar, *The Intrareligious Dialogue* (1978), and reflected in the later, revised editions of John Hick's introductory text, *Philosophy of Religion* (1973, 1983, 1990).

Finally, in the 1980s there appeared the fully developed reflections of some of these same authors: Wilfred Cantwell Smith's *Towards a World Theology* (1981); Ninian Smart's *Worldviews: Cross-Cultural Explorations of Human Beliefs* (1983); and John Hick's *Problems of Religious Pluralism* (1985) and *An Interpretation of Religion* (Gifford Lectures, 1986–87).

While these individually authored works were appearing in the 1970s and 1980s, the philosophers and historians of religion mentioned above, along with others, were also meeting annually at sessions of the Working Group in Cross-Cultural Philosophy of Religion of the American Academy of Religion to continue shaping this emerging discipline. The current volume, a partial record of their collaborative effort, is their further contribution to this new field in philosophy and religion.

II

Cross-cultural philosophy of religion offers fresh ways of thinking about and doing philosophy of religion and constructive religious thought. As noted, the thinkers who helped develop and set the agenda for cross-cultural philosophy of religion have come from both philosophy and religious studies. On the side of philosophy they are indebted to traditional Western philosophy of religion as well as to Asian and comparative philosophy. On the side of religion they have been informed by the history and phenomenology of religions and comparative studies in religion based on the social sciences. Nevertheless, cross-cultural philosophy of religion has distinctive features of its own.

As a cross-cultural approach to philosophy of religion, while frequently originating out of, it nevertheless differs from what is traditionally and usually understood in the West as philosophy of religion. In the range of data it takes into account and in the plurality of perspectives it entertains, it goes beyond the boundaries of Western philosophy and religion to draw on the methodological and spiritual resources of the world's other cultural and religious traditions.

As a cross-cultural philosophical discipline focusing on religion in particular, it also differs from what might seem to be the same enterprise under a different title, namely, comparative philosophy Asian-Western. While benefiting from the work of comparative philosophers (indeed, the scholars are often one and the same individuals), in its concern to develop criteria for the cross-cultural justification of religious truth-claims and models for constructive thinking across cultures and religions, it goes beyond the tendency of comparative philosophy to limit itself to descriptive comparison of concepts, thinkers or traditions. Use of the term "cross-cultural" (or "global") rather than "comparative" is intended to indicate the normative-constructive, not simply descriptive-comparative intent of this enterprise, above all its concern, as a mode of philosophizing, with the question of truth.

Similarly, while cross-cultural philosophy of religion would not be possible without the empirical and theoretical contributions of comparative religious studies, it differs, as normative philosophy, from the descriptive or phenomenological approach that characterizes the history of religions and other comparativist approaches to the study of religion.

Thus, the thinkers who defined this enterprise chose to avoid alternative paradigms that were (and still are) available. They did not conceive cross-cultural philosophy of religion as a species of philosophical or religious debate between proponents of conflicting first-order truth-claims. Again, it was not a matter of comparison or sharing of such first-order claims with one another as in comparative philosophy or interreligious dialogue. Nor, finally, was it their task to describe similarities and differences, or develop conceptual and structural typologies, of first-order beliefs or belief-systems among different religious traditions. These matters, as indicated, were already being dealt with by comparativists in religious studies.

Their vision of cross-cultural philosophy of religion was and is a different one. To see the distinctive character of this field we may look at the positive agenda and requirements that have shaped and continue to shape work in cross-cultural philosophy of religion and that are reflected in the structure and content of the present volume.

From its outset cross-cultural philosophy of religion has placed emphasis on the second-order or meta-issues, methodological and substantive, that arise in the attempt to do philosophy of religion or religious thought in an interreligious or cross-cultural setting. This in turn has provided the basis for developing models or paradigms for first-order projects of constructive philosophical or religious thought. Needless to say, such reflections also make possible greater theoretical sophistication in traditional comparative or phenomenological studies in philosophy of religion and religious studies as well as in the theory and practice of interreligious dialogue.

To pursue such work cross-cultural philosophers of religion have had to satisfy several criteria:

1. They have had to be philosophically sophisticated, with training either in the analytic or pragmatist traditions where philosophers are accustomed to asking such second-order questions, or in one or more of the nonanalytic traditions such as phenomenology, existentialism or poststructuralism which have sensitized philosophers to second-order questions of a hermeneutical sort.

2. They have had to subscribe to Ninian Smart's dictum that in the future philosophy of religion should be done with constant refer-

ence to the history of religions, or more broadly, phenomenological and comparative studies in religion.

3. They have had to have scholarly expertise in one or more religious traditions, including the Asian traditions, since most analytically trained philosophers of religion in the West have usually been familiar only with the Christian or Jewish traditions and not necessarily on the basis of scholarly study.

4. Finally, they have had to be dissatisfied with the way philosophy of religion traditionally has been done—not drawing on non-Western traditions or, where it has, falling into either the "conflict" or "comparison" models mentioned above.

Thus the establishment of such a discipline has required the joint efforts, on the side of philosophy, of traditionally trained Western philosophers of religion or philosophers and religious thinkers operating primarily within individual Western religious traditions as well as comparative philosophers familiar with the Asian traditions and, on the side of religious studies, historians, phenomenologists, and comparativist scholars of the world's religions and cultures.

III

The essays in this volume illustrate these new ways of thinking about and doing cross-cultural philosophy of religion by addressing such foundational topics as:

1. The definition and justification of cross-cultural philosophy of religion in a setting of religious pluralism and interreligious dialogue (part I).

2. The possibility, nature and validity of criteria of truth across religions and cultures (part II).

3. Models or paradigms for doing cross-cultural philosophy of religion (part III).

4. The hermeneutics of the interaction of Asian and Western traditions in cross-cultural philosophy of religion (part IV).

In part I, "Religious Pluralism and Cross-Cultural Truth," essays by Ninian Smart and Raimundo Panikkar address the implications of religious pluralism for the redefinition of philosophy of religion, while the essay by Harold Coward explores the implications of religious pluralism for interreligious dialogue and constructive religious thought.

Ninian Smart leads off the volume with an essay on "The Philosophy of Worldviews, or the Philosophy of Religion Transformed." Western philosophy of religion has been cut off from both modern interpretations of the Christian tradition and studies of other religions by historians and phenomenologists of religion. But while philosophy of religion needs to open out to other religions, it should also extend to other existential but non-religious ideologies and become a "philosophy of worldviews." A main task of such a philosophy is to clarify the criteria of truth as between worldviews. Smart provides an inventory of considerations relevant to the truth of worldviews, but notes that such criteria do not dictate sharp decisions. Though not forced into epistemological relativism, cross-cultural philosophy issues in a toleration of differences among worldviews. It thus assists in developing ways of thinking that are more consciously planetary. In summary, Smart argues that the philosophy of religion should be extended to the philosophy of worldviews, building upon the historical and comparative study of religions and ideologies and the phenomenology not only of religion but of the symbolic life of humanity as a whole.

Raimundo Panikkar in his essay, "Philosophical Pluralism and Plurality of Religions," focuses on the "hermeneutic of philosophies of religion." There is not just one philosophy of religion but a plurality of philosophies of religions. An attempt to overcome this multiplicity by finding an underlying unity can only lead to a loss of identity. Therefore, between a plurality *de facto* and a unity *de ratione* there must be room for a pluralism *de jure*. (By "pluralism" Panikkar means the legitimate coexistence of worldviews which are nevertheless incompatible among themselves.) After providing a typology and critique of four views of philosophy of religion, Panikkar questions whether any philosophy can ever break out of its hermeneutical circle to serve as a bridge for the encounter of religions. Panikkar suggests instead the model of "dialogical dialogue," in which truth is found not in either party but in what emerges from their encounter. In short, Panikkar argues that cross-cultural philosophy of religion is not any one philosophy of religion but an ever-open process of encounter with and philosophizing about the religious experience of humankind in its totality, truth consisting in the hermeneutic process itself.

Harold Coward, in his essay on "Religious Pluralism and the Future of Religions," notes that historically pluralism has been a catalyst in the development of religious traditions. Thus while pluralism may seem to portend crisis, it might also occasion the spiritual growth of religions. Coward examines the similarities of traditional approaches to religious pluralism and difficulties confronting religious pluralism today. If rival viewpoints proceed from starting points so disparate that little or no common ground can be established, there may be no basis for comparative understanding or judgment. But the desire for mutual understanding is too deep for this impasse to be the final word. Spiritual growth in the past has always occurred in the context of religious pluralism, not religious isolation or exclusivism. Coward therefore suggests some presuppositions and guidelines for interreligious dialogue of the future. He warns, however, that scholars should not try to formulate philosophical foundations or criteria for interreligious dialogue before it takes place. Echoing Panikkar, he argues that such will emerge, if at all, only through the process of dialogue itself. In such dialogue lies the future of religions and religious thought.

IV

The essays in part II, "Criteria of Cross-Cultural Truth in Religion," address the possibility, nature, and validity of criteria of truth across religions and cultures. Ninian Smart outlines several normative approaches and criteria of cross-cultural truth in religion. William Wainwright then focuses on criteria of truth in religion drawn from the field of metaphysics, while Mary Ann Stenger examines criteria of truth taken from various fields in religious studies.

Ninian Smart, in his essay on "Truth, Criteria and Dialogue between Religions," assesses several approaches to the possibility of cross-cultural understanding and judgment—that only within a religious system can that system be understood; that each religious system is a total worldview by which all other systems are to be evaluated; that there is no neutral arena in which competing religious truth-claims can be settled; that, on the contrary, religious systems can be verified or falsified by appeal to public facts; that public facts together with "less public" ones can make religious systems more or less plausible; that faith is a personal reality transcending religious systems; or, finally, that all religions point to the same truth. He then evaluates various criteria of truth which might render one system more (or less) plausible than another. He concludes that while such criteria are cross-culturally applicable, they offer few conclusive arguments or proofs. Epistemological certainty is elusive in cross-cultural philosophy of religion. This recognition is an important step toward enabling religions and philosophical reflection upon them to come to terms with the plural religious and ideological world that confronts them today.

William Wainwright, in an essay on "Doctrinal Schemes, Metaphysics and Propositional Truth," reviews several arguments against the importance of propositional truth in religious contexts—that oppositions between religious beliefs are only apparent; that propositional truth is relatively unimportant in religion; or that it is inappropriate to use the category of propositional truth at all in religious contexts. Wainwright replies that since some forms of religious truth presuppose propositional truth, questions of propositional truth properly arise when religious doctrines are compared and that such questions are subject to standards of rational adjudication. He then evaluates various criteria of metaphysical truth—formal, explanatory and pragmatic—concluding, with Smart, that while there is some agreement about them, they are vague, indeterminate and difficult to apply. However, though reason alone may be insufficient to resolve doctrinal disagreements, it does not follow that it is unnecessary or that it should not play an important role in one's cross-cultural judgments. Rather than conclude that there is no (propositional) truth in such matters, it might be wiser to broaden our conception of reason.

Mary Ann Stenger begins her essay on "Religious Pluralism and Cross-Cultural Criteria of Religious Truth" by citing examples where cross-cultural judgments are in fact made (Jonestown, sexist religious language, conflicting doctrinal claims), pointing up the need for cross-culturally valid criteria to justify these judgments. Turning to religious studies rather than metaphysics, Stenger considers criteria employed by scholars from four areas of religion: sociology (Peter Berger), theology (Gordon Kaufman), philosophy (John Hick) and history (Wilfred Cantwell Smith). Their criteria include rational assessment and moral evaluation, personal and historical experience, power of transformation, humanization, and acceptability to insiders and outsiders. Stenger argues that such criteria provide a way of judging some truth-claims to be more valid than others and that, though their concrete application may reflect particular cultural traditions or historical situations, their scope is universal, making them cross-culturally applicable. An important feature of Stenger's essay is her claim that such criteria can themselves undergo further development as a result of changed historical, cultural, or religious circumstances.

V

The essays in part III "Models of Cross-Cultural Truth in Religion," offer several paradigms for thinking about truth in a cross-cultural or interreligious context. William Christian sketches the logic of oppositions of religious doctrines, Joseph DiNoia analyzes the logic of religious doctrines about other religions, Norbert Samuelson explores the difference between internal and external evaluations of religious truth-claims, and Mary Ann Stenger presents Gadamer's hermeneutics as an alternative model for interreligious dialogue and cross-cultural truth.

William Christian, in his essay, "The Logic of Oppositions of Religious Doctrines," gives a pithy statement of what philosophers can contribute to the cross-cultural understanding in religion. In addition to a logical analysis of the internal structure of doctrinal systems, their more important contribution might be an analysis of contrasts and connections between doctrines. On the former point, there is often more to the logic of a body of doctrine than a religious community notices, so that even a philosopher outside that religion, by providing a logical analysis of the structure of its doctrinal system, can contribute to intra- and interreligious understanding. As to the latter point, it is highly implausible that logical analysis of the doctrines of various religions would lead to the conclusion that they are all saying the same thing or all logically isolated from one another. It is more likely, as arguments between religions assume, that there are logical connections between one religion's doctrines and those of another. Oppositions are more interesting cases than consistencies because they are more informative. They constitute at least prima facie evidence that two religions are not, after all, saying the same thing.

Joseph DiNoia, in his essay "The Doctrines of a Religious Community about Other Religions," analyzes the logic of traditional and recent positions that religions have adopted in response to religious pluralism and their encounter with other religions. Such responses must meet several criteria. They must be consistent with the doctrines of their own tradition but must also evaluate the proposals and adherents of other religions and adopt appropriate attitudes and policies. For example, they might recommend study of the doctrines of other communities, consideration of them as serious religious alternatives, or rethinking of their own doctrines as a result. This might also develop principles of cross-cultural judgment beyond the criteria internal to their religion. This could involve appeal to data about other religions and claims from nonreligious fields like metaphysics. The result might be the formulation of a general theory of religion as such. DiNoia gives a close and detailed analysis of the logic of a number of such traditional and reformulated doctrines about other religions. He cautions, however, that this should not be understood as an argument on behalf of a particular theory or theology of other religions.

Norbert Samuelson, in his essay "The Logic of Interreligious Dialogue," argues that truths of interreligious dialogue are not truths of philosophical debate. He bases this claim on a distinction between propositions and speech acts. The former, if true, are true in an absolute sense, whereas the latter are true relative to a speech community. Interreligious dialogue is concerned primarily with the truth of speech acts and only secondarily with propositional truths. Thus criteria drawn from tradition, as well as those based on reason, may be appealed to in judging religious claims. Such evaluation can be either internal or external. "Internal" means the rules of judgment are set within the context of a particular religious community. "External" evaluation involves factors independent of such a context. Since the meaning of religious claims depends upon their linguistic context, none can be judged only externally. Internal evaluation takes precedence. Though one religion may pass judgment on the claims of another, what constitutes a legitimate judgment of truth will not be a simple matter. There are several options (rejection, modification, translation, conversion) in cases of conflicting religious truth-claims.

Mary Ann Stenger, in her essay on "Gadamer's Hermeneutics as a Model for Cross-Cultural Understanding and Truth in Religion," argues for an alternative to models focused on the logic of conflicting truth-claims or the differentiation of internal and external criteria. Gadamer's concepts of the horizon of understanding as open-ended, the dialectical structure of experience, and the conversational or dialogical structure of the hermeneutical process imply openness to the truth-claims of other religions and the possibility of evaluation and change through encounter. The universality of language, its infinite capacity to transcend the horizons of any particular world, makes possible the development of criteria of truth that, while respecting the differences of religious traditions, are cross-culturally valid. Such criteria are not posited a priori before a dialogue occurs but emerge through the hermeneutical process of encounter itself. Instead of being fixated on doctrinal conflicts, we should interact with them, recognizing the limits of our own perspectives and being open to possible truth from opposing views. This fusion of horizons is never absolute or final but constitutes the starting point for new cross-cultural and interreligious reflection.

VI

The essays in part IV, "Hermeneutics of Cross-Cultural Truth in Religion," offer concrete examples of the hermeneutic interaction of Asian and Western horizons. From the side of epistemology, Conrad Hyers sees the mystical/prophetic dichotomy as arising from the ambiguity of religious experience itself, while John Fenton attacks the use of mystical experience as offering a bridge between East and West. From the side of metaphysics, Frederick Streng argues for the pluralism of Asian and Western ontologies and structures of transformation, while Ashok Gangadean builds a comparative hermeneutics drawing on Western and Indian traditions of logic and ontology.

Conrad Hyers, in his essay on "Rethinking the Doctrine of Double-Truth: Ambiguity, Relativity, and Universality," sees religious pluralism as arising from the fundamental ambiguity, hence "double-truth," of religious experience itself. Conflicts among religious interpretations arise from the ambiguity between the *mysterium tremendum* and the *mysterium fascinans* as bipolar modes of experiencing the religiously ultimate. The difference between prophetic and mystical interpretations is the basic axis of this ambiguity in religious experience. Differences between prophetic and mystical traditions result from emphasis upon one or the other side of the polarity. Recognition of this ambiguity provides a basis for accepting and resolving conflicts between the two interpretive traditions, both of which are meaningful and valid responses but partial and incomplete apart from each other. The ambiguity of religious experience and the hermeneutical "double-truth" that arises from it are what are universal, not some common experience or transcendental unity. Criteria for cross-cultural justification of religious truth-claims based on this hermeneutic require that such claims therefore be neither absolutized nor reduced to cultural relativities.

John Fenton, in his essay on "Mystical Experience as a Bridge for Cross-Cultural Philosophy of Religion: A Critique," attacks the claim that mystical experience is the ineffable essence of religious experience, transcending all linguistic and cultural differences and serving as the common or universal bridge for a cross-cultural hermeneutic. Fenton's counter-thesis is that the language of mystical traditions about mystical experience entails weak rather than strong ineffability, that language about mystical experience discriminates valid from counterfeit mystical experiences, that there is a pluralism of kinds of mystical experience and language, and that such differences are not accidental but intrinsic and constitutive of the mystical path and its goal. Phenomenological similarities among mystical experiences are often incidental to their more basic differences, appearing significant only when abstracted from their respective contexts. The attempt to bypass metaphysical or theological differences among mystical traditions by appealing to a universal or transcultural "essence" of mystical experience is thus false to the data. The "bridge" for a cross-cultural hermeneutic of mysticism must be plural and complex, not single and simple.

Frederick Streng, in an essay on "Structures of Ultimate Transformation and the Hermeneutics of Cross-Cultural Philosophy of Religion," argues that religious worldviews function not only to describe the ultimate nature of things but also to express the ultimate value of existence. Moreover, they are not grounded in any single type of religious experience but constitute a complex or family of different and overlapping ontologies and structures of transformation. Understanding both the plurality and double function of such worldviews is central to a cross-cultural hermeneutics. Streng supports this claim with a comparative analysis of three representative Western and Asian ontologies and their correlative structures of spiritual transformation. Focusing on the dialectic of positive and negative terms in each, he shows how similar terms, such as being and nonbeing, function differently in different ontological and soteriological contexts. This irreducible pluralism in religious ways of thinking and valuing means that cross-cultural philosophy of religion should take into account the differences not only in modes of doctrinal speculation among religious ontologies but also in the modes of spiritual transformation which they shape and reflect.

Ashok Gangadean, in his essay on "The Hermeneutics of Comparative Ontology and Comparative Theology," argues that the incommensurability of religious worlds appears to make cross-cultural understanding impossible, whereas the transcendental unity of religions reduces interreligious dialogue to monologue. He turns to comparative ontology to find a basis for comparative theology. Comparative ontology is not itself an ontology but a metadiscipline which attempts to understand transitions between first-order ontologies. The categorial principle of Western logic—that what makes sense in one ontological world does not make sense in another—results in a hermeneutical impasse: multiplicity of incommensurable worlds and systematic ambiguity of basic terms. This disqualifies traditional Western logic as a hermeneutic for comparative ontology. Indian logic, especially that of Nagarjuna, recognizes that natural language is already trans-categorial, neither hermetically sealed nor hermeneutically bound, perpetually ready for transformation, ready to liberate reason itself. Thus, a hermeneutics of comparative theology is not only an intellectual discipline; it can also be a path toward spiritual liberation.

VII

As an overview of the essays in this volume shows, cross-cultural philosophy of religion is as pluralistic in its approaches and concerns as the variety of religious and cultural worldviews with which it deals. Its unity is to be found, as indicated before, in shared assumptions concerning the theoretical agenda and areas of scholarly expertise that have shaped and continue to shape the discipline and that are reflected in the structure and content of the present volume.

The unity of this volume may be found in certain recurring themes, questions raised, and solutions offered. The central thematic concern is the nature, possibility and criteria of hermeneutical understanding and/or epistemological truth across boundaries of religions and cultures. This leads to a consideration of such related questions as the nature of pluralism and dialogue, cultural particularity versus transcendental unity, internal and external criteria of truth, propositional versus nonpropositional modes of truth, relativism and rationality, relative and absolute truth, the ineffability or, alternatively, systematic ambiguity of religious experience and language, and finally, multiple concepts of reason and even of logic itself. Methodologically, perhaps the most striking and important difference is that between a logic-based or "conflict" model and a hermeneutically based or "dialogue" model for formulating the central themes and answering the fundamental questions of a cross-cultural philosophy of religion.

As stated at the outset, this volume of essays is the result of the collaborative deliberations of philosophers and historians of religion who have helped to establish the discipline. It may thus serve as an introduction to cross-cultural philosophy of religion. However, since this field is still in its formative stages and since, in keeping with its nature, it is a pluralistic not a monolithic one, the following essays also constitute an invitation to join in its further development.

PART I

Religious Pluralism and Cross-Cultural Truth

1

The Philosophy of Worldviews, or the Philosophy of Religion Transformed

Ninian Smart

I

The philosophy of religion has greatly concerned itself with some old questions, about God and immortality, about miracles and evil, and in the last several decades much too with the question of the rumored vacuousness of religious utterance. Speech about God by some has been tied to pictures and parables and forms of life. But basically the agenda has been Western theism. This is what above all has exercised Wisdom, Flew, Hick, Hepburn, Phillips and others. The tradition remains dominated, from the rear, by the idea of natural theology, or by something called theism, or more particularly Christian (sometimes Jewish) theism. But whose theism? From two directions the philosophy of religion has been too much cut off from some significant realities.

In one direction the notable split between Christian theology (especially) and analytic philosophy of religion arises from their differing intellectual roots. Overwhelmingly the former's (in modern times) lie in the German-speaking world—think of Barth, Bultmann, Bonhoeffer, Pannenberg, Rahner; while the latter's lie in the Anglophone—as witness my list above, not to mention such masters in the background as James, Peirce and Russell. Often the philosopher of religion deals, at the intellectual level, with a system of ideas much simplified in comparison with the complexities of modern systematic interpretations of Christianity (or Judaism).

In the other direction there has been a tendency for the philosophy of religion to ignore practice, or to put it another way, to ignore the history of religions. Maybe "forms of life" come nearer, but the fact is that Christianity is living sacrament as well as theism, symbolism acted out as well as philosophy of life, ikon as well as argument. A more intimate bond between the philosophy of religion and the study of living religious practices would have been welcome.

The danger thus has been that philosophers deal in a somewhat denatured theism, or perhaps it would be better to say, a somewhat bony one—the anatomy is there but not much of the physiology. Also, in looking so much to Western theism, the challenge to it of other perspectives, notably Buddhist and Hindu, has been less considered than it should have been.

The fabled Martian arriving on the planet and inspecting among other things our intellectual resources might also be struck by a strange thing. Journals one would note, devoted to the philosophy of religion. The more advanced essays therein might discuss the question of truth as between religions. But over Cambodia one would not look down to perceive Christians struggling spiritually with Buddhists. One would find Marxist rural anarcho-syndicalism destroying temples and monks. In Tibet one would see the clash of ancient religion and Maoism. In Romania one would note subversive Baptists. In Sweden one would see Christianity softly overwhelmed by social democracy. In brief, one would think that as far as rivalry goes (and this is an index of competing truth-claims, perhaps) religions and ideologies were tugging against each other, and that really from a practical point of view it was odd that such a struggle was rarely depicted in journals of the philosophers of religion. The logical scientism of Flew would be but one of the many, sometimes more powerful than it, challenges to theism, itself a pattern of only one main kind of worldview.

One might be further puzzled at how blithely people could come to put religion in a sort of ghetto, considering so many professed not to be able to define it. But even accepting a certain consensus that one can use the word sensibly of certain mainly traditional systems of belief as distinguished from secular ideologies including liberal atheism, it must surely remain a question as to whether worldviews of differing kinds do not, despite their contrasts, share some fundamental properties in common.

Let me name a few. My list represents overlaps. I am saying, "Importantly some religions and some ideologies are thus", not "All and all". So:

- closely relating theory and practice
- not being straightforwardly verifiable or falsifiable
- calling for dedicated commitment
- possessing an account of human history
- implying ethical principles
- possessing a doctrine of human nature
- being capable of intellectual and practical development
- having an eschatological orientation
- possessing a cosmology
- having a theory about the genesis of religion

Let me simplify: religions and ideologies both guide persons regarding the meaning of life. Moreover, since theology is very often the product of struggle at the interface between a religious tradition and secular ideologies, and since the history of religions reveals remarkable contrasts between religions in both belief and practice, it would seem that the opening out of the philosophy of religion to theologies and religions itself pushes us onward in the direction of an even more plural range—the range of both religions and ideologies, the range of *existential worldviews*, as they might jointly be called.

(It is a great shame that there is no simple word for such *Weltanschauunggen*. *Sasanas, darsanas, margas* are suggested by India, and other cultures could supply other terms. The briefest, least objectionable English word seems to me to be "worldview." But it is far from the hint of praxis and of faith, or the smack of sacrament or angst. Nor is there an easy way out by neologism—something which Hellenizes perhaps that mix of theory and value, of belief and feel, of faith and rite which the systems in question tend to incorporate.)

In brief, it is perhaps rather sad that so little of the philosophy of religion has been aimed at a wider range. What I am now proposing is that it would be better called something like "the philosophy of worldviews." Of course, this represents a somewhat radical suggestion in that it implies something too about religious studies. But I will not here pursue my suggestion in its longer ramifications.

II

Now a desideratum of such a philosophy of worldviews, if it is to be realistically tied to worldviews as they actually exist in the world, is analysis of the structure and history of such systems. There is a close analogy with the philosophy of science, which in recent decades has so much benefited from a close relationship with the history of science. From history of course we can learn various lessons: that, for instance, it is not easy to pin down certain religions to an essence—consider the great fluidity of Christianity and in its differing way Buddhism; that nevertheless at differing times variant doctrines may fulfil much the same existential function; that many aspects of religion and ideology have to be considered as dynamic—ready for development; and so on. From history and from the comparative study of religion we can begin to piece together the so-to-speak logical structure of systems—how the differing dimensions of religion, such as doctrine, myth, ritual and experience are bound to one another in relations of implication and suggestion, of expression and definition; also too how within the range of doctrines in a system they are mutually related and organically influence one another.

Let me illustrate briefly with just one example of such structural interconnections. "In the beginning was the Word . . ." Think of how in this amazing passage a new perspective is opened up on the old doctrine of creation, now interpreted anew in relation to the Incarnation. The meaning of the doctrine now has changed. It is no longer Creation-of-the-world-to-the-power-history-of-Israel, but rather Creation-of-the-world-to-the-power-history-of-Israel-to-the-power-Incarnation. If you have a red stripe and a white stripe and add a blue stripe, lo! there is the French flag; a green stripe and lo! there is the Italian flag. The reds and whites change their meaning according to their companionship. One might say that doctrines, in St. John, are organically related. More, they come to tie in with what may be described as an historical myth, the passage of Christ from Galilee to his meaningful and tragic end in Jerusalem, and to his overcoming of the tragic in his resurrection.

Moreover, for most Christians the meaning of the Incarnation is not just to be gleaned from the good book and from the expositions of doctrine, it is also to be understood more intimately in experience and in the Eucharistic sacrament. Thus if the Word described in St. John is the Christ of faith as well as the Jesus of history, his identity is understood transactionally, and so not only is there a bond between doctrine and doctrine and doctrine and myth, but also between doctrine and sacrament, myth and experience, and so forth.

Structurally, therefore, the analysis of a religious system points to a suggestive web of interconnections. The relations are rarely ones of entailment, but there are various kinds of weaker yet highly significant kinds of mutual dependence. Systems are *organic* systems, to put the matter briefly, and in their lives they can grow or shrink.

Often a religious or political question is: How much in the way of limbs can an organism lose and still live?

So there is a vital task of structural analysis and comparison to be undertaken by the philosophy of religion, or at least *for* it. For obviously a main question, "What are the kinds of evidences for and against the truth of a religious claim?," will vary in its impact and answer according to the actual organic version of a religious faith under inquiry.

There is a kind of dialogue which informally involves itself in such organic analysis. The Christian, say a Catholic, who engages in serious conversations with a Marxist is probing to see how far there are collisions and tensions between the two systems. More formally, one aspect of the task was undertaken in William Christian's *Oppositions of Religious Doctrines*. What is needed is a sort of comparative systematics. But of course it is not just doctrines and to some extent myth and ethics, such as are the typical pastures of systematic theology, that such analysis must be kept to, for it must also relate, as we have seen, to sacred and other practice and experience.

It is at this point, though, necessary to propound a caveat and make a distinction. Sometimes a systematic theology is not so much descriptive as constructive. It is the fashioning of a new Christian (or Jewish, etc.) system of belief: a new worldview. Likewise in dialogue often the mutual exploration leads beyond existing positions to new ones, on both sides. Excellent such explorations and new articulations of a worldview are, but they should not be confused with descriptions of existing systems. Doing theology is not the same as analysing theologies. One should be clear about this, not only for the sake of truth but also clarity as to what stage one is at. So far I am saying: let the philosophy of religion take seriously the comparative structural, or better, organic analysis of worldviews. The analysis, with the aid of history, can be diachronic as well as synchronic.

I am not saying that such a concern for realism of analysis is absent in modern philosophy of religion. It is not, however, very prominent. It incidentally represents a way in which philosophical concerns are to be integrated very closely into those of the history of religions. But in accord with my plea for a broader range than traditional religious systems for us to work on, the history of religions must go beyond religions. We are caught up in worldview history and worldview analysis: *Weltanschauungswissenschaft*, one might say.

So far I have been talking in the plural. Religions, not religion; ideologies, not ideology; worldviews, not worldview (note, by the way, the incongruity of this last term). But does not the history of religions offer more than histories or comparisons of systems? Of course, and especially if we look towards the influential Chicago school. For one thing it offers an account of key structures and elements within the world of myth and experience. We can look at it as a kind of organ comparison. Just as the hearts and livers and tongues of differing animals can be much alike, so there are elements within the organisms which comparative worldview analysis explores which are markedly similar. To take a heterogeneous list: symbolisms of height, attitudes to the Earth, fertility cults, shamanistic rites, mystical experiences, techniques of contemplation, the numinous experience, rites of passage.

The exploration of religious symbolism, including acted symbolism, can begin perhaps to shape a kind of grammar of religion, and indeed much else besides. The interest today shown among anthropologists, such as Clifford Geertz, Mary Douglas and Victor Turner, in the symbolic structures both of religion and "ordinary life," points towards ultimately the creation of a science of symbolic behavior, which would also include that found within the ambit of secular ideologies.

Unfortunately again we are in some quandary because of available language. Terms such as "symbol" and "symbolic" have unfortunately drifted in the direction of the "mere" or unreal. Speaking of something as a *mere* symbol denigrates it, and often so-called symbolic gestures are substitutes for the real thing—the rude sign instead of the physical assault. Consider, to take a modern "secular" example, a Chinese guide telling visitors the statistics of pig production in a particular commune. He does so, we suppose, proudly, and with more than a hint of revolutionary fervor. Evidently the pigs are meaningful: they are charged with special value. They are pigs with haloes, we may say. Why? Because they symbolize something. They are part of making the better life for the ordinary peasant. Producing pork is a small part, but a vital part, of the process of clothing the peasants in dignity. Pigs are also symbols of joint enterprise, and of the change wrought by the liberation and all that that has subsequently meant. Are they just symbolic? Are they "substitutes for the real thing"? Not at all. Plastic models of pigs would not do (like straw surrogates for human sacrifices). Pictures of pigs, it is true, can have symbolic impact, but only because the pigs are real or represented as such. Throw away the pigs and keep the pictures—this does not serve. So in many cases x is symbolic because it is a real x. Perhaps therefore we ought to use differing language to talk about such cases, which after all permeate our very daily existence: clothes, gestures, smiles, furniture, spires, skyscrapers—they all talk, wordlessly, but deeply.

There is, then, a continuum between the formality of much religious ritual through to the rites and expressive acts of daily life. If it is reasonable to extend the philosophy of religion so that it more explicitly becomes the philosophy of worldviews, so the history of religions has a more general destiny: the inquiry into the grammar of gesture and symbolism. That there is no such continuum is in my opinion part of an ideology which seeks to partition off religion, either defensively so it can have its own norms and be *sui generis*, or aggressively so that "serious" persons can neglect it as being traditional and cut off from the vital concerns of secular living.

Moreover, the grammar of symbolic action is an ingredient in our understanding the structure of worldviews. To take a simple example: Why should the heliocentric theory have been resisted? Partly because of its damaging the symbolic value expressed in the notion of humans being at the center. Consider the emotional impact of such notions as *revolution*, *class warfare*, *progress*, *growth*, *people*, *national identity*, and many others of the common coins of current political and economic discourse. There is a major task of analysis to unravel the modes whereby things and acts are specially charged with existential meaning, for it is such symbolic meaning which provides the bridge between pure cosmology and a world picture, between pure history and a philosophy or theory of history, between scientific and value-free descriptions and expressions of the symbolic substance of things. Even a kind of agnostic nihilism has to reject meaningful patterns: it does not simply fail to affirm them.

No doubt such remarks are obvious enough, but we sometimes in the field of religion do not take their implication seriously enough. For if they are correct, then the field of religion includes a field beyond religion in the conventional sense. Perhaps we could say that the domain of the study of religion should be seen as that of the spiritual in general: the way we respond more deeply to our world. That is part of what Tillich had in mind in talking of human beings' ultimate concern (though the *ultimate* bit was hardly, even loosely, quantifiable, and must just be hyperbole).

III

However, it is more from the lateral pluralism of worldviews that the main task of the philosophy of religion seems to me to emerge. I shall first put that briefly, and then go on to an inventory of considerations and topics that seem to me to arise. The task, then, briefly is to clarify the criteria for determining the truth as between worldviews. I am assuming that worldviews are not totally compatible, and there is a sense in which the view that they are compatible (such as neo-Vedanta) is itself an additional worldview. Naturally, therefore, a prior task is the comparative analysis of the structure of worldviews. This is the very heart of the comparative study of religion, plus of course a consideration of atheistic and other anti- or nonreligious systems of belief. An immense task? Naturally, but there are many workers in the field, and the subject is as yet rather young.

The question of criteria is a high-order one, though admittedly this claim has to be modified somewhat when we recognize that a theology, for instance, may have a philosophical component, a view of how one tells what the truth is. Still, broadly the distinction of levels can I think be maintained, perhaps more as a kind of heuristic device or as a mode of orientation. Also one needs to notice that it is not just a question of criteria of truth, but of truth wedded to practice, and so a matter of criteria of correctness or appropriateness. Since also action is mediated by symbolism and feeling, we have to pay attention to the living or vibrant quality of a system or tradition.

So then let me outline an inventory of considerations relative to the truth of worldviews.

1. First there is, of course, consistency. But *applied* consistency does not typically involve straight contradictions. Whereas that God is one and God is three on the surface is a contradiction, already we note something peculiar. It does not say "There are three Gods," and when we come to consider how the tension is resolved in the idea of the three Persons, we no longer can point to contradiction clearly established, though there remains tension. So one might ask: How much internal tension does a worldview contain? Other things being equal, the less tension the better, though it has to be said that a rich system, covering different facets of human experience, is liable to have some strong tension.

Internal tension itself may encourage formulae designed to stabilize it, but the stability of the formulae themselves may be in question. This is very much the history of Christian orthodoxies and heresies. Fix up the tension in the God-man idea in one direction, and some such divergence as Nestorianism may emerge.

2. Tension may also relate to the interface between the received beliefs and values of a traditional worldview and the discovered

truths and emerging values of contemporary society. Consider the tension concerning evolutionary theory and conservative interpretations of the Bible, or the tension between Stalinist Marxism and modern biology. More obviously, in regard to values, but the same applies also to truth-claims, it may turn out that the tension is a consequence of the falsity of contemporary views. Thus there is a clash between most liberal and women's liberation views on abortion and Catholic views, but it might be that the latter's views are the correct ones. Again, the Confessing Church experienced more tension with the values of German society in the thirties than did the German Christians. Since values are typically debatable, open to intuitive decision often, tension itself has a debatable disvalue. Similarly it may turn out that a traditional religion is right about some matters of science. For instance, traditional Buddhism believed in many world systems, or as we might now say, galaxies. This is a point in favor of that tradition, when one comes to see it over against the tiny little cosmological cage in which the Jewish and Christian imaginations were long confined.

3. Both in regard to beliefs and values there is also what may be described as an epistemological tension, or so it may appear. Science does not appeal to revelation or the experience of enlightenment. There are of course some well-known debates on this score, and ways of abolishing the tension. For example, religion has to do with personal existence, not the objective world. Or, revelation and natural knowledge are in harmony, but since knowledge changes, so our worldview is constantly in need of revision. (On the latter view, the adaptibility of a worldview becomes a sign of truth or acceptability.)

4. There is a special valuational side to such tensions and resolutions of tension. It is not just that some range of data has to be seen in conjunction with some other range. It is also that one is existentially more significant than another, seen from within the perspective of the worldview which is making sense of the data. Thus Jewish theology has to make sense of the Holocaust, but sympathetic as the Buddhist may be, she/he is less concerned with the traumatic or other passages of history.

In fact, there is a whole area of priority decisions where it is hard to know how to judge. Thus Christianity may claim to be historical, its revelation woven into the fabric of history. But how much *weight* should be attached to historicity and the historical? Again, Buddhism has a contemplative experience at its heart. Generally its *bhakti* or devotionalism is subsidiary to that. But for much of Christianity, such a weight placed upon the contemplative side is regarded as excessive—for example, among Calvinists. Looked at from the angle of religious experience, the history of religion is a ballet of different kinds: prophetic, mystical, shamanistic, psychedelic, conversional. How much weight to place upon each of these varieties? Both epistemologically and spiritually, that is, both as regards authority and application to one's own life, the answers will be important, since the differing experiences tend to lead in differing directions, of calm, fervor, dualism, monism, fullness, emptiness, worship, meditation, ethical resolve, quietism, and so forth. It may be that a criterion is comprehensiveness. For instance, can both devotional fervor and contemplative calm be held within the fabric of one faith? (It is indeed hard to resist the application of this test, which makes certain forms of Christianity, Islam, Hinduism and Buddhism, for instance, superior to others.)

5. Not only is there a possible tension between religions in regard to the weighting of types of religious experience (for instance, Theravada Buddhism does not take seriously prophetic utterances expressive of relationship to a personal God, while the nontheistic contemplative style of the Theravada often is not taken seriously by more prophetically oriented believers, such as Wahhabis and many conservative evangelicals), there is also the question of the seriousness with which *any* such experience should be taken. Are they valid and are they desirable? The Marxist might doubt that they are.

It is here that there is a criterion of the persuasiveness of a given metaphysical or quasi-metaphysical framework for worldview-commitment. Thus though Marxist materialism has its symbolic side, as we have noted, it also does express a certain ontology. The denial of the transcendent represents a challenge to most, though not all, religious worldviews. But the resolution of the challenge is itself a strange matter, in that it will in great measure depend on the weighting of experience and the weighting of data. Let me put these things in another way. Without entertaining the possibility of the transcendent, one rules out religious experience as a valid avenue to the truth, but the possibility of the transcendent is taken seriously because religious experience is.

6. Since ethical insights are partially independent of worldview, another criterion of truth relates to the ethical, or more generally, social fruits of differing systems, both positively and negatively. Of course, fruits vary and are shaped by their trees. Preference, therefore, will again figure in the weighting of fruits. How does a dozen avocadoes compare with a crate of oranges, or a gallery of saints with a procession of arhants?

At this point an objection, long simmering, might be raised. In fact, two objections. First, since religion is often seen as a matter of revelation, of being chosen rather than choosing, this elaborate parade of criteria is beside the point. Second, maybe a religion in any case is not universal, but really for a particular group.

To take the second point first, let us consider two cases. The religion of an ethnic group, such as the Gikuyu or the Toraja: is it not just for Gikuyu or Toraja folk? The Torajas do not want to sell their faith to humankind at large, they just want to keep it in the face of outside pressures. But of course those very pressures are universalist, and to combat those forces a modification of tribal religion is needed, a kind of universalist modification to the effect: "Our religion is true too and reflects the Truth in a way peculiarly suited to our history and temperament."

Another noted case is that of Judaism, which some could interpret as the religion of a particular group. Even so it is a *world* religion in a pregnant sense, for it contains within it a view of world history relevant to all human beings, and exhibiting the special place of the Jewish tradition within that divinely controlled pattern.

As for the point about revelation: so be it. One criterion of the truth of a worldview is its capacity to exhibit a sensitive epistemology. It may well be that if there is a God, then by revelation the heart of his truth must come to humankind. Revealed authority is epistemologically appropriate, what one might expect. Still, the fact is there are rival revelations. It is at this point that the criteria I have already pointed to will come into play.

Let me illustrate by a parable. I do not create Scotland or Canada or Italy, but supposing I am choosing which country to live in, do I not want to balance up the various good and bad points, the arguments for and against? We have not merely to do this, but to blend our results and make a choice. So with revelations or more generally worldviews. For we are indeed in the modern world faced with a rich and daunting choice. To this I shall return.

7. Meanwhile, let me add a further point about psychology which is tangential to our previous discussion of religious experience but vitally important for all that, for it links up with the question of fruits. Worldviews include beliefs and feelings about the nature of human beings, about whether we are intrinsically good or bad, whether our troubles originate from sin or ignorance or both, where we stand in the universe—naked apes or what? Such anthropologies jibe or fail to jibe with experience and with ordinary life, and so have the profoundest effect upon our ordinary behavior in relation to reli-

gion and values. The testing of the plausibility of diagnoses of our condition is of course extraordinarily complex. It is partly a matter of science, usually rather speculative, for example, concerning the evolutionary origins of certain human traits such as the prevalence of war and violence; partly a matter of individual experience; partly a matter of metaphysical perspective.

And since religious traditions incorporate ritual elements such as worship, sacraments, and so on, then the logic of the ritual dimension has to make sense in regard to anthropology (in this sense of the term: again, a new expression is needed for, so to speak, one's humankind-view as an element in a worldview—one's *anthropism*, perhaps). In other words, there is probably a highly vital link between the symbolic grammar to which I referred before and the application of ritual religion to the world. (Incidentally, we should not neglect the ritual elements in secular worldviews.)

8. My discussion of criteria hitherto implies a kind of interplay, even rivalry, between worldviews. For instance, the whole discussion of religious experience is vital to the claims of all the major religions, and the question of validity, with attendant questions about the status of Freudian and other psychological accounts of such experience, is clearly relevant to the secular ideologies. This of course introduces the following factor: every tradition in a planetary world needs to have a theory about the others, even maybe the negative theory that they are all blasphemous delusions. This itself generates a criterion, namely, the test of the degree of plausibility of such theories (very often they break down on the facts).

This need for some "theory of the others" is part of a more general demand: that in these latter planetary days, in particular, when histories have flowed together in the great estuary of world or planetary history, a worldview needs to have a theory of its place in planetary history. A universal destiny implies something of a universal accountancy. It is true that a religion like Jainism may think itself to be in an age of great decline as predicted by its own scriptures. This is itself a theory of history (though how far old Indian ideas of *kalpas* and *yugas* can stand up to modern scientific knowledge of the wide reaches of the geological and biological past is open to doubt). Again, the degree of tension involved in maintaining, say, a Christian theory of history will be relevant to the truth of Christian belief.

From the foregoing it will be clear that criteria do not dictate, for the most part, sharp decisions. The questions of truth as between worldviews are fluid, malleable. Even if biology refutes Lysenko, this does not by itself refute Stalin, and even if Stalin be in disgrace, this does not refute Marxism. Even if historians refute some of the Gospel claims, this does not destroy the Gospel. This does not of course mean that *decisions* cannot be sharp. Joining a monastery, being twice born, leaving the Party—these are crisp enough decisions or events, when they come, but their basis, epistemologically, is bound to be impressionistic. Epistemologically we are not of course forced into a kind of relativism, which in any case is self-defeating. But I think we are impelled towards a certain toleration, seeing that there can in religion rarely be proofs.

The philosophy of worldviews, by exploring the criteria, itself of course from its higher level has an effect on the lower. Undoubtedly some uniquenesses vanish in a comparative world. But more importantly that world, in dictating criteria, provides an altered agenda for Christian or other theology, Buddhology, Marxist philosophy and so forth. This makes systematic theology more difficult, but richer, of course.

And incidentally, since it is faiths which humans live by, part of their lives, the philosophy of worldviews must have a crucial place in general philosophy. We are of course still very far from understanding how beliefs influence actions, so there is much to explore in the relationship between the philosophy of worldviews and ethics.

IV

Personally, I believe that what I have here sketched as the task of the philosophy of religion and more broadly the philosophy of worldviews is of extraordinary importance at the present time in world history. Maybe I can expatiate a little on why this is so. For important though it is in this kind of philosophizing to preserve a kind of higher-order neutrality and an even-handed empathy, it in no way follows that the results of one's thus calmer cerebrations do not have some important, disturbing and exhilarating implications. In what follows I sketch such consequences as I perceive them.

The first consequence is that our intellectual enterprises, in so far as they reflect on the nature and destiny of human beings, need to be consciously planetary. The remarkable histories of Chinese, Indian and other thought, the achievements of varied cultures—these can all now be tributaries towards the fashioning of a worldview. The element of toleration liable to arise from a recognition of the softness of criteria naturally tends toward a federal and to some extent eclectic approach to worldviews. Indeed, though there are oppositions of religious doctrines and imperatives, there are areas of non-contradiction, for religious systems, being organic, are not clusters of entailments, not geometries of the spirit. By consequence, there are always insights which can be woven into one's own tradition or movement. It is true that some worldviews are not very tolerant or open, but again it does not follow that the perceptions behind them cannot be learned from. So I do not see all religions and ideologies merging in a fuzzy haze. This is neither logically appropriate nor humanly likely. But there is a strong argument for a federalism of persons of good will.

Second, the philosophy of worldviews forcibly suggests that, since ongoing religions and ideologies need to "place" themselves in world history, to contemplate, that is, their planetary destiny, so there is a humanistic need to revive concern for this kind of history-making.

Third, the philosophy of worldviews reminds one how much the practical and the theoretical are interwoven in humankind's systems of belief in a way which leads to a gap between epistemology and commitment, that is, between the softnesses of evidence and the deep meaning of a movement or tradition. Certitude combines with impressionistic grounds, as with a person "certain" a given horse is going to win. This in turn means that the philosophy of worldviews is also about communities, nations, parties, groups. It is not just about beliefs or about propositions which an individual as individual can adopt or reject. Thus a kind of liberal atomism of belief is not a good conclusion out of the pluralism of humanity's worldviews. There needs to be a federalism of groups as well.

Furthermore, as philosophy of worldviews wrestles with the analysis of myth and of that charged facticity which somehow bridges the gap between object and feeling, it will increasingly remind us of the symbolic character of so much human belief and action. Herein lies, in my view, the clue to a new approach to politics as well as to ethics. Maximizing human dignity, which is the best we can strive for in these spheres, implies considering not just what material things, bureaucratic institutions, work conditions and so on, do for people, but why they mean to people. The student of religion has an important function in extending our understanding of the symbolic phenomenology of everyday life.

But enough of my sermon.

I hope I have argued clearly enough that the philosophy of religion should be extended to be the philosophy of worldviews, and that it should be the upper story of a building which has as its middle floor the comparative and historical analysis of religions and ideologies, and as a ground floor the phenomenology not just of religious experience and action but of the symbolic life of human beings as a whole.

2

Philosophical Pluralism and the Plurality of Religions

◻

Raimundo Panikkar

As long as there is not a single universal language, there will never be just one philosophy of religion.[1] Languages are more than nominalistic tools to handle independently given realities. The old myth of the Tower of Babel speaks of the apparently constitutive human dream of a single language. Yahweh sees this dream as the symbol of Man wanting to be equal to God, and in fact with the Tower of Babel, Man did want to reach Heaven.[2] But Yahweh shatters this constant human temptation to build a single monolithic world by confusing humanity's *logos*. Instead of constructing a new neocolonialistic tower, we can perhaps make inroads of communication, even of communion, among the human huts of our various limited worlds. The danger of a disembodied intellect is in losing the sense of human scale and falling into dehumanizing ideologies.

What we have in our case, in fact, is a *plurality* of philosophies of religions, just as we have many languages. Now, to become aware of any plurality leads the human spirit to wonder if there is any way to overcome the multiplicity by discovering an underlying unity. But the price of unity may be the loss of identity. The unity of the human skeleton cannot be equated with the practically infinite variety of our personal bodies. In other words, between a plurality *de facto* and a unity *de ratione* there may be room for a pluralism *de jure*. To be sure, this pluralism shatters the *myth of the logos* as the unique horizon of intelligibility, and reveals the *logos of the myth,* the *mythos-legein*, inherent in the human condition.

I. A Preliminary Hermeneutic

Taking seriously the cultural pluralism of humanity, that is, abandoning the monolinear idea of human progress, we can no longer hold the theory that explains the different religions as different degrees of approximation to the one ideal we hold of religion. This is to say that the consciousness of plurality of religions leads us to a hermeneutic of religion. But by the same token a hermeneutic of religion becomes a hermeneutic of the human interpretations of religion, that is, a hermeneutic of the philosophies of religion. We should then ask ourselves both about the nature of the concepts "religion" and "philosophy," and about the subject doing the hermeneutic. But this latter is conditioned in turn by the particular concepts of religion and philosophy that the interpreter holds to be true. A hermeneutic of philosophy of religion has to interpret not an objectively nonexistent "religion," but a given "concept" of religion which philosophers have actually developed. The different concepts of "philosophy" and "religion" have to be incorporated into such a hermeneutic. I cannot assume that my point of departure and my perspective are shared by all humanity. In point of fact the study of religion independently of the beliefs which people actually have and according only to my own criteria would not be a study of real religion but only the interpretation of something that exists exclusively in my mind.

In order to be brief and as clear as possible, I will define my concepts:

By *pluralism* I mean the awareness of the legitimate coexistence of systems of thought, life, and action which, on the other hand, are judged incompatible among themselves.

We may indeed recognize pluralism as a fact, but it is not intelligible in its contents, otherwise we would have a supersystem which would by definition destroy all pluralism. Pluralism is of the order of *mythos* and not of *logos*. There is no pluralist system. Pluralism belongs to the order of existence and not of essence. It is not a merely formal concept like plurality, but it is also not a material concept like unity.

By *philosophy* I understand a system of thought or even of action offering a structure which enables one to find the most universal form of intelligibility, given one's presuppositions.

Religion I understand as a belief in a set of symbols which express the ultimate meaning of life. In existential terms, I would simply say: religion is the *ultimate path*, that is to say, the way which people believe leads to their goal. The way of course varies in accordance with the different concepts of the goal: salvation, liberation, plenitude, void, the absurd, and so on. In Greek, one might even hazard a single word: *eschathodos*, the final way.

Lastly, I consider *philosophy of religion* as the human reflection on the nature of religion, considering the latter in its ultimate constitution.

This last definition needs some clarification. If Man is not merely an object of research but also a self-conscious subject, then no true understanding of any human phenomenon is possible if separated from what people have thought, believed and imagined about the object. In other words, Man's self-understanding belongs to that which Man is. Understanding may not always be self-understanding, but it is always understanding by the self. But I am not the only self. My understanding is not the only one, nor can it be substituted for the self-understanding of others. Thus, to come to our problem: religion includes what people have thought it is. Hence the problem is not one of a hermeneutic of religion, but one of a hermeneutic of the philosophy of religion, that is, a hermeneutic of the (philosophical) interpretations which people have given of religion. We must add that our "thing" has not necessarily been designated by the name "philosophy of religion."

Intercultural problems here are immense. Logically, "philosophy of religion" cannot exist except where "philosophy" and "religion" exist—but it can equally be maintained that "philosophy of religion" may be used to mean far more than such a denomination literally conveys. How, for instance, would one say "philosophy of religion" in Sanskrit, in Chinese, in Kisange or Sesuto? Before discussing any hermeneutic of the philosophy of religion with a pretension to universality, therefore, we need to make clear just what is meant by the phrase "philosophy of religion." I shall from now on no longer consider the different meanings of "philosophy" and of "religion", but, in a higher degree of abstraction, the different types of "philosophy of religion."

II. Four Types of "Philosophy of Religion"

In my opinion we usually use this expression ultimately intending the fourth type mentioned below, while unaware that we are still at one of the preceding levels. Our having often overlooked these four types has created confusions not only in theoretical and academic studies, but in the political, religious and cultural worlds as well. The four types may be distinguished as follows:

1. The philosophies of religions
2. The philosophies of religion
3. The philosophy of religions
4. The philosophy of religion

There is an inevitable problem of semantics here. The categories with which one seeks to elucidate a problem belong themselves to the problem. If one uses particular categories for posing a transcultural problem, one does not command an adequate language; and if one translates them, one already uses foreign categories—even assuming that the translation is right. We should therefore use names as they refer to the intentionality which gave rise to the original words. Need we speak of sense (semiology: structure or internal coherence) and signification (semantics: meaning for a subject), or referent (world) and intentionality (of the author)?

Be this as it may, I shall concentrate on the explication of my typology, leaving a hermeneutic of the language employed for another occasion.

1. The Various Philosophies of the Different Religions

These are philosophical efforts within particular cultures which try to render the religious problem intelligible from the perspective of a specific religion: particular philosophies of specific religions. This first type of philosophy of religion includes also any philosophical criticism within a religion made by the means provided by that religion. A specific example is the philosophy of Christianity in the West, even if the philosophical instruments used are not explicitly Christian. Here also belongs what is generally called theology, that is, the effort at intelligibility from within a religion itself.

Of course, any philosophical construction has a constitutive pretense to universality, but the very sphere of that universality is limited by our presuppositions. There is in any affirmation the subjacent claim that it is valid for the horizon one considers as given. But we can never define this horizon without destroying it as horizon.

However, the problem is not so simple, since the impulse to universalize is inherent in the human mind. The philosophy of Christianity, for instance, falls often in this pitfall of extrapolating its own categories of understanding. This is done even when one limits oneself to a mere questioning of other religions, without realizing that the questions are already conditioned as much by the responses expected as by the concepts used in formulating the questions. When, for example, a Christian asks if Hinduism and Buddhism also have a God, the Christian already commits an unjustified extrapolation. When writing philosophy of religion starting from a Thomist, Marxist, Theravadic or linguistic analysis of the religious fact, we have a philosophy of religion which is often applied to other religious traditions. If history did not furnish us with enough examples of the frequently tragic results of misunderstandings of this kind, one might doubt the existence of any such problem. I am inclined to think that a large number of the philosophies of religions written today still belong to this first type. Both apologetics as well as criticisms of religion mostly appertain to this first type of philosophy of religion.

2. *The Philosophies of a Religion*

This second category denotes the several philosophies of a particular religion. The rich and complex religious traditions of humanity have given birth to several philosophical systems. The philosophical pluralism at the heart of contemporary Christianity is a pertinent example, and the great Western Christian systems associated with the names of Augustine, Thomas, Descartes, Hegel and others, might also be cited. We do not have a super-philosophy but a variety of philosophical systems claiming to give us a valid philosophy of a specific religion, even though the kind of unjustified extrapolation found in the first type of philosophy may also be present here, this time between philosophies of a single religion.

In this second type the hiatus between religion and philosophy is greater than in the first type, where the philosophy of religion has only to explain and criticize religious beliefs different from those serving as its own basis. For example, for a certain Christian philosophical milieu it will not appear surprising that "pagans," "infidels" or "barbarians" should have a philosophy—of their own tradition—that helps them to understand their own religious situation. But that a post-Tridentine Catholic, a believer and a philosopher, could have an intelligent understanding of reality without also subscribing to, say, the twenty-four Thomistic theses, will not pass without posing a serious philosophical problem. The disparity between the two attitudes touches on the very nature of philosophy and religion. Each religious tradition can beget its own philosophical understanding, but something remains philosophically problematic if within one single tradition we have a plurality of philosophies. How can a Muslim, for instance, subscribe to a Hegelian or Marxist philosophy? We are witnessing here the birth of philosophical pluralism. The different philosophies have become options based upon ultimate forms of intelligibility—though naturally from the point of view of any one of these options the others may be judged erroneous, inadequate or incomplete.

This pluralism is based on at least one of the two following assumptions: (a) no philosophy can reach its own ideal of being ultimate, so there may always be the possibility of irreducibly ultimate options; and (b) religion is ever transcendent to any philosophical speculation, so no philosophy can ever exhaust the understanding of the religious fact.

3. *The Philosophy of Several Religions*

The distinction between religion and philosophy becomes sharper in the case of the exact reversal of type 2, namely, when a single philosophy serves as the instrument of intelligibility and of orthodox expression for several religious traditions. Western medieval scholasticism, for example, was employed by Judaism, Christianity and Islam alike. Modern existentialism, a philosophical attitude accepted by Christians, Marxists and atheistic humanists, would be another example. And a certain Advaitic philosophy, applied to Hinduism, Buddhism and even Christianity, would furnish a third. One could say that this type discovers a unitary language used to convey different religious intuitions.

The present quest in India for a Hindu-Christian philosophy (or theology, as many would prefer to call it) does not consist in trying to formulate or reformulate Christian concepts in Hindu terms, but in finding a common language which would permit expression of the fundamental intuitions of both traditions without doing violence to either.

The danger here is that religion may be reduced to philosophy, in this case to a sort of rationalism or latent intellectualism in which the human intellect is considered powerful enough to encompass the traditionally irreconcilable. And in fact, the majority of philosophical systems which have a cultural and multireligious vitality do seem to suffer from a certain gnosticism. "True" philosophy becomes "authentic" religion and the "genuine" substitute for the "superstition of the masses." One understands the prudence and even the mistrust with which religious authorities regard facile syncretism or eclecticism which, however well-intended, would strip religion of its most precious elements. Here philosophy may easily appear to be more fundamental than religion.

4. The Philosophy of All Religion

This fourth type represents a certain ideal of philosophy of religion, since it would offer a philosophy valid for the religious experience of all humanity. This would be a single philosophy for understanding and criticizing any religion existing on earth.

If the danger which threatens the first and second types is uncritical extrapolation, and the temptation in the third type is reductionism (reducing religion to philosophy, which is logical, since there is a common philosophical nucleus), the snare in this fourth type lies in reducing philosophy to formalism—of structure or of essence or the like—and/or in reducing religion to a super-metaphysics common to all. Certain traditionalist and metaphysical positions would appear to have fallen into that snare: the "real thing," they will tell us, is the primordial tradition, or the primitive revelation, or the primary metaphysical insights. A kind of mystical philosophy undergirding all religions may be adduced as another instance.

All the same, this fourth type may well be the inevitable model for any really profound encounter in a cross-cultural setting. Can we be content with a philosophy of religion valid for certain provinces of human experience only? Can we ignore the religions of others? Should we not try to comprehend the human experience in its totality? Should the Tower of Babel be rebuilt? Or is it, perhaps, necessary to renounce the great Babel-constructions and be content with establishing *paths of mediation*? Might these not be the ways of communication, the means of communion?

The question may be put simply, by asking if any agreement is possible among the different religious traditions of humanity. Is the philosophy of religion not the place, the bridge, necessary for the encounter of religions? Does it not have a mediating function? But the answer is not as simple as the question. We shall proceed, at best, to point out some milestones on the way.

III. Hermeneutic of Philosophy of Religion instead of Hermeneutic of Religion

If we are all imprisoned in our own hermeneutical circle— if there is nothing more than a plurality of hermeneutics and a plurality of religions—what is going to break the circle in order to open us to a comprehension of that most profound dimension of the human spirit?

In his introduction to the colloquium, *Herméneutique de la philosophie de la religion* (Paris: Aubier, 1977, p. 1), Castelli asks if there should be "Emancipation from religion, or emancipation through religion?" And he adds: "This is the question to which the hermeneutic of the new philosophy of religion is called to respond." I think that the call comes not only from the "secularization" of the West, which he underlines, but also from the religions, ancient and modern, of the world.

My response to Castelli is this: we should have emancipation from religio*n*s through religion itself, purification of concrete religions by the religious spirit of humanity. However, the religious dimension only exists in our concrete religious attitudes. For any critique of religion, positive or negative, I have to stand somewhere. And this place has to be as fundamental as religion claims to be, that is, it has to be religious too. *Hic Rhodus, hic salta*! The very thought is dizzying. Here are seven points I venture to signal.

1. The recognition that we do not have a philosophy of religion of the fourth type seems to me a first positive step in the right direction. The first condition for going beyond the confines of our traditions is perhaps to be conscious of our own limitations. Any cross-cultural enterprise should begin with the awareness that there are frontiers to cross and human rights to respect. To question my own categories of understanding, even if I cannot jump over them, perplexes me, but it redeems me from my own closed circle.

2. It is true that we do not have a philosophy of religion, but can we renounce it? The human spirit seems unable to stop short of a certain unity which appears necessary, indeed vital, to it. To be sure, it remains an ideal, the goal is transcendent: the omega-point is always beyond our reach. Certainly, we cannot remain enclosed, self-content within ourselves, but setting out to conquer others (with our own weapons of understanding) is not always the best alternative. One should also open oneself to the other, allow oneself to be invaded. But where then shall we meet? At my place? At the other's? At a third one's place? Or in the middle of the road?

3. In the ultimate encounters there is no third place, nor is there a middle of the road: there is no neutral ground. How can there be a "No-Man's" land in the land of "Man"? To believe that dialectics could offer us such a place seems to me a fallacy arising from a defective analysis of human awareness. It also contradicts a given fact: real-

ity does not have a dialectical structure. And among all the human events on earth, the dynamism of religions especially cannot be reduced to dialectical games. Human existence is prompted by such a spontaneity, freedom, providence or chaos that it defies any reduction to rules, dialectical or not.

4. Nevertheless, we cannot renounce our claim to intelligibility under the pretext that we cannot understand everything, nor can we put an end to contact and dialogue. But how is it possible, if in this dialogue nobody should impose rules of the game on anybody else? The *dialogical dialogue* is, in my opinion, indispensable as the only, or at least as the most promising, chance for a fruitful encounter.

The dialogical dialogue does not replace dialectics, but complements it. It is not based on a common confidence in the neutral field of logical dialectics, but on a true reciprocal confidence in the other, that is, in the fact that the other is a source of understanding and original perspectives just as much as I am. Consequently, he or she is worthy not only of moral respect, but also of philosophical consideration, even if I find his or her opinions quite unintelligible. The dialogical dialogue is a truly "opening of the logos" (*dia ton logon*), attaining that other sphere of human experience which is only made possible through confidence in the other *as other* and not just in *what* I understand that the other says. In the dialogical dialogue I am open to the other in such a way that my partner can discover my myths, my subjacent assumptions—and vice versa, of course. The authentic dialogue exists neither in what I say, nor in what my partner adds, but in that which takes place in the dialogue itself. Neither of us knows what is going to happen beforehand, nor have we any power over it during the process. Only when we stand-under the spell of the words happening between us can we under-stand each other. We both listen.

5. This means that philosophy of religion cannot properly be called by that name unless it has in one form or another included the religious experience of humanity in its totality. Insofar as there may be some religion, perhaps unknown to the rest of the world, that has not yet spoken of its own way of conceiving the problem, we cannot speak of a philosophy of religion which fully embraces the purport of those two words. Any analysis of the human situation is always provisional, on the way both to reaching the truth and to being overcome.

6. Paradoxically, then, the first function of the philosophy of religion will be to recognize its own limits and to keep them open, to have a constant critical attitude in the face of the above-mentioned

dangers of extrapolation and reductionism. The human phenomenon transcends us and our understanding of pluralism obliges us to accept the contingency of all our opinions, even of the philosophical and religious ones.

7. This leads us to the search for the passage from a *de facto* plurality to a *de jure* pluralism. Within the limits of philosophy a certain philosophical pluralism has been accepted: one may not agree with other ways of thought, but besides the ethical obligation to tolerate them, there is the positive conviction of the richness of diversity, hence of pluralism. What kind of world would it be if Leibniz, for example, were the only patron of philosophy—or St. Thomas, or Hegel? We may be convinced that the philosophical system of Malebranche is false, for instance, and still find that the philosophical mosaic of the West offers a panorama of extraordinary beauty, even though it may not be philosophically evident. It is sometimes difficult to recognize the rights of a particular philosophy: the *carvakas* of India are the classical example of the "villain" in this regard, while the bourgeois mentality may be the undiscussed victim of a Marxist ideology. But because it arises from an order which is greater than we are, we must admit today that philosophical diversity is not just a minor evil to be tolerated, it is a major fact to be taken into consideration.

We are much less advanced within the limits of religions. And precisely this, in my opinion, makes the problem of the philosophy of religion so important. Religious wars are still a reality: many people are not yet disposed to admit on the theoretical plane that the *de facto* plurality of religions may be recognized as a pluralism *de jure*. To recognize religious pluralism touches on a more profound level of the human spirit than the level reached by recognizing philosophical pluralism. From the point of view of a specific philosophy and/or of a particular religion, one may criticize the opinions of others, one must even denounce them if they seem erroneous or even harmful, but one should not raise one's own criteria as absolute values. In fact history shows us that often, thanks to the "errors" of "adversaries," the truth is purified more and more, and shines all the more brightly.

Religious pluralism should not be confused with religious indifference, or with a condescending eclecticism which tolerates all religions because fundamentally all of them are considered to be irrelevant. I repeat that pluralism cannot give rise to a supersystem or a superior point of view without, by that very fact, destroying itself. A system open to the understanding of other systems, or a religion as flexible, as welcoming and universal as possible, are imperatives for our times, but they are not examples of pluralism. When a certain Vedanta and Christian theology believe themselves to be tolerant because they accept the validity and even the truth of all religions, providing that they range themselves in their places and play the role which is assigned to them, this Vedanta and this Christianity are perhaps magnanimous and may even be right, but they offer, certainly, no example of pluralism.

There is a fundamental difference between pluralism and mere plurality. The most central presupposition of pluralism is the conviction that no system can exhaust the horizon of human experience, and that to want to fix the conditions or to suggest the possibilities according to which one attains the ultimate realities, implies either an excessive rationalism or the pride of believing oneself in possession of a criterion of truth which does not take into account what fragile vessels we are.

In short, the hermeneutic of religion is always a hermeneutic of the philosophy of religion, and this hermeneutic is always in process, never finished. It is not a philosophy or philosophies of religion or religions, but an ever open philosophizing in search both of its proper object and of its own subject, because the human way consists in the going, itself. The singular and the plural apply here as little as do the masculine and the feminine. The very awareness of the ultimate dimension of humanity is philosophizing about our religiousness.

3

Religious Pluralism and the Future of Religions

□

Harold Coward

The time will soon be with us when a theologian who attempts to work on his position unaware that he does do as a member of a world society in which other theologians equally intelligent, equally devout, equally moral, are Hindus, Buddhists, Muslims, and unaware that his readers are likely to be Buddhists or to have Muslim husbands or Hindu colleagues—such a theologian is as out of date as is one who attempts to construct an intellectual position unaware that Aristotle has thought about the world or that existentialists have raised new orientations or unaware that the earth is a minor planet in a galaxy that is vast only by terrestrial standards. Philosophy and science have impinged so far on theological thought more effectively than has comparative religions, but this will not last.[1]

Religious pluralism is a special challenge facing the world religions today, yet in another sense religious pluralism has always been with us. As the history of religions shows, each religion arose in a religiously plural environment and shaped itself in reaction to that pluralism. The creative tension pluralism occasions has often been the catalyst for new insight and religious development. It was out of the welter of views, the Brahmanical/Jain/Materialistic/Agnostic pluralism of his day, that the Buddha's enlightenment arose. It was in the midst of the Meccan admixture of Jews, Christians, Zoroastrians, Manicheans and others that the prophecy of Allah through

Muhammad burst forth. It was in the midst of the numerous territorial gods of the ancient Near East that God covenanted with Abraham and Moses. It was the challenge of Gnosticism and Greek philosophy that helped early Christians to identify their separateness from Judaism. And it may be said of Hinduism that plurality has been its strength right up to the present day. Certainly there were times in the history of each of these religions when the pluralistic challenges receded to the background, often signaling a period of spiritual stagnation, for example, Christianity through the Middle Ages or Islam just prior to Sufi encounter with Hinduism. And when the challenge of pluralism reasserted itself, it usually infused new life into the tradition confronted. Thus, although the challenge of religious pluralism is in one sense the crisis of our age, it is at the same time its opportunity for spiritual growth.

It is as yet too early to detect the new contents and forms that will arise from the modern challenge of religious pluralism. But perhaps it is possible to indicate some beginning outlines of the religions of the future, religions which will be able to live comfortably side by side in a global community. Let us examine the major features of the current situation, and then make some observations as to the future of religions. Section 1 contains a summary of similarities of traditional religious approaches to religious pluralism. Section 2 describes some of the difficulties confronting religious pluralism today. Section 3 indicates my own view of the future of theology vis-à-vis religious pluralism. Section 4 sketches some guidelines for interreligious dialogue.

I. Religious Pluralism: Some Common Approaches

A study of how religions have responded and are responding to the challenge of religious pluralism points up three themes or principles which generally seem to be held in common:

1. The logic by which the fact of religious pluralism can best be understood is the One manifesting as the many—transcendent reality phenomenalizing as the various religions.

2. There is a common recognition of the instrumental quality of particular religious experiences.

3. Spirituality is identified and validated by the superimposing of one's own criterion upon the other religions.

Also held in common are several difficulties posed by modern pluralism. Let us examine each of these points in detail.

1. *A Common Logic: The One and the Many*

From the perspective of philosophy or theology the logic of a source reality experienced in a plurality of ways seems to be the most satisfactory way of accounting for the facts of religious pluralism. The oldest formulation of this logic is encountered in the Vedic notion of the One which is called by many names. For Buddhism the causal law of *karma* is the one reality which the religions are trying to cope with in various ways. Judaism and Christianity share the Biblical perception of all peoples and nations as under the one God, as well as the *Logos* notion of Greek philosophy. In Islam there is the "mother Book" of which the earthly books of the various religions are copies. Contemporary scholars of religions such as Karl Jaspers,[2] John Hick[3] and Wilfred Cantwell Smith[4] also adopt this logic, as do current thinkers in the major religions. The logic of the one and the many is both the oldest and the most current contemporary explanation of religious pluralism.

The attempt to reduce all religions to one common universal—all religions are really the same—has been unacceptable to the major religions and, as Charles Davis shows, it is philosophically unacceptable because it leads to a violation of the principle of freedom.[5] A universal religion would amount to religious coercion. Unity without diversity leads to a denial of freedom. Thus plurality in matters of faith and morals should be accepted positively. With regard to the internal relationship between the One and the many, all religions would seem to agree that emphasis should be placed on the One as the creative source. The identifying of the creative or spiritual source with the One rather than the many allows the many (the individual traditions) to change without destroying the One. It is a one-sided identity relationship. This is why the richness of plurality provides the dynamic to lead the many religions back to their creative source. Thus, the center of gravity is kept in the One, without overthrowing the many. What is required is to use one's own particular religion as means of access to the deeper creative source of all religions.

2. *Religion is Instrumental*

The diversity and plurality of religion points out its instrumental function. The revelations, doctrines and spiritual disciplines of the many religions are the means by which the One is reached. The sayings of the Buddha, the monastic rules, the philosophic schools and the Bodhisattvas all function as instruments of enlightenment in Buddhism. They are the "boats" to help one across the river of *karma-samsara* to enlightenment of the other side. But once the goal is reached, the "boat" employed is left behind. Buddhism is not Buddha's sayings or the monastic institution but the enlightenment experience itself—the *dhamma* as Buddhadasa would say. Similarly, in Hinduism the Vedas, though necessary, are left behind in the realization of *moksa* or release. The Vedas are the "ladder" by which Brahman is reached. But when the instrumental function of the Vedic "ladder" has been accomplished, for the released soul at least, the Veda is no longer required. Gurus, ashrams, images and yogas are likewise instrumental in their function within Hinduism.

The scriptures, forms and practices of Western religions differ in that their instrumental function is never transcended in the experience of the devotee.[6] The Torah, New Testament or Qur'an are never transcended and left behind in the way that they may be by the Hindu or Buddhist who has achieved release. But even though they cannot be totally transcended, the function of scripture in the Western religions is to be the instrument or means by which God is revealed. In a similar way, theology, prayer, the singing of hymns and the partaking of sacraments are variously employed in the Western religions as means by which the one God is responded to, gives grace and is known, although each religion varies in its acceptance and use of these instruments.

Thus it becomes clear that much of what is commonly taken to be the core of the various religions is really a particular collection of instrumental means by which the One may be reached. Understood in this way, the various religions need not be treated as fixed, unchanging truths, but rather as developing traditions of religious instrumentality. It is the One, not the many, which is the absolute and therefore unchanging.

Problems arise within religious pluralism when it is the forms of the various religions that are absolutized rather than the One. Both Karl Rahner, within Christianity, and Nagarjuna in Buddhism, may be seen to be in common on this point, although of course their understanding of the One is quite different. Both see the religions as imperfect instrumental forms by which the One may be apprehended. To this the Jewish prophets, Muhammad and Shankara would surely give assent. Much misunderstanding between religions can be avoided if the instrumental nature of the plurality of religious experience can be grasped. In the past the lack of such awareness and the absolutizing of the instrumental forms of religion has often been the cause of religious conflict.

Wilfred Cantwell Smith has recently argued that the problem with much scholarly study of religion, especially in the modern West, is the taking of religions to be fixed, unchanging forms.[7] This absolutizing and reifying of religion has missed the cumulative and developing nature of religious traditions—a major element in Troeltsch's analysis. Smith suggests that the various religions have never been distinct entities. In their instrumental forms, as the history of religion shows, the religions have constantly borrowed from and interacted with each other. Smith suggests that if scholars gave serious study to the Chinese concept of *san chiao* (the three traditions) and the Japanese concept of *Ryobu Shinto* (two-sided Shinto), a better understanding of this aspect of religious pluralism could be achieved.[8]

3. The Superimposition of Validating Criteria

Another common feature observed in the history of religions is the practice of responding to the challenge of pluralism by superimposing one's own validity criterion upon the other religions. If, for the Christian, Christ is the validating criterion, then true spirituality within any other religion is to be identified by the superimposition of Christ upon that religion—thus Rahner's "anonymous Christians" and Panikkar's "Unknown Christ of Hinduism." For Buddhadasa, the *dhamma* is the truth of all religions. For Islam, the Qur'an is the validating revelation against which all others must be tested. Just as the Jews have been elected by God to fulfill a certain role in history, so other religions are to be understood in terms of their particular election by Yahweh. And since, for the Hindu, all paths must lead to the one Brahman, so Buddha, Christ, Muhammad and Moses may be validated as avatars of Brahman. Fundamental to religious pluralism is the fact that commitment within each tradition is experienced as absolute and is universalized by superimposing it upon the others. The reasons for this may well be found in the psychological and philosophical limits of human nature. This possibility will be explored later. An important point to be noted here, however, is that the validation criteria adopted by each of the religions arose out of "the wrestle" of each with the challenge of pluralism. The validation of traditions came after contacts with others. The criteria of Christianity, for example, were formulated after contact with Greek philosophy and Gnosticism. As we see in the history of religions, this same process can be observed in each of the religions.

II. Religious Pluralism: Some Common Problems

Before moving on to dicuss the future of religions, some common dangers and difficulties in present-day religious pluralism should be briefly identified.

The Problem of Conversion

An obvious area of difficulty is the missionary activity which occurs when the superimposition of one's own criterion upon the other is followed by efforts to convert the other. It is part of our nature as human beings that we want to share our most treasured convictions with others. Often, as in the cases of Buddhism, Christianity and Islam, that tendency is reinforced by the teachings of the tradition. Difficulty ensues when this desire and direction to carry one's preaching or teaching to others is made militant or exclusive. Militant or exclusive approaches are today being severely questioned in terms of each tradition's own teaching. In addition, once good information about the other traditions is made available, as it now is, the resulting understanding usually produces a rethinking of the missionary philosophy and method. Examples of such a result can be seen in Islamic Sufism in India and modern-day Christian theology. Pluralism will always demand that we share our particular understanding of religion with one another. If done in sympathy and respect for the integrity of the other, such sharing, as past and present examples demonstrate, can result in spiritual growth and enrichment for all. In the open experience of other traditions the possibility for conversion always exists. But, as the history of pluralism within each tradition shows, the result is more often one of the strengthening and enrichment of one's own religion. The alternative of a closed-minded attacking of others has frequently produced both internal stagnation and interreligious conflict, often violent, of the sort that all religions would now see as a negation of spirituality.

The Divergence of Theistic and Non-Theistic Religions

In reflections upon the history of religions the difficulty of the divergence between the theistic religions and Buddhism and Advaita Vedanta Hinduism (Taoism and Confucianism can probably also be included here) has continually reappeared. This problem has caused scholars of religion no end of trouble, often tempting them to solve the difficulty by uncritically imposing the concept of God on Advaita Vedanta and Buddhism. John Hick is sometimes noted as a scholar engaging in just such a "solution."

Wilfred Cantwell Smith attempts a more honest resolution of the problem.[9] Employing his corporate self-consciousness approach, he tries to demonstrate that as a general symbol for the transcendent, the term "God" could be acceptable to Buddhist scholars. The Theravadin, imagines Smith, would agree that for purposes of general discussion the notion of *dhamma* could be fruitfully compared with the concept of God in the Western religions. Buddhists have held *dharma* as a transcendent truth, one which is beyond the capabilities of words, and yet immediate and lived. In Mahayana Buddhism, the Bodhisattva as a symbol of the transcendent may be a functionally parallel term to the theistic term 'God'. For the Advaita Vedantist, it may be Brahman symbolized as *sat* (pure being), *cit* (pure consciousness), and *ananda* (pure bliss). The Buddhists and monistic Hindus might well be prepared to admit that while conceptualizations across traditions may differ, the secondary status which they accord conceptualizations in any case allows them not to be overly disturbed by such difficulties. Taken on that secondary level, the concept of God might be accepted as a heuristic term in discussion across traditions. Smith does not suggest that we all simply agree to use the term 'God' and leave it at that. He strongly urges the necessity of learning each other's languages and thought forms. Only then will the vocabulary problem be soluble.[10]

As a contribution to the process that must go on while we are learning each other's languages, he offers the following suggestion as a possible basis for discussion between theists and nontheists: "by the term 'God' one means a truth-reality that explicitly transcends conception, but in so far as conceivable is that to which man's religious history has at its best been a response, human and in some sense inadequate."[11] Smith adds that in religious history he includes, in addition to Buddhism and Hinduism, the Western classical tradition, metaphysical-humanist-idealist, where transcendence has appeared as Truth, Beauty, Justice and the Good. In case someone were to assume that the provision of an encompassing description implies also that all religions are true, or equally true, Smith responds as follows:

> That would indeed be silly. I, of course, hold that not even one "religion" is *equally* true, abstractly, in all its instances

through history; rather, it becomes less or more true in the case of particular persons as it informs their lives and their groups and shapes and nurtures their faiths.... What I do urge is that the problem of religious truth is in principle not different but in practice much improved if one takes the whole of religion rather than a sector of it as the question's field.[12]

Although the history of religions would seem to generally support Smith's interpretation, there is one point on which we might find it necessary to differ. Smith strongly urges that "our understanding of each other's concepts be anchored in history, even for history-transcending and self-transcending concepts such as 'God'."[13] While this assertion will be acceptable to Judaism and Christianity, it would seem unacceptable when applied to Islam, Hinduism and Buddhism. While Judaism and Christianity explicitly experience God's truth in and through history, it seems most unlikely that the Muslim, Hindu or Buddhist can share this perception. While admitting that there is history in religion, that is, traditions do change through time, for them the truth is not "anchored" or revealed in that historical process, but in the reality that is behind or beyond it. As Smith urges, we must learn and respect each other's language and thought forms. In this instance his training as a modern Western historian has perhaps prevented him from following his own advice.

The Conflict between Religious Equality and Inequality

Yet another difficulty in contemporary religious pluralism is the conflict between constitutional statements of "equality" (e.g., in the United States and India) and religions which understand persons to be at different stages of spiritual realization and thus not equal (e.g., the law of *karma* in Hinduism and Buddhism). When such a conflict arises, as it now has in India, the requirement of equality may legally override the teachings and practices of a religion such as Hinduism and thereby violate religious freedom. Since constitutions calling for equality usually also enshrine the principle of religious freedom, a serious internal contradiction results. At this point, the politicians, the law-makers, usually throw up their hands and pass the problem on to the courts. Since the problem is not a legal one, but a conflict of views or presuppositions (e.g., egalitarian humanism versus the *karma* theory of Hinduism, in the case of India), it is really a classic pluralism type of problem. Here the experience and wisdom of religions could helpfully inform the modern humanist or secularist. The problem and principles of religious pluralism are in many ways parallel to those of present-day cultural problems.

The equality problem is only one of many occasioned by modern cultural and religious pluralism. For instance, Islam perceives itself as a state religion. Yet if it were to attempt to absorb or take over a nation such as the United States or Canada, which are constitutionally multicultural, it would be perceived as subversive. Again, religious and secular traditions and perceptions would clash. This fact requires that Islam, as it increasingly finds itself a minority in pluralistic host cultures, reinterpret its perception of itself as a state religion.

The Problem of Reactive Exclusivism

A threat to the creative contribution of pluralism to religion is that at times some members of religions react to the challenge of pluralism with a militant exclusivism (e.g., Christian or Islamic fundamentalism). Such a reaction is always to be regretted in that, as the history of religions suggests, it usually breeds spiritual stagnation and "religious violence," as the history of modern Iran demonstrates. As in a family, the accepting of differences in the context of mutual respect and appreciation can be a powerful catalyst for good. Egocentric narrow-mindedness is always destructive, and is the opposite of true religion in any tradition.

Having examined some of the factors—similar approaches and potential difficulties—evident in the current situation of religious pluralism, let us now turn to some suggestions for the future of theology and interreligious dialogue in the situation of religious pluralism.

III. Religious Pluralism and the Future of Theology

Within modern Western thinking it was Schleiermacher who inaugurated a "bottom–up" approach to religion. This had the effect of drawing attention to the universal nature of religious experience in its many different traditions—thus the relativizing approach of Ernst Troeltsch. In addition to turning attention away from metaphysics, rationalism or revelation (top–down approaches), the focus on the humanity of religion has had the effect of highlighting some of the limitations in human nature that must be taken seriously in all future religion.

Future Theology and the Limits Inherent in Pluralism

For the purposes of this discussion, let us give the term theology a broad, general meaning, namely, religious knowledge or truth in all of its pluralistic forms. Although this may seem uncomfortable for a Buddhist or monistic Hindu, we would ask them to agree to such a heuristic interpretation for purposes of our current discussion. The question to be examined is: "What are the limits to be respected in all future theologizing?" Within the Christian religion Karl Rahner has discussed this at length. He demonstrates that pluralism requires a shift from the scholastic method of the past to a new approach as yet not fully grasped. But as a first step toward future theology, some important limitations can be stated—limitations which will apply to future thinkers in any religion.

Theology, says Rahner, can no longer follow the simplistic pattern of the past where the problem of pluralism was overcome by application of the principle of non-contradiction. When two theological positions were seen to be contradictory alternatives, then, according to the principle of non-contradiction, since both could not be right at the same time, a decision could be taken one way or the other as to which was the right one. In this way the pluralism or the contradiction would be overcome. This was the pattern which typified the scholastic theology of the past. It is a pattern which can no longer serve in the face of the challenge presented by the encounter of religions. As Rahner recognizes, theology finds itself in a new situation:

> The pluralism of which we are speaking here, rather, consists precisely in the fact that it is quite impossible to reduce the theologies and their representative theses to a simple logical alternative in this manner, in the fact that they exist side by side with one another as disparate and mutually incommensurable.[14]

In the above quotation Rahner is speaking of the pluralism that he finds currently to be the case within Christian theology alone. It is a pluralism which is insurmountable because no common basis can be found between the various theological schools upon which to arrive at a comparative understanding and logical judgment between alternatives. If Christians find this to be the case between the various theologies put forth within Christianity itself, how much more will such a difficulty obtain when the competing claims of the various religions are considered?

The inescapable pluralism of all future theology is seen to have two limiting dimensions. First, there is the fact that rival viewpoints may adopt starting points so different that little or no common intellectual ground can really be established. And without the basis of this common ground, individual propositions cannot be discussed in such a way as to arrive at a positive "right" or "wrong" judgment. Although the two partners in the dialogue may anticipate similarities and differences in their positions, the lack of a common ground, says Rahner, "means that the representatives of the different schools cannot achieve, even indirectly, a position in which they can explain to one another consciously and unambiguously in what precisely the difference between their respective intellectual outlooks consists."[15] Here Rahner is pointing to the experience which he has, and he thinks others have, when one's partner in theological dialogue constantly proceeds from different starting points than one's own, uses terms differently, and assumes points as established which are alien to one's own thinking. This results in no conclusion being reached and the discussion being broken off for lack of time or other reasons which make it impossible to continue. In any case the lack of a common intellectual basis, preventing the reaching of conclusions, is a limit which necessitates pluralism in theology.

A second limiting dimension which Rahner identifies as necessitating theological pluralism has to do with the finite nature of the human mind. All the various theological positions and full knowledge of the various world religions can no longer be mastered by any one mind. Even if a single world civilization or religion were to emerge, says Rahner, there would still be interior differences which would manifest an increasing pluralism of theologies with respect to "their methods, their structural developments, their outlooks, their terminologies, and the practical trends to which they give rise. These differences will be so great that as theologies it will be quite impossible for them to be covered by, or subumed under any one single homogeneous theology."[16] This means, then, that there cannot be any *one* theology, even when one's gaze is restricted to a particular religion. If, by reason of the limited capacity of the human mind, dogmatic judgments cannot be made within one religion, how much more must that be the case when theological reflection takes place within the larger context of the many religions. Within the context of world religions theological pluralism is the rule.

Both of these limitations will have to be taken seriously by scholars functioning within a particular tradition or within the context of world religions. Since the time of Nagarjuna[17] in the East and Immanuel Kant[18] in the West, the intellectual limits of the human mind have been known, if not always respected. But perhaps more important for theologizing in a pluralistic context will be the first limitation noted above—the lack of a common intellectual basis upon which dialogue or debate may be conducted. A theologian of one of the Western religions, that is, Judaism, Christianity or Islam, will quickly encounter this difficulty if he or she begins to think through the concept of creation with a Hindu or the notion of God with a Buddhist. A common intellectual ground just does not seem to exist. Understanding, albeit partial and blurred, seems to come only when one suspends or brackets one's own viewpoint and attempts to adopt the assumptions of the other and "see" the universe through those alien concepts.

But here too certain psychological limits arise and must be taken seriously by the theologian. In any intellectual exercise in which the theologian attempts to "see" with the concepts of another religion, the psychological dynamics of one's own mind will never allow one to be completely objective or neutral in one's perceptions. The first impulse will be to identify similarities between the position of the other and one's own. Usually this signals an act of intellectual reductionism, or what Freud termed *projection*.[19] Instead of a real similarity having been identified the theologian has simply indulged in the self-protective mechanism of saying, "Oh yes, I see what you mean by that; it is exactly the same as I mean by this." One projects one's own viewpoint onto the person of the other religion and then claims to discover that it is the same as one's own. Of course, this is very comforting in several ways. It suggests that there is only one truth after all, that one has it (probably in full*er* or full*est* measure, and thus implicitly or explicitly claims superiority for one's own view), and therefore no change is required. A making of what is more likely the true discovery, namely, that real difference does exist, naturally produces emotional insecurity and doubt about whether one's theological position is absolute.

This universal human characteristic of ego-attachment to one's own position has been given much attention by Nagarjuna and other Madhyamika Buddhists. They approached the problem as follows. Since human beings are by nature ego-attached to their own view or theological position, no amount of counterarguing from an opposed position will have any effect. The theologian in question will simply reinterpret an objection or counterposition in such a way as to fit his or her own system. In other words, by the mechanism of projection one will attempt to force the other off their presuppositions and onto one's own. And since the other will be attempting to do the same (both are ego-attached to their positions and cognitively cannot let go), an endless and unhelpful debate will ensue. With this psychological insight in hand the model developed by the Madhyamika Buddhists for theological debate was simple and devastating. The Madhyamika entered the debate with no theological position of their own. Their aim was so completely to understand the position of their opponent that they would be able to find the internal inconsistencies inevitably present in every theological system and then, by *reductio ad absurdum*, bring the whole thing crashing down around the ears of their opponent. To be defeated by one's own system brings on a severe psychological shock, one which might even convince the theologian to give up theologizing for good. Once a theologian puts down the pen and lets go of the favorite concepts, the way is cleared or emptied of intellectual obstacles so that one could finally "see" reality as a pure perception and live one's life appropriately.

The Madhyamika and Freudian analyses both make clear that any attempt to absolutely conceptualize reality is inevitably tied to the finite limitation of one's cognitive processes and the self-centered distorting emotions attached thereto.

When the above limitations are taken seriously and applied to current theological models, a helpful critique results. For the Christian, for example, it means that there is no longer any ground upon which a theologian can make absolute claims for a particular theological position. For example, Hans Kung's argument that one should be a Christian because Jesus of Nazareth is "ultimately decisive, definitive, and archetypal for man's relations with God, with his fellow man, with society"[20] is found to violate the limits of theologizing on at least two counts. The first problem, of course, is that Kung is making the very kind of absolute claim to knowledge that the finite limits of the human mind rule out of court. Second, as Paul Knitter has pointed out in his careful assessment of Kung's argument, it is based on a badly blurred view of other religions.[21] In spite of Kung's warning to other theologians that they must not reach theological conclusions without a clear knowledge of the other world religions, Knitter's analysis shows Kung's own understanding to have been seriously distorted by the basic a priori of his thinking, namely, that Christ is the final norm for all religions.[22] Kung has engaged in Freudian projections (seeing Christ as the unknown fulfillment of all other religions) and intellectual reductionism (incorrect and simplistic understandings of other religions, so as to fit them into his own categories).

Kung's approach is that of a Christocentric theologian. Whereas all religions are recognized in varying degrees to be particular manifestations of God, Christianity is seen as the only religion which fully or most fully manifests God and therefore must serve as the criterion for all others. Theological approaches which presuppose a universal *logos* as foundational for all religions and then identify the *logos* as Christ are simply a variation on the same theme and suffer from the same failings of psychological projection and intellectual reductionism. If, for example, a Jew were to be told that the basis of Judaism was the *logos* of which Jesus Christ was the criterion manifestation, the response to such a theology would likely be that the theologian in question had never really understood the Jewish religion and indeed was taking a Christianized version of Judaism to be real Judaism. Christians frequently have the same sort of response when told by a Hindu that Christianity is fully encompassed within Hinduism as yet another particular manifestation of the one Brahman. It is not surprising that the Christian finds it difficult to recognize Christian belief and practice in such a Hinduized version of Christianity. In all of these examples theological limitations have not been respected and the result proves itself to be unacceptable when seen in the context of religious pluralism.

Another approach developing from the modern humanistic emphasis resolves the problem by moving in the opposite direction. It attempts to overcome the difficulty by seeing Christianity along with the other world religions as simply various manifestations of one common humanity. This is the method frequently taken by theologians who have been seduced by the psychologists, sociologists or historians of religion. It is also a reductionism, but this time in the opposite direction. Instead of seeing the various religions has merely particular manifestations of the one divine, this solution reduces the transcendent experiences of the various religions to being no more than particular expressions of a common humanity. In the first, the human diversity of religious experience is reduced to a common transcendent reality; in the second, the plural experiences of the transcendent are reduced to a common human experience.

The implications of this discussion would seem to be that the Madhyamika Buddhists are right. When the limitations on theologizing are taken seriously, all future theologizing in the sense of establishing ultimate claims to knowledge must cease. Is the correct vision for the future one in which thousands of theologians of the various religions all around the world simultaneously put down their pens? What then—silence? While the Madhyamika Buddhist might approve, as well as modern sceptics and positivists for different reasons, silence must be rejected as the correct vision for the future of theology and religions.

The Future of Religions in Dialogue

The inherent desire to conceptualize and share religious experience is simply too deeply ingrained in human nature to render silence an acceptable answer. In fact the Madhyamikas have been far from silent. To be precise their prescription of silence was only intended to apply to claims of *absolute* knowledge. As long as that limitation is honored then discussion of any sort, including theological discussion, could take place. As a first step, then, let us attempt to indicate some of the presuppositions upon which the interreligious dialogue of the future should be grounded. These presuppositions are drawn inductively from our prior analysis of the present situation in religious pluralism:

1. That in all religions there is experience of a reality that transcends human conception.

2. That that reality is conceived in a plurality of ways both within and between religions, and that the recognition of plurality is necessary both to safeguard religious freedom and to respect human limitations.

3. That the pluralistic forms of religion are instrumental in function.

4. That due to our finite limitations and our simultaneous need for commitment to a particular experience of transcendent reality, therefore our particular experience, though limited, will function in an absolute sense as the validating criterion for our own personal religious experience.

5. That the Buddha's teaching of critical tolerance and moral compassion always be observed.

6. That through self-critical dialogue we penetrate even further into our own particular experience of transcendent reality, and possibly also into the transcendent reality of others.

Let us consider each of these in more detail.

1. The first presupposition simply states the recognition found in each of the major religions, namely, that God, Brahman or *Dhamma* is a transcendent reality over and above the mundane, which cannot be fully conceptualized. It does not judge as to whether transcendent reality is the same or different across religions. Such a judgment would be absolute and would exceed the limits of human knowledge. It is therefore best left to God, Brahman or *Dhamma*. The statement does, however, distinguish dialogue as religious; that is, although acceptable to all religions, it is not a statement the humanist or materialist could accept. This distinction would seem to be challenged by Wilfred Cantwell Smith, who argues for the inclusion of the humanist, although he restricts inclusion to the rational humanist.[23] Certainly the merits of a dialogue involving all the possible pluralities within the global community is deserving of careful study. But, even if such a global dialogue were deemed advisable, there would still be a need for a separate caucus composed of those who could in some sense share an experience of transcendent reality.

2. The second presupposition arises from the limitations on theologizing discussed above, and the fact of religious pluralism witnessed in the history of religions. It safeguards against claims of absolutism of a kind that would cause religious dialogue to self-destruct. It also safeguards religious freedom.

3. The third presupposition, following from the second, gives importance to the instrumental function of religious forms through which religious experience takes place, namely, that the revelations, doctrines and spiritual disciplines of the many religions are the means by which transcendent reality is reached. By implication the plurality of instrumental forms also points up the variety of spiritual dispositions in persons, a fact which the religious absolutisms of the past have, to their detriment, often ignored.

4. The fourth presupposition is perhaps the most important and the most difficult. On the surface it might appear to conflict with presupposition 2, which safeguards the plurality of religions. But the absolutism ruled out in presupposition 2 is the sort that would impose the experience of one's own religious commitment upon all others as ultimate truth. By contrast the term absolute in the fourth supposition is used simply to describe the felt nature of commitment to the transcendent through a particular personal experience of religion. It is a recognition that deep religious commitment is necessarily felt as absolute, and as such functions as the validating criterion for all of one's personal experience. This, however, does not impose it on others or rule out the recognition that in other persons there is

a similar absolute commitment to a particular experience, which (presupposition 2) will be different from one's own. As Jaspers correctly observes:

> The language of transcendence, then, is spoken only in particular languages. . . . In such . . . the truth which is heard is absolutely true, yet the speaking and hearing is such that it cannot be taken as universally or normatively true, but must admit the possibility of other, even of opposed truths.[24]

Thus, one is able to honor one's own commitment as absolute and at the same time respect the different absolute commitments of others. In this way the limitations outlined above are respected, yet the necessity for absolute religious commitment to a particular religion is allowed. In a dialogue situation it would mean the preservation of our differences in dignity and mutual respect.

5. The fifth presupposition describes the character of mutual respect as one of critical tolerance and moral compassion. Standing secure in our difference we are encouraged to constructively criticize and so learn from one another. Our criticism is to be constructive, tolerant and undergirded by a moral compassion toward others. In such an atmosphere pluralism provides the opportunity for spiritual self-judgment and growth. It suggests that all theologizing activity should, as it were, be overheard by theologians of the other religions. The resultant theology would be more honest and humble than we have often been accustomed to in the past.[25]

6. The sixth presupposition states that spiritual growth arises not from religious isolationism or exclusivism, but rather in the context of religious pluralism. The history of each major religion demonstrates that in all cases the creative periods were those marked by the challenge of pluralism. It also squares with the experience of those now seriously engaged in dialogue, namely, that the result is an enriching and deepening of one's own religious experience. Whether such spiritual deepening can reach a sense of a shared experience of transcendence or, as Tillich puts it, a point where particularity breaks through to spiritual freedom and to a vision of the spiritual presence in other expressions—that possibility remains for future dialogue to explore.

A basic prerequisite for such future dialogue is that all participants have good information about each other's religions. This is probably the single biggest obstacle to the success of religious dialogue. The majority of people today are illiterate of their own religion as well as the religions of others. In this regard the academic discipline of religious studies has a major role to play if future dialogue is to succeed. Intellectual knowledge of the facts of all religions is needed, but alone that will not be sufficient. We will not be able to empathize with the sense of transcendent reality that the forms of each religion seek to convey if only surface or intellectual knowledge is all that is achieved. True empathy and understanding requires that we learn each other's languages, for therein lie the important nuances of transcendent experience that are often lost in translation. Thus, the educational prerequisite for future dialogue is a stiff and serious one, requiring dedication and effort from all who would partake.

In the past many efforts at dialogue have failed because this prerequisite has not been observed. Groups of well-meaning Jews, Christians, Muslims, Hindus and Buddhists have held polite and gracious gatherings and returned home without having significantly entered into each other's thought forms. Although such meetings have produced a pious respect for others as fine religious persons, they have not generated the deep self-criticism and spiritual renewal (presupposition 6) which future dialogue must achieve. If serious study, including knowledge of each other's languages, is to be obtained, it is here that religious studies departments have an important and timely contribution to make. In Canada, the United States, Australia, England and Europe, universities have good offerings of this kind. But in India a serious weakness exists. While the opportunity is well-provided for the serious study of Eastern religions, including Sanskrit, Tibetan and Chinese languages, the same cannot be said for opportunities to study Western religions and the languages of Hebrew, Greek and Arabic. Until this fundamental deficiency is corrected, Indian participants will be hampered through the lack of prerequisite requirements for effective dialogue. The establishing of religious studies departments in which equal opportunity is provided for the study of all major religions and languages is an urgent need in Indian universities. Let us go one step further and hope that in the future seminaries throughout the world would also see this as a necesssary prerequisite for theologizing.

In his book, *Towards a World Theology*, Wilfred Cantwell Smith gives careful attention to the importance of language in future religious dialogue. While agreeing that knowledge of each other's languages is essential, he takes the further step of suggesting the need for some common operational or generic terms in which communication across religions can take place. He proposes the construction of conceptual categories to facilitate dialogue, and attempts a beginning by redefining the terms 'faith', 'salvation', 'theology' and 'God'.[26] Now while we have in this present discussion already made similar moves to facilitate discussion (e.g., our general use of 'theology' above), there is a very real danger in such an approach. Knowing the penchant of scholars to create their own cognitive universe through the construction of generic terms, there is a very real danger that the construction of such categories ends up as a metalanguage, which is yet one more thought form to add to those already existing. Of course, this need not happen if scholars are careful not to give ontological status to their descriptive categories. The best safeguard against such a danger would be to let the various religions speak in their own languages and thought forms as much as possible. If in the courses of dialogue useful and acceptable operational terms arise, as they undoubtedly will, then the process of communication will be aided. But for scholars to set out self-consciously to construct the generic forms for future dialogue (as Smith seems to propose) is dangerous and ill-advised.

The above presuppositions and prerequisites are but a beginning attempt to formulate the requirements for future dialogue. As such they are necessarily sketchy, incomplete and in places probably misconceived. But they represent one attempt to reflect self-critically on the experience of the past, and on that basis to formulate some guidelines for dialogue. For in such dialogue lies the future of religions.

PART II

Criteria of Cross-Cultural Truth in Religion

4

Truth, Criteria and Dialogue between Religions

Ninian Smart

I. Possible Positions

1. *Only within a system can that system be understood. Given that a person cannot be committed to more than one system, there can be no way of evaluating one religion over against another.* This is one interpretation of Wittgensteinian fideism.

There are several objections to this position:

a) Good work in anthropology and the history of religions abounds. For example: *Nuer Religion*; Mircea Eliade on yoga; Howard Smith's *Confucius*; Gombrich on Sri Lanka; and so on. Further there are sensitive dialogical approaches. For example: John Taylor on African religion; Kenneth Cragg's *Sandals at the Mosque*; and so on.

b) The notion of understanding is degree-bound—poor, good, better, shallow, profound, and so forth. This first thesis supposes it to be "all or nothing at all" across system boundaries, even if it may allow degrees of understanding within a system.

2. *There is no neutral arena in which competing truth-claims could be settled. Each religious system defines a total worldview into which other systems are somehow fitted and in accord with which they are evaluated.*

Again, there are several objections to this position.

a) Religious systems in fact need to respond to changes in "secular" knowledge and social desiderata. These can become pointers to criteria. For example, does faith F fit better or worse than faith G with modern science and human needs in a period of modernization and development?

b) If faith F presents C as a criterion of truth, then faith T may turn out to do well or badly by that criterion. If well, then that is a ground for respecting criterion D put forward by T, and so something like an inter-system consensus about criteria cannot be ruled out.

c) If the second thesis is correct, then the choice of a worldview would be arbitrary, and the notion of the truth of a worldview would evaporate. (This would also seem to be a consequence of the first thesis.)

3. *There is no **absolutely** neutral arena.*

This appears to be the truth contained in the second thesis, and may be part of what the first thesis was trying, ineptly, to say. The reason partly has to do with *weight*. Thus faith F and faith G may agree that the historicity of certain claims is a test of the truth of a faith, but it may be very lightly regarded by F and heavily emphasized by G. Again, the systems are only thinly deductive, so that confirmation of one element does not spread deductively to other elements. For this reason I used the expression "doctrinal schemes," not systems, in *Reasons and Faiths*.

4. *Systems can be verified or falsified by appeal to public and empirical facts.*

There are objections to this thesis as well.

a) Maybe aspects of a system could be verified or falsified, but most systems are schemes with organic flexibility. Public facts might make a faith more or less plausible, but one could scarcely speak of verification, and so on.

b) Some important evidence, for example, religious experiences, is not easily made public, and are themselves weighed by interpretations deriving from within the system. Thus at most it could be said:

5. *Public facts can make a system more or less plausible, as can also the "less public" facts.*

Often the matter of plausibility is rather indirect. Thus the discovery of intelligent life on other worlds would make traditional Christianity uneasy. How many Christs do you have to have, and then about uniqueness and so on? Likewise with historical scepticism regarding allegedly alleged facts in the New Testament.

6. *Faith transcends the religious systems, and is a personal relationship.* This is a thesis put forward in differing forms by Wilfred Cantwell Smith and Rudolf Bultmann.

Here, too, there are objections.

a) Faith in what? If an unknown X, then all religions point to the same (empty) truth. But that does not settle whether or not one should face Mecca when praying, and so on.

b) If the faith is specified, then that specification will arise through a system, and the thesis only transfers the question to a different level. (I have argued this point at some length in my *The Yogi and the Devotee*.)

7. *All religions express and point to the same truth, so the only mistake is false exclusivism.*

There are objections to this position as well:

a) Essentially it is a variant on thesis six, but Cantwell Smith and existentialist theology tend to be more personalistic, while the Indian neo-Vedanta and Aldous Huxley's perennial philosophy are more impersonalistic and *atman*-oriented.

b) It cannot be shown than even the "experts," that is, saintly and insightful persons in different systems, agree on thesis seven, or if they did, on what the content of the "same truth" would be. Of course faiths do have *some* insights in common.

These objections seem to leave only the third and fifth theses. It might now be useful to look at those factors which would plausibilify (or the reverse) one system over against another. One may look at them in terms of various "appeals" that can be made.

II. Criteria of Truth

1. *The appeal to religious experiences* (prophetic, mystical, and so forth).

Naturally these tend to occur within a worldview, and so are colored by interpretation, perhaps inevitably. So the question of the relation between experience and interpretation becomes highly important.

Also there is the question of typology, that is, about how we classify the varieties of religious experience, and whether type T would establish something different from type U. This is likely, since one can view the varieties of doctrinal schemes as up to a point consequent upon differences in the chemical combinations, so to speak, of experiences.

But there is no doubt that this first criterion is potent and well-recognized in religions. Consider Paul's conversion, the revelations of Muhammad or the Enlightenment of the Buddha.

2. *The appeal to history.*

Naturally mere history can be relevant to the transcendent but cannot by itself clinch transcendental claims. It is the "mythic" or interpretative use of history that is vital to a faith. Still, negatively and positively, mere history can be important. If we knew nothing of Jesus, or knew that he was a murderer, it would make Christianity less plausible.

3. *The appeal to charismatic authority* (for example, a prophet).

Criteria of charisma must exist, if obscure, for we can recognize those who lack it.

4. *The appeal of ethical fruits.*

This is a complex criterion for, as with the first criterion, system S may prize apples and system T oranges. Still, barren trees are observable as well as inconsistencies. If system S preaches love, but seems practically more interested in respectable rectitude, it is a problem for it.

5. *The appeal of "modernity."*

In other words, does a faith fit with modern knowledge? This kind of appeal, on behalf of Buddhism, for instance, is made effectively by K. N. Jayatilleke in his *The Message of the Buddha*.

6. *The appeal to psychological relevance.*

In other words, does a faith help people in their daily lives? This can be extended in a social and political direction.

There are doubtless various other criteria. For example, the aesthetic properties of a religion might be relevant, other things being equal.

In conclusion, undoubtedly there are criteria, but few knockdown arguments. The same applies to ideology. Thus, epistemologically, certainty in religion is elusive, to say the least. What then of religious certitude? Often the less certain a position, publicly, the more passionate the claims to its certain truth. The interplay of religions thus has a certain threatening character. But ideals are so often threatened by realities, and it is necessary for each religion to come to terms with the fascinatingly plural religious and ideological world in which it finds itself.

5

Doctrinal Schemes, Metaphysics and Propositional Truth

◻

William J. Wainwright

I find myself in almost complete agreement with the critical remarks made by Ninan Smart in the first part of his essay "Truth, Criteria and Dialogue between Religions." I also believe that the criteria cited in the second part of his essay are relevant to the assessment of religious systems. My own comments are designed to expose a few faulty arguments put forward by some on this subject and to call attention to other criteria which can, I believe, be used to assess the truth of doctrinal schemes.

I

In this section I propose to consider arguments which have been introduced to support a set of related claims: (1) that oppositions between religious beliefs are only apparent, (2) that propositional truth is relatively unimportant in religious contexts and (3) that it is inappropriate to use the category of propositional truth in religious contexts or when evaluating religious doctrines. The arguments which I shall consider are not the only ones which have been offered, but they are the ones which are most germane to my purpose. I shall attempt to show that they are either unsound or inconclusive.

1. It is sometimes argued that because systems of religious doctrine provide different approaches to a single reality, conflicts between systems are only apparent.

This argument is open to the following objection. There are three alternatives.

a) We cannot discriminate between different approaches, that is, we cannot evaluate them as better or worse, or as more or less true or accurate or correct.

b) We can discriminate between approaches but only on the basis of "subjective" factors. A subject may, for instance, choose an approach because of its inherent attractiveness, or because of its ability to satisfy one's needs, or because one finds that one can do no other. (So a man may choose a wife because he is attracted to her, or because she fulfills needs which he has, or because he cannot help but do so.)

c) Objective discriminations can be made between different approaches.

a) If we cannot discriminate between systems of religious doctrines, then no discriminations can be made between, for example, beliefs associated with Theravada Buddhism and beliefs associated with cargo cults. I would also point out that the sort of view which we are considering typically includes a characterization of religious reality which Christians, Jews, Buddhists, and so on, approach in their different ways. This characterization itself appears to be a religious doctrine. If we cannot discriminate between religious doctrines, then there is no reason to prefer this characterization to the ones provided by Barthian Christianity or Norse mythology.

b) Consider the second alternative. I would suggest that the acceptance of this alternative precludes one from adopting certain approaches. It is not clear to me, for example, that one can consciously choose some of the traditional versions of Christianity on the basis of subjective factors. To adopt Roman Catholicism simply because one is attracted to it, or finds it satisfying, or because one cannot help oneself, and not because God has, through the church, demanded a certain response, is not really to accept Roman Catholicism at all. To be a Roman Catholic is not simply to believe, do and feel certain things, but to believe, do and feel them *for certain reasons*. Therefore, if one believes, does and feels these things for other reasons, one has not really adopted Roman Catholicism. Again, if the second alternative is the correct one, then quite different choices are equally legitimate if they are attractive to, or satisfy those who make those choices, or if those who make them find that they can do no other. It is not clear to me that this admission is compatible with the kind of commitment which has been made in, for instance, traditional Roman Catholicism.

c) If objective discriminations can be made between approaches, that is, if some doctrinal schemes are objectively more adequate than others, then the possibility of conflict reemerges. Conflicts will occur if people disagree (as they in fact do) as to which approach provides the most adequate account of the "object" of religious attitudes.

2. It is sometimes said that there are kinds of truth which are more important than propositional truth. Truth is sometimes authenticity or genuineness, or the True may be equated with the Real. In certain contexts these kinds of truth are more significant than propositional truth.

I would agree that "truth" can be used in these senses. Whether truth as authenticity or reality are more important than propositional truth is, however, a moot question. One must ask, "important for whom, in what contexts and for what purposes?" What I wish to argue is that, because these other kinds of truth presuppose propositional truth, we cannot evade the question of propositional truth by appealing to truth as authenticity or to truth as reality.

a) It does, I think, make sense to say that God (Brahman, Nirvana) alone is fully real. We can, for instance, distinguish levels of reality. Items on level m are more real than items on level n if and only if (roughly) all items at level n depend for their being upon items at level m (or at some level higher than m), but no items at level m depend for their reality upon items at level n (or at some level lower than n). In this sense dreams are less real than dreamers. Fictional characters are less real than their authors and the world of contingent being is less real than the God who calls it into being.[1] Again, the unreal may be identified with the incoherent, and the fully real with that which is free from incoherence (either because it is coherent or because it is neither coherent nor incoherent). Thus, one might argue that the world of nature is unreal because all views which try to grasp it ultimately prove to be incoherent (Madhyamika, F. H. Bradley), and/or that unitary consciousness is fully real becauses it is free from duality and can, therefore, be neither coherent nor incoherent (Walter Stace).

I would suggest that statements like "God alone is fully real" or "the Brahman alone is real" either (i) have no determinate sense, or (ii) merely express our attitudes towards, and evaluation of, God or the Brahman (our conviction that God or the Brahman is better or more significant or more wonderful than anything else), or (iii) can be explicated by (sets of) propositions in the manner suggested.

The first two alternatives are unacceptable. Statements about God and Brahman are meaningful. Furthermore, these statements do more than merely express our attitudes towards, and appraisal of, God or the Brahman. Attitudes towards and evaluations of x presuppose certain beliefs about x. When one adopts an attitude towards x or evaluates x, one commits oneself to the appropriateness of those attitudes and evaluations. Because the appropriateness of an attitude or evalution is partly determined by the nature of the object of that attitude or evaluation, this commitment involves a commitment to the truth of certain beliefs about x. It follows that those who make the above statements about God or the Brahman are committed to propositions about God or the Brahman and that they are, therefore, justified in making them only if those propositions are true.

b) "Truth" can be legitimately used in the sense of authenticity or genuineness. Essential to truth in this sense is the idea of a standard, or model, or paradigm or exemplar to which the authentic or genuine "object" conforms. To use "truth" in this sense is, then, to be committed to certain standards. Now one's adherence to these standards either has an objective warrant or it does not. If it does not have an objective warrant, the use of "true" is inappropriate. We cannot speak of genuine coins if there is no generally accepted and institutionally authorized system of coinage. It is misleading to say that the life of a Christian is true or authentic if the adoption of Christian models is only a matter of taste. If, on the other hand, these standards are objectively warranted, then some sort of justification or backing for them is in order. This justification or backing will normally include propositions. (In religious contexts, these propositions will typically be propositions which articulate a worldview and/or describe the human condition.)

In short, I would suggest that the concept of propositional truth is inextricably bound up with other concepts of truth and that, therefore, one must either abandon the concept of truth altogether or address oneself to questions of propositional truth.

3. Consider the following argument:

a) Objective truth claims (i.e., claims to the effect that one doctrinal scheme is more nearly correct than others) are in order only if there are standards which are independent of any particular system, in terms of which the truth or falsity of these claims can be assessed.

b) There are no standards of this sort. Therefore,

c) Objective truth claims are not in order.

This argument is valid and its first premiss is plausible. Its second premiss cannot be dismissed out of hand. Nevertheless, I would suggest that it is much more difficult to establish than is sometimes supposed.

a) In the first place, it is difficult to determine the degree to which standards of truth and rationality actually vary from tradition to tradition. Winch has, for example, argued[2] that in spite of the fact that the magical practices of the Azande appear to be irrational when judged from the standpoint of Western scientific culture, they enable the Azande to come to terms with the inevitable contingencies of human existence and, therefore, have their own kind of rationality. However, as John Watt points out,[3] the criterion to which Winch appeals in order to show that Azande practices are rational, namely, that is reasonable to do what is necessary in order to secure such important goods as peace and resignation in the face of life's contingencies, is not a criterion peculiar to the Azande, but is instead "a general norm of rational action."

Disagreements concerning the relative merits of specific and concrete standards, for example, that a certain kind of oracle yields accurate information, may conceal substantial agreement at more general, and abstract levels. If we are to determine the extent of disagreement, we must be provided with detailed accounts of the patterns of reasoning employed in the different religious traditions. These accounts must not only describe what is said and done; they must also bring out concealed assumptions, hidden presuppositions, unexpressed implications, and so on. For example, behind the appeal to the words of a particular scripture, person or group of persons may lie certain general assumptions about authority—for instance, that if one is not directly acquainted with certain facts, then it is reasonable to accept the report of those who are directly acquainted with them; that words which have a certain causal origin (God, Brahman) must be true or appropriate; or that sanctity of life authenticates doctrines. Or behind the appeal to certain kinds of praeternatural experiences may lie the assumption that experiences of the type in question are cognitive, and that it is reasonable to base beliefs on cognitive experiences. What is required is logical analysis, not mere description. Few have addressed themselves to this task (Bochenski, Christian and Smart are notable exceptions), but until it is completed any estimate concerning the degree of disagreement is very premature.

b) Some of the arguments which have been employed to show that substantive divergence exists are totally unconvincing. For example, the occurence of statements of the form "*p* and not-*p*" has been taken to show that a particular tradition rejects the law of contradiction. It, of course, does nothing of the kind. In order to show that a tradition rejects the law of contradiction, one would have to show (i) that both "*p*" and "not-*p*" are being construed literally, (ii) that "*p* and not-*p*" is not being used to deny that a certain type of predicate applies (cf. "God neither exists nor does not exist", where "*x* exists" = "*x* is spatiotemporally located," and "*x* does not exist" = "*x* is not spatiotemporally located, but would be spatiotemporally located if it were real," and the sentence is used to make the point that neither predicate is logically appropriate), and (iii) that the tradition consistently ignores the principle. (Even those who accept the principle occasionally contradict themselves. People are not always rational.)

c) Even if different traditions employ different standards of truth and rationality, it does not follow that there are no universally valid standards in terms of which the doctrines and arguments of those traditions can be assessed. From the fact that beliefs about values vary from culture to culture, it does not follow the values vary from culture to culture. Similarly, from the fact (if it is a fact) that beliefs about what is true or rational vary from tradition to tradition, it does not follow that what is true or rational varies from tradition to tradition. That a standard is not employed in a given tradition does not entail that it should not be applied to (within) that tradition, or that arguments and doctrines within that tradition ought not to conform to it.

Finally, let me point out that if the argument which we are considering is sound, then anything goes and there can be no (rational) grounds for rejecting the most intolerant, dogmatic or silly position. Conceptual relativists and ethical relativists are in a similar position. Ethical relativism is sometimes offered as a ground for tolerance (Ruth Benedict), but a consistent ethical relativist has no reason to condemn intolerance. Similarly, a consistent conceptual relativist has no (rational) grounds upon which to base a condemnation of (any sort of) absolutism.

II

Religious doctrines may be backed by appealing to the pronouncements of an authoritative book, person or group of persons; by appealing to cultic practice[4]; and by appealing to religious experience. I do not think that these appeals are always illegitimate. Nevertheless, they are all, except for the last, useless in interreligious contexts.[5] Are there, then, other criteria which are relevant to the assessment of religious doctrines?

I believe that Basil Mitchell is correct when he says that "in its intellectual aspect, traditional Christian theism may be regarded as a worldview or metaphysical system."[6] I am strongly inclined to belive that at least some of the doctrinal schemes which are incorporated in other religious traditions can also be regarded as worldviews or metaphysical systems.[7] Although I cannot prove this thesis, I would like to adduce three considerations which point to its truth.

1. Christian doctrines can be more or less adequately expressed in the concepts and categories of, say, Aristotelian, Platonic, Cartesian or Heideggerian metaphysics. Again, Eliot Deutsch has "reconstructed" Advaita Vedanta, detaching it from its traditional setting.[8] The fact that Christian doctrines can and have been expressed in metaphysical terms and that Advaita lends itself to a reconstruction of this sort *suggests* that Christianity and Advaita are at least implicitly metaphysical.

2. William Christian has pointed out that "a course of action recommendation is acceptable without absurdity only if the course of action can be carried out."[9] I would call attention to the fact that certain relevant courses of action can be carried out only if certain doctrinal statements are true. One cannot successfully pursue a path which leads to a recognition of one's identity with Brahman if Brahman is unreal. One cannot order one's life in conformity with God's will if God does not exist. Most philosophers would classify "God exists" and "Brahman alone is fully real" as metaphysical statements.

3. Some religious doctrines appear to be incompatible with certain metaphysical views. Thus, traditional Christian theism appears to be incompatible with naturalism, Spinoza's pantheism and McTaggart's idealistic pluralism. If some religious doctrines actually do

conflict with certain metaphysical claims, then (*a*) they are at least partly metaphysical in character, and (*b*) they are at least partly susceptible to evaluation by metaphysical criteria.

The last point is the one I wish to pursue. If doctrinal schemes are, at least in part, metaphysical schemes, then perhaps interreligious disputes can be adjudicated by appealing to the criteria which are used to evaluate metaphysical systems.

What are these criteria? Consider the following.

1. An adequate metaphysical system must be consistent and free from logical error.

2. A metaphysical system is inadequate if it is self-stultifying.[10] A worldview is self-stultifying if its assertion implies that it cannot be known to be true. For example, any metaphysical system which denies the possibility of metaphysical knowledge is self-stultifying. (Positivism may be self-stultifying in this sense.) A view is self-stultifying if its assertion denies its own truth conditions. For example, any view which asserts that all views are false is self-stultifying. Views are self-stultifying when the explanations which they incorporate adduce the very sort of thing which those views purport to explain. For example, theistic systems which explain contingent being by deriving it from another contingent being may be self-stultifying in this sense. And so on.

3. An adequate metaphysical system must be coherent. It must not only be consistent, it must also "hang together." The system's components must be relevant to one another and the view as a whole must display a certain amount of systematic articulation.

4. An adequate metaphysical system must be comparatively free from ad hoc hypotheses, that is, from hypotheses which have only been introduced to enable the system to cope with counterevidence.[11]

5. Other things being equal, a simpler system is preferable to a more complex system.

6. An adequate metaphysical system must not include elements which are "contradicted by well-established data."[12]

7. A theory's scope must be taken into consideration. For example, Pepper argues that all data are relevant to a metaphysical hypothesis, and that a metaphysical hypothesis fails in scope when it is forced not merely to reinterpret its data (consciousness, moral

experience, science, etc.) but to deny any reality to it.[13] In any case, other things being equal, one metaphysical system is more adequate than another if it explains more things or accounts for a wider range of human experience. Among the facts which are included within the "relevance range" (Yandell) of religious doctrines are the existence and order of the world, humanity's moral and religious experience, its spiritual aspirations, extraordinary instances of sanctity, numinous experience and mystical consciousness, claims that revelation has actually occurred, and so on.

8. An adequate metaphysical system must provide illuminating explanations of the data within its scope.

9. Systems can also be judged by their fruitfulness, that is, by their ability to integrate new data and new insights from the domains of science, art, morality, and so forth.

10. Tillich argues that philosophical theories must be judged by "their efficacy in the life process of mankind,"[14] and according to Ferre an adequate metaphysical system must be "capable of 'coming to life' for individuals . . . becoming . . . a usable instrument for coping with the total environment." It must, he says, have a "capacity for ringing true with respect to those who use it," enabling them to "cope successfully with the challenges of life."[15]

It is possible to subsume some of these criteria (namely, the second, fourth, sixth and ninth) under others.[16] If we do so, we will be left with six criteria, three of which are formal (consistency, coherence and simplicity), two of which concern a system's explanatory power (scope and explanatory adequacy), and one of which concerns the existential effects of adopting a system. Problems are clearly connected with these criteria.

a). Some (consistency and coherence) exclude very little. Most interesting metaphysical systems are reasonably consistent and coherent.

b). Some are vague and/or admit of several interpretations. "Hanging together" and "exhibiting a reasonable amount of systematic articulation" are inherently vague notions. Again, it is unclear whether a system's simplicity should be determined by the number of its basic assumptions or by the number of its basic concepts, or by some combination of the two. Nor is it clear how we count assumptions or concepts.[17]

c). Some are difficult to apply. It is difficult, for example, to determine the efficacy of a system "in the life process of mankind." In the first place, unless one possesses wide sympathies and a great deal of (historical, sociological, psychological and theological) information, one is not even in a position to apply this criterion. In the second place, one must be careful not to prejudge the issue by appealing to values which can only be defended by appealing to tenets peculiar to only some of the systems which are being evaluated.

d). In at least one case, the very meaning of the criterion is unclear. It is generally agreed that an adequate metaphysical system must explain or "illuminate" the facts within its range. In view of the importance of this criterion, it is surprising to find that little has been said about the nature of metaphysical explanation or the conditions under which a metaphysical system can be said to illuminate the facts.

(i) Does a metaphysical theory illuminate the facts if it succeeds in creating a "feeling of grasp" or comprehension? Of course, no theory will attract adherents or continue to be retained which fails to produce a feeling of grasp or intelligibility. At the same time, the feeling of grasp is a very untrustworthy guide.[18] Is any one person's feeling of grasp as good as anyone else's, or should we only consider the impressions of those who meet certain conditions? And if so, what conditions? Intelligence? information? sympathy? imagination? moral seriousness? wide experience?

(ii) Or perhaps a metaphysical system explains a set of facts if those facts can be deduced from the system. Classical attempts to derive the possibility of revelation from a consideration of the nature of God and the human condition provide a quasi-deductive pattern of reasoning which allegedly illuminates the fact of revelation (though notice that the fact of revelation is not entailed by the explicans, but merely the possibility of the fact). Theodicies may provide other examples. Given that the premises of an Augustinian-type theodicy are true, certain evils will occur (those entailed by finitude) and the occurrence of other evils (that is, those caused by the abuse of free will) is not unlikely.

(iii) A metaphysical system might be said to illuminate the facts if it succeeds in integrating a set of apparently unrelated facts. A Thomistic, Barthian or liberal Christian anthropology provide different ways of integrating historical, psychological, sociological and moral facts. Thus, to oversimplify, these facts might be seen either as an expression of humanity's drive towards transcendence or beatitude, or as an expression of our sinful self-reliance, or as the result of an interaction between an innately good human nature and a corrupt environment.

(iv) Or perhaps metaphysical systems illuminate the facts by providing answers to what Toulmin has called boundary questions. Boundary questions are questions which arise at the border of, say, science or morality but are not themselves scientific or moral questions. Examples of such questions are "Why is there any being or order?" or "Why should I be moral?"

In short, while there is some agreement concerning the criteria which are to be used in assessing metaphysical systems, these criteria are vague, indeterminate and difficult to apply. Furthermore, as Smart points out, there is no agreement as to the relative weight which should be assigned to them. It is not, therefore, surprising that intelligent and informed people can employ these criteria and come to radically different conclusions.

In view of this situation it is tempting to argue in the following way:

1. The function of rational ("intersubjective," "objective") criteria is to produce an agreement on questions of truth (adequacy, reasonableness). Therefore,

2. Criteria which when fairly applied fail to produce agreement are not (fully) rational or objective.

3. The criteria for assessing metaphysical systems, even when fairly applied, fail to produce agreement. Therefore,

4. These critera are not (fully) rational or objective.

(1) is plausible and appears to imply (2). If truth (as distinguished from opinions about truth) does not vary, and the fair application of a set of criteria, S, leads A to judge that p and B to judge that non-p, then the fair application of S has led at least one person who uses S into error. Disagreement does, I think, indicate a functional failure.

Is (3) true? We should not accept it too hastily. It can be argued that in order to employ these criteria with any hope of success, one must possess not only intelligence, but broad experience and wide sympathies, and certain mental and moral habits (intellectual honesty, a tolerance of complexity, etc.). Again, because of the complexity and delicate character of the evidence, it is never entirely clear that both disputants have precisely the same facts in view (Newman is very instructive on this point). When disagreements occur it is, therefore, very difficult to determine whether the criteria have been employed with equal skill and sensitivity (i.e., with equal "fairness"). (3) may be true, but its truth is not easy to establish.

III

The first section of this essay was designed to support the contention that propositional truth is important, that questions of propositional truth quite properly arise when the doctrines of one system are compared with those of another, and that those disputes are subject to rational adjudication. The second section of the essay is concerned with some of the difficulties involved in actually adjudicating these conflicts, and with the suspicion (which these difficulties create) that reason is unable to resolve them.

Are we at an impasse? In the *Phaedo* (C88c–91c) Plato exhorts us not to dispair of reason when confronted by the collapse of arguments which we have trusted (e.g., naive and uninformed arguments for the superiority of one religion), and by the inevitable difficulties to which rational inquiry leads. We should also remember Aristotle's advice, namely, to expect no more precision or certainty than the subject matter admits of (*Nichomochean Ethics*, bk. I, sect. III). In particular, we must avoid two mistakes:

1. Even if the relevant criteria are not fully adequate (and what counts as adequacy should be partly determined by the subject matter) and doctrinal disagreements cannot be resolved by reason alone, that is, even if the adoption of a worldview inevitably involves a decision to venture beyond the evidence, it does not follow that these disputes need be a-rational, or that anything goes. That reason is insufficient does not entail that reason is unnecessary or even that it should not largely determine one's decision to adopt a worldview.

2. It is unreasonable to insist upon a degree of rigor which we do not expect in our own disciplines. For example, it is sometimes assumed (e.g., by Plantinga) that a good argument is not only sound but such that all of its premises would be accepted as true by any (fully informed) rational being. I would suggest that very few (no?) significant arguments in philosophy, the history of religion, biblical scholarship, law or literary criticism (etc.) meet these standards. Furthermore, as Mitchell has persuasively argued,[19] the criteria which are used in historical research, literary criticism, and at certain points in science (the choice of a scientific paradigm such as Newtonian mechanics or Aristotelian physics) are subject to

difficulties similar to those investigated in the second section of this essay. We can, of course, conclude that there is no objective (propositional?) truth in these areas or that disputes over the interpretation of an historical event or literary text or scientific paradigm are a-rational. In my opinion, it would be wiser to broaden our conception of reason.

6

Religious Pluralism and Cross-Cultural Criteria of Religious Truth

□

Mary Ann Stenger

In recent years contemporary theologians and philosophers of religion have been confronting many of the same issues that historians of religion have wrestled with for years as part of their methodological discussions: definitions of religion, ways of knowing or understanding diverse religious traditions, possible categories for comparison, problems of language in explaining ideas cross-culturally, normative judgments entering into descriptions of religious traditions, and so on. The normative issues of cross-cultural comparison and judgment in particular require extensive treatment and form a necessary part of the agenda of cross-cultural philosophy of religion. In this essay, I shall focus on the issue of criteria for making evaluative judgments of religious truths from diverse religious traditions.

In the first section I shall look at how the problem of criteria arises in the setting of religious pluralism. In the context of the effort to maintain pluralistic religious truths, we face the question of how one can judge some experiences or claims as false. By what criteria can we judge cross-cultural religious phenomena and truth-claims? Next, I shall analyze some recent attempts to offer criteria for judging various religious expressions and experiences cross-culturally. The third section will provide a critical evaluation of the above criteria with a focus on their cognitive adequacy in relation to the tension between a relativistic approach and an approach using a more absolute criterion. In a final section I shall offer my own thoughts about criteria for cross-cultural truth in religion.

I. The Problem of Criteria of Cross-Cultural Religious Truth

Ninian Smart, as an historian of religion, finds the descriptive study of religion important in furthering worldwide human understanding. But as a philosopher of religion, he also asks the normative question of evaluation: "We need to be critical as well as appreciative. But by what criteria? That, of course, is the crucial question."[1] Thus, the issue of truth and the basis for judging religious phenomena constitutes a major challenge for philosophy in a cross-cultural religious context.

A popular response to the plurality of religious traditions in our world is "To each his/her own," a response which attempts to bypass the question of judgment and truth. One can adopt a form of cultural relativism, asserting the rightness and truth of one's own religious position in relationship to one's own personal and cultural situation and tolerantly allowing for others' differing views. One thereby suspends judgment of others' religious positions, assuming they have little or no relevance to one's own situation but much relevance to others' own personal and cultural contexts. One can feel a rather smug comfort in having truth for oneself and yet of being enlightened enough to allow that others may have truth for themselves. Perhaps we may go along naively suspending judgment on others' religious truth-claims until events or cultural changes occur which shake that naiveté and cultural relativism, and we find ourselves making judgments of truth and falsity. By what criteria are we judging, and can those criteria be cross-cultural or only relevant to a particular personal religious cultural context?

Let us consider three examples where judgment occurs and cross-cultural conflicts arise. These will be used later to discuss concrete applications of criteria of religious truth, but for now they help point to the need for such criteria.

1. *Jonestown.* The tragedy of Jonestown was related to the religious beliefs of its followers. For them Jones was a messenger from God, and his commands were to be followed, even to the point of death. But the response of many people to the deaths in Jonestown was not a continuation of "to each his/her own". What criteria do people use in judging the religious beliefs of that religious group? Some

Christians might say, based on their own internal criteria of true revelation, that it was a misreading of God's revelation. But can there also be nonsectarian, cross-cultural criteria which could be used to judge the religious beliefs and activities of the Jonestown group?

2. *Sexist religious language.* Some people have rejected past symbols of the ultimate which are patriarchal and have called for nonsexist expressions of the ultimate along with inclusive references for the followers. Others have seen such patriarchal expressions as essential to religious expression and truth. We can talk of cultural factors in such responses, but we can also ask for criteria of religious truth which would apply cross-culturally and not be as dependent on those cultural factors.

3. *Conflicting religious views.* Some Christians argue for a permanent soul, while some Theravada Buddhists reject a permanent soul. An *advaitin* philosophical approach which sees Brahman as the only ultimate and deities such as Vishnu, Krishna or Shiva as belonging to a lower level of reality conflicts with the viewpoint of a worshipper of Krishna who sees Krishna as the Supreme Lord, ultimate in himself. Some Jews see Jesus as a great teacher, perhaps even prophet, but disagree with Christians who see Jesus as the incarnate Son of God, both fully human and fully divine. These conflicts point to the need for cross-cultural discussion but also for criteria which could apply to differing religious traditions and be more than the expression of one tradition's point of view. Even if people agree to differ, they may also want to agree on a criterion which would find some religious truth-claims unacceptable.

This problem of criteria for religious truths can be formulated in the following questions:

1. Are all religious phenomena and truth-claims within various descriptive categories equally true examples of religious experience and equally valid?

2. On what basis can a person judge between conflicting statements and ideas from different historical or cultural situations?

3. Is there or can there be a criterion for judging cross-cultural religious phenomena which is more than an expression of the subjective state and historical situation of the knower?

Let us turn to some recent suggestions of cross-cultural criteria for judging religious phenomena and truth-claims.

II. Possible Criteria of Cross-Cultural Religious Truth

Each of the four thinkers treated in this discussion comes from a different academic specialty in the study of religion: sociology (Berger), theology (Kaufman), philosophy (Hick) and history (Smith). Yet each addresses the normative issue of evaluation cross-culturally and proposes possible criteria.

Peter Berger

The "inductive" approach which Peter Berger argues for in *The Heretical Imperative*[2] is open-ended enough to look at religous phenomena from both West and East. The approach focuses on experience "as the ground of all religious affirmations" (p. 62), where "experience" is understood as including one's own individual experience and, more broadly, the experiences embodied in varying religious traditions. With such openness come problems of religious certainty which Berger addresses.

The first issue is how to identify or judge "false" religious experience. After rejecting a moral criterion for judging truth, Berger prefers a rational criterion whereby one evaluates the insights claiming to come from a religious experience on the scale of reason (p. 148). This rational judgment includes relating the religious experience and accompanying insights to other human experiences and knowledge.

The second issue deals with the basis for preferring one religious tradition rather than another. Here Berger calls for comparing various religious alternatives and then making a personal subjective decision, taking account of one's traditional roots but also one's openness to all other religious traditions (p. 150).

A third problem of religious certainty is the desire to feel certain that what one proclaims or accepts as truth is really truth. Berger's response is to argue that in this finite world one only experiences religious certainty momentarily (p. 152). Religious certainty is a matter of an experience which transcends the relativizing character of other life experiences, an encounter with the ultimate, but the certainty is very fragmentary.

With that basic approach to religious certainty as background, Berger discusses the coming contestation of religions from the West with the East. By "contestation" Berger means more than a mutual exchange of ideas for increasing mutual understanding (the descriptive level). Rather, he means involving oneself with the truth-claims of other religious traditions in an open-minded way, with the possibility of changing one's own worldview (the normative level). Berger characterizes the contestation of East and West as the contestation of two distinct types of religious experience: "confrontation with the divine" (West) and "interiority of the divine" (East) (p. 168). He then asks: *"How could it be possible that both types of religious experience are true?"* (p. 170). Berger does not attempt to answer this in any final way, but one would assume that his answer will result from his use of the inductive method together with the specific suggestions of a criterion of rational evaluation in relation to personal decision and experience.

Gordon Kaufman

In *The Theological Imagination*[3] Gordon Kaufman calls for a rethinking of Christianity's claim of finality and a new thinking about its relationship to other religious traditions. He discusses three positions which have dealt with this issue but sees all of them as inadequate. The position that the Christian faith holds final religious truth while other religious traditions may be close to or preparatory for that truth in varying degrees does not recognize the sophistication of other traditions nor the difficulty in specifying *how* these other traditions approximate the Christian (pp. 173–74). The cultural-religious relativist position is rejected because it does not accept an ultimate unity of religious truth, a unity which Kaufman thinks is crucial if the religions can legitimately claim that *truth* was their basic concern (p. 174). A third position recognizes each religious tradition as representing a partial view of ultimate reality and truth, a position which gives up Christianity's claim to finality and superiority but does recognize ultimate truth as the goal (p. 175). Kaufman disagrees with all three positions because they tend to assume that for the purpose of judging religious faiths, we are now in a position to determine their correct and permanent relationships to each other, that history, as far as religious truth is concerned, has already come to its final period (pp. 175–76).

Kaufman's alternative position stems from his view that theology today must assess the present situation, look to the future, and determine what beliefs and ideas from the past are still adequate and workable for the present and future. The key question that Kaufman pulls from his assessment of the present and estimate of the future is: "How shall we build a new and more humane world for all of the peoples of the world?" (p. 181). This question becomes a criterion of theological beliefs and ideas, including those from the non-Christian religious traditions. This criterion of humanization approves what is necessary or helpful in building a humane world order and rejects what hinders such a humanization of our world. Under this criterion, there would be a refocusing and reconstructing of theological concepts and practices cross-culturally (p. 197).

Kaufman, then, deals with the plurality and relativity of religious phenomena by focussing on the human level and the need for a more humane order as a common point shared by all religions. The criterion of humanization recognizes that common point as a cross-cultural basis for judging religious truth.

John Hick

In recent writings John Hick has used cross-cultural comparisons of religious ideas and figures to show some structural similarities and to emphasize to Western Christians that they must be open to religious truth outside their own tradition. Throughout his discussions Hick operates with the view that there is one infinite divine reality behind all differing religious images and visions. On the one hand, this leads him to argue that it is "unreasonable for any religion to claim to be alone authentic, dismissing all the others as false."[4] On the other hand, he recognizes that "it is entirely possible that more adequate and less adequate images of God operate within different religious traditions."[5] His discussion has begun to move from comparisons and a call for openness to the more difficult and challenging question of evaluation.

In "On Grading Religions" Hick attempts to grade religions as total traditions, rather than looking at particular religious phenomena, and finally concludes that that is not a realistic task.[6] In part because of the diversity within each tradition, Hick sees the different religious traditions as "equally productive" in transforming humans from focusing on the self to centering on Reality or the Ultimate (ibid., p. 467). But on the way to reaching that conclusion, Hick does analyze evaluative approaches and criteria which may be helpful in judging particular religious phenomena, even if not finally productive in judging religious-cultural totalities.

Hick analyzes three criteria that operate when people acclaim and accept a divine mediator in the founding of a religious tradition. First, the moral criterion, based on a universal ordinary moral sense of humankind, asks: Is the mediator basically good rather than evil, and does his/her teaching offer a better moral vision than the existing common morality? (pp. 458, 460). The second criterion focuses on the ability of the mediator to present a new vision of reality that stimulates people to follow it: Is the new vision ultimately good and is a new and better life possible through it? (pp. 459, 460). The third criterion centers on the people responding: Are the people transformed and thereby assured that the Divine has in fact been mediated to them? (p. 460).

One can also consider the historical-cultural actualizations of the mediator's teachings and visions, which will include both good and evil, positive and negative elements. Hick proposes rational evaluation of the cognitive, theoretical elements of a religious tradition, and moral evaluation of the historical-cultural actualizations of religious beliefs (p. 461), but both lead to the conclusion of positive and negative, stronger and weaker examples in each tradition. One can also ask whether the basic religious vision continues to be "soteriologically effective" or life-transforming, but any final verification of that is eschatological (pp. 461–62). In the end, Hick does not find any of these criteria sufficient to adequately compare and fairly assess religious traditions as a whole. However, I think these criteria may be more successfully applied to specific religious phenomena and therefore deserve our consideration in dealing with the issue of judging religious truths.

Wilfred Cantwell Smith

Wilfred Cantwell Smith argues that religious truth does not lie in the religions but in persons.[7] Looking at religious persons cross-cuturally, one can argue that one person's life and religion may be more true or more false than the religious life of another person, but that truth or falsity depends on the personal life which is lived in a specific context, not on the context itself.[8] Such a judgment of a religious person is not a judgment of the religious tradition or context itself.

Even when Smith moves from the truth of religions as existential, personal truth to the truth of religious statements, he continues his personalist emphasis by insisting that statements be related to the lives and faith of persons and be agreeable to those persons as well as to outsiders.[9] In *Towards a World Theology* he expresses the principle of verification in this way: "No statement involving persons is valid . . . unless theoretically its validity can be verified both by the persons involved and by critical observers not involved."[10]

But Smith is interested in more than verifying descriptions of religious persons when he calls for a world theology which thinks of all religious persons as members of one world religious community.

The goal for this world theology is the building of a world community (p. 129). This universalist thrust is balanced with Smith's insistence that participation in one particular religious community will not be superceded and that the particular faiths must not be diluted (p. 125). He attempts to maintain this universalist-particularist balance with a form of the insider-outsider criterion. A test of the truth of a world theology will be based on whether it does "justice to the facts of human religious history, on the one hand, and, on the other, to the faith, experience, insight of both Christians (or whichever group from which it emerges) and the others" (p. 153). The shared challenge of building a common world provides a common basis for applying the insider-outsider criterion and for participating in the formation of a world theology.

Underlying this concern for the insider-outsider is Smith's view of truth as both particular and universal. Truth for Smith is personal and humane and therefore also particular; it is apprehended by particular persons in specific historical situations. But truth is universal in that the truth itself transcends the historical level and the specific formulation of it (p. 190). The insider-outsider criterion attempts to do justice to both aspects of truth and still allow for some critical evaluation.

Preliminary Comparison

Summarizing the above discussion, we have the following criteria suggested for judging cross-cultural religious truths:

1. Berger's criteria of rational evaluation in relation to personal decision and experience.

2. Kaufman's criterion of furthering humanization.

3. Hick's criteria of rational and moral evaluation of religious phenomena, including assessment of the transforming power of a religious vision and its mediator.

4. Smith's criterion of acceptability to both insiders and outsiders, emphasizing personal religious truth and concern for building a world community.

With these criteria, all four thinkers advance beyond the position of some earlier thinkers which asserts the superiority and absoluteness of Christianity. Although some thinkers, such as Schleiermacher, Troeltsch and Rahner, had recognized some truth in non-Christian religious positions, they tended to see this truth as preliminary (Schleiermacher and Troeltsch) or anonymously Christian (Rahner). Berger, Kaufman, Hick and Smith attempt to treat religious truths from varying traditions on the same level. Their discussions do not begin with the assumption of the superiority and absolute truth of Christianity, though all four find it necessary to deal with that position in their writings.

A second point of comparison is that all four thinkers conceive of the absolute as transcending any particular religious-cultural embodiment. For Berger, Hick and Smith this seems to provide a common point among diverse religious traditions. Although agreeing with that conception of the ultimate, Kaufman focuses on the interest in the human as the common point that all religions share.

Third, all four thinkers view religion as more than belief, as including moral, psychological, historical, cultural and social factors. They see these factors as contributing to the diversity of religious traditions as well as to the development of criteria for judging religious phenomena. Although the question of criteria is a cognitive issue, the suggested criteria attempt to deal with other aspects of religion as well.

Finally, one can contrast Smith's strong insistence on individual religious persons with Hick's attempt to evaluate religions as a whole. Even when Hick concludes that such a grading of religions is not possible, he still speaks of the religions as totalities. Smith, on the other hand, prefers not to talk about the totality of a religious tradition but rather about specific persons from the religious traditions. Berger's characterization of East and West shows an attempt to look at religious ideas and practices more broadly than the usual delineation of traditions, but his criteria for judging religious truth are dependent on individual persons. Kaufman's interest in history (past, present and future) and humanization shows an attempt to combine a concern for individual persons with a broader worldview of religious traditions.

In the next section the evaluation of these criteria will focus on their cognitive adequacy and workability within particular religious traditions and yet transcending that particularity.

III. Evaluation of Criteria of Cross-Cultural Religious Truth

The evaluation of the criteria from these four thinkers will address the questions and examples raised at the end of section I as part of the problem of criteria.

1. *Are all the religious phenomena and truth-claims within various descriptive categories equally true examples of religious experience and equally valid?*

The answer to this question depends on whether one looks at the religious phenomena in terms of particular experiences, events, writings and persons, or as whole traditions. All four thinkers want to be open to all religious phenomena, but that does not mean accepting all as equal. The criteria that they offer along with the process of applying them provide a way of evaluating particular phenomena and truth-claims so that some would be more true or valid than others. At the same time, all four thinkers are hesitant about dismissing a major religious tradition or "grading" them as religious totalities. Hick's claim "that the Real, the Ultimate, the Divine is known and responded to within each of these vast historical complexes"[11] puts all the major traditions on an equal footing soteriologically and in relation to truth. Smith's call for religious persons in all traditions to have a role in the formation of world theology suggests an equality in the discussion and evaluation leading to broad-based theological truth. For all, the criteria suggested work better when applied to particular phenomena rather than to the traditions as whole entities.

If one agrees that the religious phenomena and truth-claims are not all equally valid, then one must move on to the question of the basis for judgment and evaluation.

2. *How, on what basis, can a person judge between conflicting statements and ideas from different historical or cultural situations?*

This question not only involves the issue of what criteria can be used in judging, but also the issue of the cognitive basis for the criteria and judgment. A traditional basis for criteria evaluating non-Christian religious traditions has been some form of religious authority for Christians (scripture, tradition or church authority). Although many aspects of the Christian tradition are and have been a strong influence on these four thinkers, all of them formulate their criteria with a much broader basis than religious authority. As Kaufman states, and as the others might well agree, "All claims to truth made simply on the grounds of religious authority are in question."[12] Rather, the various forms of religious authority constitute one part of the total experience and reflection which provide the basis of judgment for particular persons.

Generally speaking, all four develop their criteria on the basis of rational assessment, moral evaluation and personal experience.

While one might argue that Berger gives more weight to reason, Hick to moral evaluation, Kaufman to the intellectual level (but also to practical evaluations) and Smith to the existential level, all of them use some forms of rational assessment and moral evaluation. The element of personal experience is important for all four thinkers, but the particular understanding of personal experience makes a difference in the grounding of the criteria.

The element of personal experience shows up in Berger's discussion of subjective decision and the momentary certainty of encounter with the ultimate. Included within that personal experience is the individual personality and particular situation of the person, including one's religious roots. This element allows for the influence of the historical-cultural situation, but Berger does not make a strong correlation between theological truth and the historical-cultural-psychological situation.[13]

Hick begins his discussion of grading religions with a discussion of the fact that the majority of people evaluate the traditions of the world in accord with the tradition into which they were born. Certainly that "genetic confessionalism" is one aspect of the historical-cultural relativity and plurality of our present religious situation. But even when Hick is describing an individual's acceptance of a particular faith as based on the moral evaluation of the mediator and the transforming power of the new religious vision, he is primarily interested in the individual as an example of a cross-cultural religious structure rather than as a particular representative of a specific historical-cultural-personal situation.

In contrast, both Kaufman and Smith emphasize the historical-cultural situation, although Smith is more interested in the individual person than Kaufman. A concern for persons is implied in Kaufman's criterion of humanization, but the individual-psychological aspect of the personal is not stressed. For Smith, to talk of the personal is to include the individual's existential response to the ultimate and the particular historical-cultural-religious roots of the individual.

To the extent that the criteria reflect personal experience, are the criteria too subjective? If any of the thinkers were proposing judgment of religious phenomena based purely on the emotional or psychological state of the person, independent of the subject's relation to the historical-cultural situation and reasons, then the criteria would be too subjective. But all of them see a role for reason, which is intersubjective, and all of them connect the personal to the historical and cultural situation, providing an additional degree of intersubjectivity. Both Berger and Hick could stress this connection to the historical-cultural situation more, but they do not ignore it.

The intersubjective elements of reason and history help to balance the subjective elements that influence our normative thinking and evaluation of religious phenomena. The ongoing discussion and application of the criteria also provides a more objective context for judging. Smith's insider-outsider criterion and Kaufman's humanization criterion depend on the agreement and common judgment of many people, not just one personal subject.

Recognizing the role of the subjective and historical situation in the formation of criteria, we can ask whether truly cross-cultural criteria are possible.

3. *Is there or can there be a criterion for judging cross-cultural religious phenomena which is more than an expression of the subjective state and historical situation of the knower?*

Implicit in this question is the tension between a relativist approach and a more absolutist approach, and that tension involves several issues:

a) The ability of the criterion to have both a universalist thrust as well as recognition of the importance of particular religious persons and traditions.

b) The extent to which the criteria reflect a Western-Christian approach.

c) The recognition of historical and cultural change.

d) The relationship of the criteria to the ultimate.

a) Do the criteria offered have a universalist thrust as well as a recognition of the importance of particular religious persons and traditions?

All four thinkers show a universalist thrust in their development of criteria to be applied cross-culturally and in their concern for cross-cultural religious truth. For both Kaufman and Smith, there is an explicit universalist hope of building a more humane world community. For Berger, the contestation of East and West shows a search for the universal within and beyond the two approaches. For Hick, the universal of Reality or the Ultimate underlies the various religious structures, such as response to a mediator or theoretical works. But there is a point where Hick's discussion of the criterion of moral evaluation of the mediator could be more universal. Since not all religious traditions focus on persons as mediators, but may focus on things (rock, object of nature, book), words or events (fire, sacramental action) as mediating the divine, one could broaden the discussion of mediator to speak of symbol or hierophany. Such a move would enable Hick to deal with more religious traditions and develop more universalist criteria.

On the other side of the question, we have already discussed the role of particular religious persons in each thinker's approach. But we can ask whether the criterion and approach can respect the individuality of the different religious traditions. Berger's characterizations of East and West do not preserve the integrity and individuality of the religious traditions nor the plurality within them. However, his discussion of the process of evaluating religious truths does not depend on such characterizations and could be followed while maintaining both the openness to all and the individuality of the different religious traditions. Kaufman's criterion of humanization assumes a common interest of the religious traditions in the human order, but the application of it may well involve a recognition of the individuality of the different religious traditions. While all may have an interest in the human, how the criterion of humanization will work will depend on the definitions of human found within the varying religious traditions, not all of which may agree with Kaufman's understanding of building a more humane world. Hick's view that all the great world religions "are equally productive of that transition from self to Reality which we see in the saints of all traditions"[14] may not recognize sufficiently the diversity of the religious traditions, but the criteria he discusses can take account of those differences in terms of moral and rational evaluation and the understanding of soteriological transformation in each tradition. Smith is the most careful about maintaining the tension between his universalist thrust for a world theology and his particularist concern with religious persons. That tension is expressed quite clearly in his insider-outsider criterion and the relationship of a world theology to the specific religious traditions.

b) Do the criteria offered overemphasize a Western-Christian approach?

Certainly the Western-Christian background of these thinkers shows up in some elements of their discussions of criteria, but it does not dominate those discussions. Hick's focus on the mediator reflects a Western-Christian orientation even though some other traditions may focus on a mediator as well. Kaufman does show elements of humanization within Christian faith and tradition, but he does not explicitly develop the criterion of humanization from those elements nor does he identify Christianity with those elements. The criterion of humanization implies a refocusing and reconstructing for Christian theology as well as for other religious views. When Smith speaks out of his Christian background he balances it with a call for others to participate in the same way from their own religious traditions in order to achieve a world theology. The insider-outsider criterion provides one way to avoid an overly Western-Christian approach. All four thinkers operate out of a Western-Christian background, but all make efforts to avoid that particularist emphasis in developing criteria for judging religious phenomena.

c) Do the proposed criteria take account of historical and cultural change?

All four thinkers see our present religious situation as changed from the past, in part because we are more aware of religious pluralism and positive elements in religious traditions not our own. All also look to a future which will be more open to that pluralism, thereby offering new religious possibilities and perhaps a more humane world community. But Berger's East-West characterizations and Hick's view of present religious traditions as fairly settled options suggest a static view of religions.[15] On the other hand, both Kaufman and Smith express a more explicitly dynamic view of truth. They see the present situation as a development from the past, a need to address the present, and an openness to the future. This includes a recognition that a present response may need to be modified and developed in relation to the future. Berger's concluding comments suggest that approach also, but his discussion of East and West needs an explicit acknowledgment of that openness.

The criteria offered can be applied to differing historical situations as well as differing cultural situations, but we also need to recognize that the criteria themselves may change with historical and cultural changes.

d) What is the relationship of the criteria proposed to the ultimate?

Each thinker recognizes the cultural relativity of our present religious situation, but each also accepts an absolute toward which religious experience can direct people. Presumably one purpose of the criteria offered is to help judge whether claimed religious experiences and ideas do direct toward the ultimate or not.

Because all four thinkers want to remain open to the diversity of views of the ultimate, they do not discuss particular characteristics (personal, impersonal, transcendent, immanent) of the ultimate as part of their proposed criteria for judging religious phenomena. It was mentioned earlier that all view the ultimate as transcending any particular cultural-historical embodiment. This does not mean that the ultimate cannot be revealed or encountered through finite vehicles, but such an experience would provide momentary absoluteness; it would not transfer absoluteness to particular historical-cultural structures, objects or ideas. Accordingly, the criteria for judging religious phenomena focus on the historical-cultural embodiments or expressions of the ultimate and human responses to it. Yet the relationship of this finite historical-cultural level to the ultimate is important in judging religious truth.

Berger addresses the relationship to the ultimate in his discussion of experiences of momentary certainty, encounters with the ultimate that "carry within them an intrinsic conviction of truth."[16] Such momentary experiences of the ultimate and of truth will always be relativized, but not voided, by finite human expression of them, and even more by openness to truth in the future and in a broad range of cultural expressions. Such an approach avoids absolutizing particular experiences or expressions of the ultimate, but also allows for an openness to the ultimate.

In discussion preceding his development of the criterion of humanization, Kaufman addresses the relationship between the absoluteness of God and the relativity of human finitude. He argues that an emphasis on the relativity of human thought, truth claims and activities is important for preserving the absoluteness of God.[17] It is interesting, then, that the criterion which Kaufman advances is so strongly humanistic and could be developed quite apart from any recognition of the absoluteness of God or the ultimate. Although one can make strong arguments for the relationship of God or the ultimate to humanization from various religious traditions, one can and people do talk about humanization totally apart from that relationship.

Although Hick sees all the major religious traditions as equal ways to the ultimate, he does not focus on the relationship to the ultimate in the criteria he discusses. He does, however, consider people's assessment of the transforming power of a religious vision, and that could be part of an evaluation of the relationship to the ultimate. But of course false religious visions could have great transforming power for people. Hick does not address that possibility nor the possibility of people absolutizing the finite in their religious response.

Smith's emphasis on personal-existential religious truth points to a relationship with the ultimate at the base of one's criteria of religious truth. That relationship can be some form of the revelation of God to particular historical persons, but what is revealed is God, not particular words, truth-claims, religious structures or specific practices, although these may be symbols or mediators of God.[18] This statement can serve to guard against absolutization of the finite and needs to be added to the criteria of personal religious truth and acceptability to insiders and outsiders.

The concern with the relationship to the ultimate is an important element in avoiding both a relativist and absolutist approach to the issue of truth. The recognition of an absolute, the ultimate, avoids a pure relativism, but the accompanying recognition of the relativity of all finite religious phenomena avoids an absolutism also.

All of the issues raised in relation to the third question point to the need to maintain the tension between a relativist and absolutist approach in dealing with cross-cultural religious truth. As we have noted, all four thinkers try to balance their concern for universal truth with a concern for particular personal religious truth (less true in Kaufman's case). Also, all four maintain the ultimate over against and in relation to the particular historical religious phenomena. The universalist thrust, along with the affirmation of an ultimate, is an attempt to achieve a truth which is more than an expression of the subjective state and historical situation of the knower. The criteria proposed attempt to achieve this truth or recognize this truth in religious phenomena, but these criteria are always relativized in terms of the present historical situation, the ultimate itself, and the dynamic nature of truth.

4. *Can the proposed criteria judge some religious experiences or truth claims as false?* (Application to earlier examples)

In the first section of this essay the specific examples of Jonestown, sexist religious language and particular cross-cultural conflicts of belief were used to raise the questions of criteria discussed above. It is important to consider briefly the application of the proposed criteria to these examples to see whether they have advanced us beyond our original problem.

1. *Jonestown.* Using the criteria of moral evaluation and an assessment of the transforming power of a religious vision, many of the people who belong to Jonestown probably would have judged Jones and his insights quite positively. But the response of many outsiders after the deaths were known would indicate that the insider evalua-

tion would not accord with the moral evaluation by outsiders. Although one might be able to achieve insider-outsider agreement on descriptive historical statements, one would have far more difficulty in achieving insider-outsider normative agreememt.[19] The element of rational assessment discussed by Berger and Hick would probably yield a negative judgment of Jonestown for many, along with a negative moral evaluation. Similarly, the criterion of humanization would give some support to the view that Jones' claims were false or immoral, since many would agree that the results of those claims were inhumane. One problem I see here, however, is that Jones offered his followers a vision which many of them (and perhaps many others, looking only at the vision and not at other aspects of Jones or Jonestown) found to be more humane that their present living situations. The inhumanity and exploitation seem much clearer after the tragedy than when looking at his prior vision and earlier practices. When applied to this example, the use of the suggested criteria and the results depend greatly on the personal-historical situation of the person judging.

2. *Sexist religious language.* Personal-cultural factors certainly play a role in evaluating sexist religious language, as we well know from responses to that issue within various Christian and Jewish communities today. Rational evaluation alone may not be sufficient to evaluate the language, but moral evaluation or application of the criterion of humanization may judge sexist religious language negatively, since language which excludes half the human race would not be helpful in working for a more humane world. If one broadened Hick's discussion of assessing the transforming power of a mediator to include religious symbols, one could make a strong argument that patriarchal symbols have lost their transforming power or block the transforming vision for many persons. But there are also others for whom the transforming vision is essentially tied to such patriarchal expressions. Using Smith's insider-outsider arppoach, one would have to have considerable dialogue and discussion, but even then agreement does not seem likely, since the personal-cultural factors are expressed so strongly on this issue. If Smith hopes to work for a world theology with broad-based suppport, such an issue will be important.

3. *Conflicting religious views.* All four thinkers call for ongoing discussion and cross-cultural dialogue to increase our understanding of the positions of others. Some conflicts may be resolved through discussions which clarify what is meant by various terms and concepts, but not all conflicts and differences will be resolved in that

way. One can offer rational assessment of the claims and beliefs in these examples (Christian permanent soul vs. Theravada Buddhist nonpermanent soul; *advaitin* Brahman as ultimate reality vs. Krishna as ultimate for his worshippers; Jesus as a great teacher to some Jews vs. incarnate Son of God for Christians), but since there is sophisticated philosophical and theological argument available for these various positions, as Hick has pointed out, the conflict will not be easily resolved by that means. One could try a moral evaluation of the historical outworking of these beliefs, but that would not necessarily invalidate the beliefs themselves since there are many historical outworkings which in fact do not truly reflect the beliefs they claim to be based on or which are not necessary concomitants of the beliefs. Ongoing cross-cultural discussion of these issues may lead to the agreement to disagree, dependent on personal decision and historical-cultural background.

Kaufman and Smith might also suggest that such posing of cross-cultural truth-claims as "conflicts" is not helpful. Because Smith wants to focus on personal religious truth, he is less interested in propositional truth. Kaufman prefers to focus on the pressing need to build human community rather than on resolving conflicting truth-claims.[20] Berger and Hick also want to give some weight to the personal religious response to the ultimate, but they also show more interest in the truth of religious affirmations and propositional truth.

Consideration of the application of these criteria to specific examples shows that some evaluation of religious phenomena can be made, but that our historical-cultural-personal situations play an important role in that evaluation. If our present historical-cultural situation demands more awareness and more tolerance of differing religious viewpoints, perhaps that will play a strong role in our ongoing evaluations and advance us toward cross-cultural truth.

IV. Conclusions about Criteria of Cross-Cultural Religious Truth

The normative question of judging religious phenomena and truth claims cross-culturally will continue to challenge us in future cross-cultural studies. We want to be open to religious truth expressed in a variety of ways and to be tolerant of the persons and lifestyles of varying religious traditions. Yet we do not want to be totally relativistic and allow any position as true. So we are faced with judging religious phenomena and developing criteria for judgment.

The criteria of rational assessment and moral evaluation are used commonly in evaluating truth-claims, whether religious or not. They may be more helpful in cross-cultural evaluation in the future if cross-cultural discussions focus on understandings of reason, moral goodness, moral evil, and so on, in an effort to transcend our particular cultural-historical backgrounds in applying these criteria. Similarly, the criterion of humanization may reflect a universal interest in the human, but concrete understandings of what constitutes a humane world may differ substantially. Smith's insider-outsider criterion seems to work more easily on the descriptive-historical level than on the normative level, although some agreement on the normative level is important for developing a world theology. Cross-cultural discussion may help to further understand and reduce conflict, but may also serve to clarify basic differences.

If we look to the future, some insights and developments from Paul Tillich's discussion of theological truth may be helpful in developing cross-cultural criteria. In another place I have used Tillich's discussion of the truth of faith and the nature of religious symbols to suggest some basic criteria for theological statements.[21] These criteria can be divided into criteria for the subjective side of truth and criteria for the objective side of truth. Such a division may help clarify discussion about the difference between existential truth and propositional truth, or the distinction between a more analytical judgment of truth and a personal judgment of truth.

On the subjective side of truth, we are concerned with the response of persons to religious symbols (including events, objects, ideas, theological statements, truth-claims). Does the religious symbol make the ultimate accessible and understandable for a group of people? Is the symbol accepted as meaningful and true by a group of people? These questions are asking whether a religious symbol evokes a response, is effective, or conveys transforming power for a group of people. If the answers to those questions are "no," then we can not (or no longer) call the symbol true. These questions allow for the possibility of historical-cultural change as well as personal change in response to certain symbols. They also allow for the great diversity of personal religious responses that we have within different religious traditions as well as among them. From a descriptive point of view one can come to understand how various symbols work in other traditions and see that they are effective and transforming for persons. But that does not mean that they will become normative or transforming for us. Once one has determined that these subjective conditions of religious response to particular symbols have been met, one still has the difficulty of distinguishing or judging among the many religious symbols that are alive and effective for persons. Discussions of existential truth or personal judgments of truth focus on this subjective side of truth, but need to put that together with the objective side of truth to have more productive evaluation.

On the objective side of truth, we are concerned with the content of the religious symbol or phenomena which should in some way express the ultimate. Does the symbol point beyond its finite form to the ultimate? Does it participate in the power of the ultimate? If we follow the stance of the four thinkers discussed, namely, that the ultimate transcends all historical-cultural embodiments of it, then we do not have easy access to any absolute authority which can answer these questions for us. But perhaps there is a criterion which will work to "protect" the ultimate and express that stance and therefore also give us some help in judgments on the objective side of truth.

In several places Tillich uses a paradoxical form and content to express the ultimate and avoid idolatry.[22] His criterion for avoiding idolatry points to the finite nature of all religious expression and to the ultimate as transcending such finitude and yet as being expressed through it (in a limited way): "That symbol is most adequate which expresses not only the ultimate but also its own lack of ultimacy."[23] On the one hand, such a criterion avoids reduction of the ultimate to the finite, and on the other, it avoids absolutization of the finite. True religious symbols should avoid both of these alternatives. Some might argue that Kaufman reduces the ultimate dimension to the finite with his criterion of humanization, though that is not his intention (his other discussions of the ultimate avoid that reduction). On the other hand, one could apply the criterion against the absolutization of the relative, such as occurred in response to Jones in Jonestown or in the identification of patriarchal language as the only true way to express the ultimate. Although every religious symbol involves the use of something finite to express the ultimate, the finite should not be identified with the ultimate itself. We can use such a criterion both within a religious tradition and among various religious traditions as a guardian of the stance that the ultimate transcends any particular historical-cultural embodiment. Although the criterion by itself cannot adjudicate the cross-cultural conflicts posed in the third example, it can serve as a guide to being open to differing religious viewpoints and as a guardian against absolutizing one's own religious viewpoint.

As we look to future development and application of criteria, we need to work for metacriteria, criteria which are applicable within particular religious traditions but also applicable cross-culturally. The development of such criteria will demand serious discussion of terms to produce clear cross-cultural understanding. All of the criteria discussed here—rational evaluation, moral evaluation, assessment of transforming power, subjective-existential response of persons, humanization, acceptability to both insiders and outsiders, and the paradoxical criterion for avoiding idolatry and reduction—do not have to be tied to a particular religious tradition, though their concrete application may reflect a particular tradition or personal-cultural-historical situation. Still, I suggest that they provide a good beginning for discussion and further development.

In judging religious phenomena we are sometimes confronted with so-called quasi-religions (cults, secular movements which take on ultimacy, and so forth) as well as major religious traditions. If we broaden Hick's discussion of mediator to symbol, then we can apply the criteria discussed here to these quasi-religions. Again, such application will depend on serious discussion, insider and outsider, of the meaning of terms and concepts.

These suggestions for criteria of truth are not final answers to the problem of judging and evaluating cross-cultural religious phenomena. Their adequacy or inadequacy will become clearer in the process of applying them and discussing them in the ongoing cross-cultural interchange of religious ideas and philosophical approaches. Both the religious phenomena and truth itself are dynamic, and therefore the criteria for judging them must be open to development and change in the future.

PART III

Models of Cross-Cultural Truth in Religion

7

The Logic of Oppositions of Religious Doctrines

◗

William A. Christian, Sr.

What can a philosopher, *qua* philosopher, hope to learn by studying various religious communities?

Some of the topics a philosopher can investigate, with reasonable hope of learning something, concern the internal structure of the doctrines of a community. Others concern contrasts and connections between different bodies of doctrines. In other words, we can study bodies of doctrines one by one, and we can study them two by two.

I

To introduce a topic of the first sort, consider what Irenaeus, the second-century bishop of Lyons, has to say in his treatise *Against Heresies*. He has much to say about the setting of human life. He speaks of the creation of the world and the history of its redemption. And he has a good deal to say about how human beings should conduct their lives in this setting. But, along with these propositions about the world and these proposals of courses of action, Irenaeus brings in considerations of a different order.

He must do this because he wants to argue that certain Gnostic doctrines are not authentically Christian. So he cannot be content with ridicule and invectives, though he descends to these at times. And he cannot be content to argue from general standards of truth or from general standards of moral rightness, though he argues in those ways at times. He has to appeal to more specific standards. For his direct objective is to show that the Gnostics have gone astray from the authentic teachings of the Christian church.

So he needs a framework for arguments on questions of the form: "Does [some sentence] *s* express a Christian doctrine or not?" These questions cannot be argued unless there is some nonarbitrary way of dealing with them. They call for rules and principles to guide judgments. The following are some of the parts of the framework Irenaeus develops for such questions:

1. *s* is not a Christian doctrine unless it is in accord with the scriptures.

2. Passages in the scriptures (like passages in Homer) ought to be interpreted in their contexts.

3. Apostolic tradition amplifies and confirms what the scriptures say.

4. Bishops can be relied on to preserve apostolic tradition.

Now Irenaeus means to speak for the Church. So he must be putting forward those rules and principles as Christian doctrines. And, since their function in this situation is to guide judgments on whether something is a Christian doctrine or not, we might say of the framework as a whole that it is proposed as a doctrine about doctrines.

Similar situations, with similar requirements, occur in the histories of other religious communities. For example, the Buddhist doctrine of the "Four Great Authorities" in the *Mahāparinibbāṇasutta* sets up a procedure for determining whether or not some reported saying of the Buddha is to be accepted as genuine. Doctrines about abrogation of previously binding rules, in Judaism and more importantly in Christianity and in Islam, have similar functions.

Second-order doctrines of a somewhat different type cluster about notions of a twofold truth, or two kinds of truth, or two or more kinds of meaning texts may have. These occur in the teachings of all the major religions. Distinctions are drawn between truths of reason and truths of revelation, or between truths veiled in metaphors and explicit truths, or between conventional and commonsense truths and ultimate or absolute truths. Often these distinctions bear directly on hermeneutical questions, and hermeneutical doctrines are clearly cases of doctrines about doctrines.[1]

This feature of the bodies of doctrines of religious communities, namely, that they include second-order doctrines, is by no means a new discovery, but it might well make the pulse of a philosopher beat faster and prompt one to study its various occurrences.

To return to questions like the one Irenaeus was addressing, questions of the form "Is s a doctrine of R?," where R stands for the name of some religious community or other, produce an interesting set of consequences. If someone who is not a member of that community sets out to answer a question of this type, it seems that two courses are open. One may undertake to speak only at second hand, strictly as a historian, let us say. But one may find that the historical facts are not clear. Or one may find that a strictly historical answer is not sufficient, since one is studying a living community still in the course of developing its doctrines.

If so, and if one still undertakes to say whether some sentence expresses a doctrine of that community or not, then one must shape one's own judgment in accord with that community's framework for such judgments. One would have to do what a member of that community would have to do. One would have to accept, for the time being, those of its second-order doctrines which are relevant to the question. Then perhaps we could put the difference between one's position and the position of a member of that community as follows: If a member of that community claims that some sentence expresses a doctrine of that community, he or she is thereby committed to accepting that sentence, but if our nonmember claims that some sentence expresses a doctrine of that community, he or she is thereby committed to accepting, as a framework for argument, only the relevant second-order doctrines. One is not committed to accepting the community's first-order doctrines, doctrines about the world and conduct in it, or any second-order doctrines which are not relevant to the question.

These consequences may well give pause to those philosophers who, on the one hand, do not feel called upon by their own religious community (if they have one) to speak for it and, on the other hand, do not wish to speak for other religious communities. But a philosopher can study the logic of questions of the form, "Is s a doctrine of R?," without undertaking to answer them. We can learn something by considering possible values of s which may turn out not to be doctrines of R, even implausible ones, though plausible ones are needed to keep us on the main track. Furthermore, generally there is more to the logic of a body of doctrine than that community itself has had occasion to notice. Somewhat similarly, generally there is more to the logic of physics than physicists have had occasion to notice.

II

Now let us touch on a topic of another sort, one concerning contrasts between doctrines of different religions. Conceivably, after studying the teachings of a number of religious communities, we could come to the conclusion that they are all saying the same thing. Or, conceivably, we could conclude that these bodies of doctrines are all logically isolated from one another. But before we could come to either of these broad (and, I will add, highly implausible) conclusions, we would have to deal with a number of particular cases. We would have to study many pairs of doctrines of different religions.

What would it mean to say that there are logical connections between one body of doctrines and another? Let us say that one body of doctrines is connected with some other if (i) some doctrine belonging to one is the same as some doctrine belonging to the other, or if (ii) some doctrine belonging to one depends for its acceptability on some doctrine belonging to the other, or if (iii) some doctrine belonging to one is opposed to some doctrine belonging to the other. Arguments between proponents of different bodies of doctrines have to lean heavily on connections, or supposed connections, of these different kinds.

Let us take (ii), the case of dependence. To say that what is said in some sentence depends for its acceptability on the acceptability of what is said in some other sentence is to say that if the latter is not acceptable, the former is not acceptable. But we need some distinctions to see how this would work in the case of doctrines of different religions. These may be brought out by use of the following schemas.

1. $s1$ depends on $s2$.

2. $s1$ is a doctrine of $R1$. $s2$ is a doctrine of $R2$.

3. ($s1$ is a doctrine of $R1$) depends on ($s2$ is a doctrine of $R2$).

The first point to notice is that statements of form 1 are independent of statements of form 2. If what is said in some sentence depends on what is said in some other sentence, it does so whether or not either sentence is a doctrine of some religious community. For example, suppose that for $s1$ we read: (*a*) Jesus is the Messiah whom

God promised to send. And suppose that for $s2$ we read: (b) God promised to send a Messiah. Then it seems clear that the first of these (a) depends on the second (b). If God did not promise to send a Messiah, then Jesus is not the promised Messiah. So far nothing has been said about whether either sentence is a doctrine of some religion. It is indeed plausible that (a) is a Christian doctrine and it is plausible that (b) is a Judaic doctrine. But whether or not these statements of form 2 are true, it could still be true that (a) depends on (b). We can be right in some statements of form 1 and wrong in statements of form 2.

The second point to notice is that statements of the form 3 are quite a different matter. These say that if some $s2$ is not a doctrine of $R2$, then some $s1$ is not a doctrine of $R1$; for example, that some sentence expresses a doctrine of the Christian community only if some other sentence expresses a doctrine of the Judaic community. Statements of this form are highly problematical, though we do not have to go into that now. The main point is that statements of forms 1 and 2 do not depend on them.

To sum up, if someone claims that a certain doctrine of one religion depends on a certain doctrine of another religion, they would have to argue on two different fronts. They would have to argue that what is said in some sentence is acceptable only if what is said in some other sentence is acceptable, arguing here for a statement of form 1. And they would have to argue independently that these sentences express doctrines of different religions, arguing here for statements of form 2. If they do not want to argue for statements of form 2, for reasons mentioned above, or for other reasons, then they must content themselves with plausible cases and modify their claim so it would take the following form: $s1$ depends on $s2$, so if $s1$ is a doctrine of $R1$ and if $s2$ is a doctrine of $R2$, then this doctrine of $R1$ depends on that doctrine of $R2$. But in any case they would not have to argue for any statement of form 3.

The main points I have made about (ii) dependence, with the aid of schemas 1, 2 and 3, hold for cases of (i) identity and cases of (iii) opposition as well. But some differences should be noticed. It seems that there could not be identities of second-order doctrines, doctrines about doctrines. The reason is that a fully explicit second-order doctrine of a community mentions that community essentially. So no sentence could express both a second-order doctrine of one community and a second-order doctrine of another community, though there could be close parallels. But this does not count against identities of first-order doctrines. It is plausible that the sentence "God is merciful" expresses a Judaic doctrine and it is plausible also that this sentence expresses a Muslim doctrine.

Oppositions are in some ways the most interesting cases. Certainly they are more interesting than consistencies. They are more informative, we might say. If we know that two sentences are consistent, and if we know that one of them is acceptable, we do not yet know whether the other one is acceptable or not. But if we know that two sentences are opposed, and if we know that one is acceptable, then we know that the other is not acceptable. That is why, if we know that two doctrines of different religions are consistent with one another, we have not yet found a connection between the bodies of doctrines to which they belong. But if we know that the doctrines are opposed to one another, then we have found a connection. Also, an opposition is prima facie evidence that in their bodies of doctrines these religious communities are not saying the same thing.

8

The Doctrines of a Religious Community about Other Religions

◻

Joseph A. DiNoia

A member of a religious community might have occasion to ask of the teachers in the community: What do we have to say about other religions? What is the value of their beliefs and ways of life as compared with ours? How are we to regard other religious people? How are we to act towards them?

Such questions might arise in circumstances of actual contact and interaction between the members of one community and the adherents of other traditions. Or they might reflect a more hypothetical interest, kindled perhaps by the study of the religious literature of distant cultures or by philosophical inquiry into the place of religion in human affairs. A religious community's answers to questions like these would turn on considerations close to the center of its scheme of doctrines. In a general way at least, these answers would have to account for the claims that other religions were understood to make about a range of human concerns not unlike that covered by its own important teachings. In addition to providing an overall account of the worth of other religious traditions, a community's answers to these questions might also have to include some appraisal of the spiritual state of the adherents of other religions and some advice about the policies and attitudes appropriate in their regard.

Religious teachings which have arisen in response to questions about these matters are of considerable philosophical interest. In this essay I shall analyze the logic of those elements in the discourse of religious communities in which something is taught about other religions and their adherents. I shall draw mainly upon the Christian scheme in presenting illustrations of doctrines of this sort, but I understand the analysis of the logic of such doctrines to be applicable to the study of any well-developed religious scheme in which teachings about other religions occur.[1]

I

A notable feature of the world's major religions is that each fosters a comprehensive pattern of life in its adherents. In the course of fostering their distinctive patterns of life, religious communities generally teach something or other. Whether rules for meditation or credal formulas, the elements of discourse in religious communities which propose some truth for belief, some good as worth seeking, or some course of action for adoption, are being designated here as *religious doctrines*. Doctrines are those forms of speech which are normative for the rest of a community's discourse.

A religious community's doctrines taken as a whole can be designated as its body or *scheme* of doctrines without implying any rigid or constant ordering of these doctrines. Often the doctrines of a religious community are only implicit, in the way grammatical rules are in the skillful use of language. Even when explicated, they may hang together rather loosely and be susceptible of ordering in a variety of ways.

One of the functions of theologians and their counterparts in nontheistic communities is to study the connections among their community's doctrines and suggest some orderings of them. In the course of doing so, these experts often employ claims from nonreligious fields of inquiry like biology, ethics or metaphysics in order to show the links between the doctrines of their community and "all there is."

When a religious community proposes something to be believed, undertaken, or valued in a certain way, it claims at least by implication that what it teaches is true, right and good. A person is a member of a religious community to the degree that he or she accepts the teachings of that community and therefore these claims about them.

II

Normally, the distinctiveness and integrity of a religious community's pattern of life and scheme of doctrines and the spiritual states of outsiders do not arise as pressing issues. But interaction between its members and the members of one or more other religious communities is likely to stimulate concern over such issues. In the history of religions such interaction has occurred in the great variety of circumstances prevailing in warfare, conquest, trade, missionary undertakings, and the like. Such interaction prompted most of the major world religions to develop some teachings about their counterparts, either individually or en bloc.

Where a religious community ($R1$) has had occasion to teach something with regard to other religious communities ($R2$, $R3$, etc.) and their members, the class of sentences in its characteristic discourse which express such teachings are here designated as its *doctrines about other religions*. Generally speaking, in this set of teachings the scheme of doctrines of $R1$ is developed in such a way as to evaluate alternative proposals in $R2/R3$ concerning matters covered by $R1$'s central doctrines, to appraise the spiritual states of the members of $R2/R3$ in view of whatever $R1$ proposes as the true aim of life, and to command policies and attitudes to be adopted in regard to $R2/R3$ and their members. These purposes require that the central doctrines of $R1$ be interpreted and developed in ways that will generate teachings about other religions which are reasonably consistent with these central doctrines and suited to circumstances of interaction (if there be any) between the members of $R1$ and the members of $R2/R3$.

Doctrines about other religions in $R1$ articulate implications which its central doctrines have under specific circumstances depending on whether other religions *qua* religions (as systems of belief or patterns of life) or the adherents of other religions (as fellow human beings or "unbelievers") are in view. $R1$'s doctrines about other religions *qua* religions assert something to be true or to be valued about them, or recommend some course of action to be undertaken in their regard. Examples of such doctrines are:

1. Other religions teach some true and right doctrines.

2. Other religions can advance their members toward the attainment of the true aim of life.

3. The traditions of other religions should be studied and esteemed.

It should be noted that $R1$'s doctrines about other religions *qua* religions could refer to all other religions as a group (as in 1–3 above) or to $R2/R3$ singly, as in examples such as:

4. $R2$ is fulfilled (or superseded, or abrogated) by $R1$.

5. $R3$ is a thoroughly corrupt religion.

Within the larger class of doctrines about other religions in $R1$ it is possible to distinguish a subclass made up of doctrines about the members of other religious communities. Doctrines of this sort assert something to be the case or to be good about the religious and moral states and dispositions of the members of other religious communities, or propose some course of inward or outward action to be adopted in dealings with them. $R1$'s doctrines about the members of other religious communities could refer to all such persons as a group or to members of some particular religious commuity. Examples of such doctrines are:

6. Members of other communities could perform good actions conducive to the attainment of the true aim of life.

7. The members of $R3$ should be persuaded of the errors of the doctrines they hold.

8. Engage in dialogue with the members of other religious communities.

The distinction between doctrines about other religions *qua* religions and doctrines about the members of other religious communities can be useful in clarifying the different ways a community's central doctrines come to bear on the development of its doctrines about other religions. (I shall illustrate this point later in this essay by presenting some examples of Christian doctrines of this sort.)

Like other teachings in $R1$, including some important ones, its doctrines about other religions may not have received official formulation in its creeds and codes but may nevertheless have acquired certain standard uses which apply beyond the concrete circumstances which occasioned their emergence. First, doctrines about other religions which were originally elaborated in order to guide $R1$ in its dealings with $R2$ may supply precedents for its relations with $R3/R4$ and their members. Further, $R1$'s doctrines about other religions may eventually serve to shape its assessments of all groups, teachings and individuals that do not fall within the bounds of its membership and of adherence to its teachings. In this way $R1$'s doctrines about other religions come to be applied to thought systems which are only in a borderline sense "religious" and to individuals who adhere to such systems or profess allegiance to no explicitly religious community or body of beliefs and practices. In addition, although $R1$'s doctrines about other religions are for the most part addressed to its own members and to questions they may raise, such doctrines may have uses in apologetical arguments constructed in order to persuade nonmembers to approve or favorably entertain $R1$'s doctrines. Lastly, $R1$'s doctrines about other religions can have important "internal uses." $R1$'s doctrines about other religions can function to explicate the point of central doctrines in $R1$ in times when it has very limited contacts with the members of other religious communities. Such doctrines can be propounded and developed without reference to any existing communities and mainly to disclose the point of some central doctrines in $R1$.

In this next section I shall illustrate and amplify some of these logical points in the course of drawing attention to some doctrines about other religions in the Christian community.

III

Consider the following example of a Christian doctrine about other religions:

$C1'$. Other religions teach some true and right doctrines.

The Christian scheme can be understood to support this assertion with a variety of considerations. In the first place, the doctrines of revelation and inspiration could be invoked in order to affirm that God can bring it about that some elements of the Christian pattern of life might occur outside the visible Christian community. Whether or not this is actually the case would call for observation and generalization. But Christians could teach that true and right doctrines may occur in other religions without adducing examples of such doctrines and without proposing any theory to explain their presence in existing (or extinct) religious traditions. Even in the absence of direct acquaintance Christians could assert $C1'$ as an implication of central Christian doctrines about the freedom, omnipotence and universal providence of God. In view of such doctrines it would seem inconsistent to many Christians to fix limits on the scope of God's action such that only the Christian pattern of life would be regarded as embodying true beliefs or fostering aspects of a good life.

Thus the doctrine that other religions may possess true or right teachings ($C1'$) articulates an implication of central Christian doctrines about the unrestricted power of God to enable human beings to discover the truth about God and to live in accordance with that truth. But $C1'$ would presumably need to be qualified by other important Christian doctrines about the more focused activity of God in the election of the people of Israel, in the ministry and destiny of Jesus Christ, and in the presence of the Holy Spirit in the Christian community. According to these doctrines God has made Godself known in a special manner in particular times and places and has provided the means by which human beings can achieve, with greater assurance than would otherwise be possible, the true aim of life, that is, union with God and participation in the life of the Trinity. A primary function of the doctrine of revelation in the Christian scheme is to articulate the nature and consequences of this special communication on God's part. In view of the Christian doctrine of revelation (and other doctrines as well), $C1'$ would need to be qualified and reformulated in an assertion like the following:

$C1$. Other religions teach partial truth in comparison with the fullness of truth taught in the Christian community.

The logic of the Christian scheme appears to entail that any acknowledgment of truth and values of other religious traditions be qualified in this way.

The nature of this qualification and its dependence on central Christian doctrines (in addition to the doctrine of revelation) can be observed more directly by considering the following expression of a common Christian doctrine about other religions *qua* religions:

$C2$. Other religions are surpassed by Christianity.

If, as the Christian scheme seems to teach, the true aim of life is salvation as union with the Trinity, and if membership in the Christian community is the divinely willed means given to attain this aim, then it would not be consistent with central Christian doctrines to ascribe to other religious communities a value equivalent to that ascribed to the Christian community. Thus, although central Christian doctrines affirm the universality of salvation, they also assert that the Christian community has privileged public access to knowledge about this aim of life and the means to attain it. Any ascription of value to the doctrines, institutions and forms of life of other religious communities would have to be qualified by ascriptions of inherent, intrinsic and contributory value to the Christian community and to membership in it. $C2$ could be expressed in statements employing a variety of related but logically independent concepts among which the following figure prominently: invalidation, supersession, fulfilment and perfection. Each of these concepts can be employed in elaborating Christian doctrines about other religions in ways that would appear consistent with central Christian doctrines which ascribe a unique set of valuations to the Christian community.

Another Christian doctrine about other religions develops implications of central Christian doctrines about the providence and universal salvific will of God:

> $C3$. Other religions could play some role in the divine plan of salvation.

According to this doctrine, other religions could be said to exercise a preparatory role with regard to Christianity in world history, or in the history of particular cultures, or in the lifetimes of individual human beings. Insofar as the partial truth in other religions (so an argument for $C3$ might proceed) can be dispositive for the emergence or acceptance of the fullness of truth in Christianity, other religions could be said to be encompassed in the order of grace and salvation.

For the purposes of illustrating the logical points I made above, the Christian scheme could thus be viewed as yielding three main doctrines about other religions *qua* religions which acknowledge the partial truth ($C1$) and providential role ($C3$) of other religions without prejudice to the attribution of special properties to the Christian community in comparison with other religions ($C2$).

Let us turn now to some examples of Christian doctrines about the members of other religious communities. I stress that my discussion of these examples is meant to contribute to the philosophical study of the logic of doctrines about other religions. I do not intend to advance proposals, much less to construct arguments for them, in the Christian discipline of "theology of religions."

Each of the world's major religious traditions seems to claim that the aim of life it proposes is the one most worthy of pursuit by all human beings without exception. A claim of this sort appears to be implied by the respective basic religious valuations which are ingredient in the doctrinal schemes of these traditions. To ascribe an unrestricted inherent or intrinsic value to some existent, as do Christianity and Islam, for example, or to some state of being, as does Theravada Buddhism, for example, is to propose that something be valued in a certain way not only by the members of a particular religious group but by human beings generally. It would be odd, though naturally not impossible, for a religious community, in view of its definition of that on which its pattern of life is centered, to manifest indifference with regard to the courses of action and particular valuations and beliefs which are understood to foster attainment of the true aim of life. Hence Christians teach some version of the claim that there is no salvation outside the church and the pattern of life it fosters, and Theravada Buddhists teach that there is no attainment of *nibbana* except in the following of the Noble Eightfold Path. It is not a sign of arrogant exclusivism that religious communities are consistent and serious in their teachings about the true aim of life and the means regarded as necessary to attain it.

The seriousness with which a religious community regards the aim of life it recommends imparts considerable urgency to questions about the chances outsiders have of attaining it. In Christianity, as in other religions, there are teachings which address these questions. Such questions need not be felt with particular urgency, to be sure, if a religious community were to assume that all religious communities foster identical aims of life, or that the different aims they propose are all worthy of pursuit, or that any of the patterns of life they foster conduce, whether equally or not, to the attainment of the true aim of life. Whether rightly or not, the central doctrines of the Christian community, and arguably of other major religious communities as well, seem to rule out such assumptions. Hence Christian doctrines about the members of other religious communities, and about outsiders generally, tend to focus prominently on other religious persons' prospects of attaining the aim of salvation despite their persistence in patterns of life which seem to point them in other and possibly wrong directions.

In view of the unique valuation of the Christian community, expressed for example in $C2$, it is not surprising that Christian doctrines about the members of other religious communities should attempt to account for their possible salvation in part by asserting the possibility of a virtual or hidden association with the Christian community on their part. Consider the following statement of such a doctrine:

> $C4$. Members of other religious communities could in some hidden way be members of the Christian community.

According to central Christian doctrines about the universal salvific will of God, all human beings who ever lived, including those who lived before the appearance of the Christian community, are called to participate in a relationship of union with God. Some construals of Christian doctrines about these matters take it that the very existence of the universe and of humankind within it is to be attributed in the first place to the divine intention to enter into union with human beings. If the universal human condition is such that persons could not attain their true and divinely willed destiny without benefit of divine aid, then this aid, given in Christ in a decisive way, must be accessible to all persons who have ever lived. Hence there are the Christian doctrines that human beings who attain their true destiny do so only in virtue of the grace of Christ and thus only through some sort of affiliation with the community in which this grace is uniquely (though not exclusively, according to some Christian theologians) found.

Many important Christian doctrines about the members of other religious communities seek to account for the possibility of a virtual or hidden association with the Christian community on the part of nonmembers. Consider the following examples of Catholic formulations of such doctrines:

    *C*5. Members of other religious communities could possess an implicit faith which could become explicit in Christianity.

    *C*6. Members of other religious communities could perform good actions having salvific value for them.

*C*5 draws upon a standard distinction made in Christian doctrines about the sacraments and means of grace between ordinary and *in voto* (i.e., effectively desired) reception of sacramental grace and on the classical concept of implicit faith. *C*6 articulates the persistent Christian recognition of the many instances of morally upright conduct on the past of persons who are not Christians and in addition ascribes contributory (or "salvific") value to such conduct. Christian doctrines such as these express a valuation of a certain range of religious and moral states and dispositions by ascribing to the members of other religious communities a virtual membership in the Christian community.

In addition to giving a general account of other religions and their adherents in the light of central Christian doctrines, doctrines about other religions in the Christian community may function to guide its members in their dealings with the members of other religious communities. In other words, in addition to doctrines about other religions which convey assertions and valuations, there are some which recommend courses of action. Such practical doctrines about other religions in the Christian community urge or enjoin the adoption of certain attitudes and policies with regard to other religions and their adherents. Examples of such practical doctrines about other religions are:

> $C7$. Christians should engage in dialogue with members of other religious communities.
>
> $C8$. Christians should proclaim the gospel to the members of other religious communities.

Practical doctrines such as these get their force from central Christian doctrines and from the valuations and assertions conveyed in doctrines about other religions *qua* religions and about the adherents of other religions.

In addition, interaction between the members of other religious communities and Christians is likely to stimulate the development of doctrines about particular religions. Consider, for example, the specific recommendations which are implicit in the recommendation to engage in dialogue with other religious people:

> $C7a$. Christians should study and esteem the doctrines of other religious communities represented in dialogue.
>
> $C7b$. Christians should entertain the proposals and arguments of other dialogue participants as serious religious alternatives.
>
> $C7c$. Christians should be open to the possible developments of their own doctrines which might be suggested in the course of their study of other religious traditions and in dialogue with their adherents.

Such recommendations imply that Christian dialogue participants will have developed some doctrines about particular religious communities or interpreted standard Christian doctrines about other religions in ways that are applicable to the doctrines, institutions and ways of life of the actually existing religious communities whose members are encountered in the course of dialogue (or in other forms of interaction like collaboration or missionary ventures).

These remarks about practical doctrines about other religions in the Christian community suggest some amplifications in the general account of the logic of doctrines about other religions which has been advanced up to this point in this essay.

In circumstances of interaction between members of $R1$ and members of $R2/R3$, assessments of particular features of the discourse and practice of these other communities are likely to be required. Detailed appraisals of this kind would presumably need to move beyond considerations suggested by $R1$'s central doctrines and doctrines about other religions in order to develop suitable principles of judgment. In developing such principles $R1$ would need to appeal to explicit information about the doctrines of $R2$ or $R3$ as well as to internal doctrinal considerations of its own and to claims from nonreligious fields of inquiry like metaphysics and ethics. In this way, members of $R1$ would be equipped to assess the universal claims implicit in the basic religious valuations, main practical doctrines, and central beliefs of $R2/R3$.

Doctrinal considerations thus serve to shape the style of $R1$'s interactions with $R2/R3$. Conversely, interaction with other religious communities can have a significant impact on the internal development of $R1$'s doctrines. Interaction with other communities and the consequent need to elaborate doctrines about other religions which are consistent with central doctrines may provoke thoroughgoing reappraisals of $R1$'s central doctrines and stimulate new understandings of their meaning. Furthermore, changing circumstances may require reformulation of standard doctrines about other religions in $R1$. In part this is because the connections between such doctrines and $R1$'s central doctrines are not hard and fast. For example, a particular doctrine about other religions might be consistent with one central doctrine in the scheme of doctrines in $R1$ but conflict (perhaps not obviously) with another. If changing historical circumstances or interaction with other religious communities or other factors bring such inconsistencies to the fore, then decisions would be needed as to whether or not particular doctrines about other religions well and truly express authentic doctrines in $R1$.

IV

Distinctive formulations of doctrines about other religions are likely to be proposed in connection with different orderings of $R1$'s central doctrines by its expert members (theologians and their counterparts in nontheistic communities). Such formulations may give expression to already existing doctrines in $R1$ about other religions or may be interpretations of some central doctrines which subsequently come to be accepted as well-formed doctrines in $R1$ about other religions. Such formulations can be distinguished from the more or less standard traditional teachings which are embedded in $R1$'s scheme of doctrines, and from authoritative formulations of such teachings (if there be any) which emanate from official sources in $R1$. An overall systematic account of the doctrines in $R1$ about other religions (such as a "theology of religions" in the Christian community) would presumably incorporate most if not all of the main formulations of such doctrines which have been elaborated in the history of $R1$ as well as suggest some new ones. A well-developed overall account of $R1$'s doctrines about other religions would normally explicate the connections between these doctrines and $R1$'s central doctrines as well as appeal to other fields of knowledge, especially in order to propose some principles of judgment by which the particular doctrines and forms of life in $R2/R3$ could be appraised.

Given the fairly loose structure of most schemes of doctrines, there is likely to be a considerable degree of flexibility in the way $R1$'s doctrines about other religions are proposed and developed in particular orderings of its central doctrines by its expert teachers. For example, a particular doctrine about other religions may figure more prominently in one ordering of doctrines than in another. Again, some orderings of the doctrines of $R1$ may seem to work with the unexpressed rule that all explications of the doctrines of $R1$ must be undertaken with a view to $R1$'s doctrines about other religions and their adherents, while other orderings may not refer to any such doctrines. Again, the connections between such doctrines and central doctrines may be explicated differently in alternative orderings of $R1$'s scheme. Variations like these could be fruitfully studied in the course of comparative analysis of particular orderings of the doctrines of $R1$ by philosophers of religions or others interested in the logic of religious discourse.

Because $R1$'s doctrines about other religions may exercise important functions in disclosing something of the overall logic of its doctrinal scheme, distinctive formulations of such doctrines by expert teachers in $R1$ may be proposed with a view to projected rather than actual interaction between members of $R1$ and members of $R2/R3$. Rather than the relationships between $R1$ and $R2$ and $R3$, what may be in view here is the relationship between $R1$ and R. Here R may designate a summary of the main features thought to be basic to all actually existing religious communities ($R1, R2, R3,\ldots$), or a stipulative definition of the structures of an ideal R, aspects of which are partially instantiated in $R1, R2, R3, \ldots$, or a dimension of the innate or acquired dispositions of human persons, or a structure or set of structures in the organization, legitimation and maintenance of social and cultural systems. To put this point more succinctly, in this case $R1$'s doctrines about other religions are formulated with a view to some general theory of religion. Such formulations may be developed mainly for internal purposes, in order to clarify the point or draw out certain implications of some central doctrines in $R1$. Formulations of this kind may or may not prove serviceable in the circumstances of interaction between $R1$ and $R2/R3$. Their usefulness would depend upon such matters as how adequately they account for de facto religious communities.

I shall illustrate this point of some of these aspects of the logic of a community's doctrines about other religions by referring to some Christian doctrines of this sort.

The Christian doctrines about other religions which I formulated earlier as $C1$–6 originated in the Christian community as doctrines expressing valuations and assertions about particular religions and their adherents. Thus, the literature in which they were first propounded manifests extensive and detailed knowledge of the classical and ethnic polytheisms, the royal cults, the mystery religions and the sophisticated religio-philosophical systems, represented by developments of Platonism and Stoicism, for example, prevalent in Hellenistic societies. In this early literature the acknowledgment of the partial truth in doctrines like $C1$ and the rejection of errors of other traditions and patterns of life are framed in terms of specific judgments about the beliefs and practices of particular cults and philosophical schools. Authors like Justin Martyr in his *Apologies*, Clement of Alexandria in his *Protrepticus*, *Pedagogus* and *Stromateis*, or Augustine, especially in the *City of God*, write with respect or disapproval as the case may be about doctrines with which they have been acquainted first hand or to which they themselves at one time adhered.[2]

The Christian community's teachings about Judaism's providential relationship to it are generalized in this literature to explicate the invalidation, supersession and fulfillment of all the religions of classical antiquity in doctrines like $C2$, specifically with regard to their particular theistic, ethical and soteriological doctrines. Ascriptions of a providential role to other religions, and expressions of confidence about their adherents' eternal salvation (in $C3$–6) reflect the conviction on the part of early Christian writers that most of the men and religions in their experience seemed to seek the salvation which Christ alone could assure them.

The doctrines about other religions which were to become standard in the Christian commuity were thus originally propounded in circumstances of religious interaction in which explicit attention to the doctrines and forms of life of particular traditions was unavoidable. In the literature of this period formulations of $C1$–6 almost always have specific referents in view. The literature of Christian antiquity abounds in formulations in which doctrines first propounded in reference to Judaism came to be applied to the other religions and religious philosophies with which Christians were engaged in dialogue and debate.[3]

But in much of subsequent Christian literature doctrines like $C1$–6 are for the most part propounded independently of valuations and assertions having for their specific referents any religious traditions or their adherents. This development is understandable. Throughout most of its later history the Christian community rarely experienced circumstances of religious interaction comparable in intensity to those of late antiquity. Not until well into modern times would such circumstances again obtain on a broad scale.

During most of its history the Christian community's interaction with other religious communities was usually quite limited in scope. Hence its theologians had little occasion to take the doctrines and patterns of life of other religions specifically into account in developing Christian doctrines about other religions. With the gradual eclipse of classical polytheism, with the establishment of Christianity as the religion of the empire, and with the Christian appropriation of many of the religious and philosophical ideas of the Hellenistic world, only the Jewish community retained a significant religious identity in the midst of the enveloping Christendom. During large portions of Christian history Islam appears to have been regarded as something of a Christian heresy rather than a distinctive religious tradition.[4] The religions of the nomadic tribes at the edges of civilization were thought to represent versions of the thoroughly corrupt polytheism increasingly on the wane throughout the empire itself and were dealt with accordingly. Well into the Middle Ages and beyond, therefore, Christian doctrines about other religions were regularly invoked to clarify the point of central doctrines or to authorize energetic and far-reaching missionary endeavors. The prominence of formulations of $C2$ along with generally negative assessments of other religions and convictions about the near impossibility of attaining salvation without explicit faith lent considerable urgency to the Christian missionary enterprise. Where they occur at all, acknowledgments of the worth of other religions in doctrines like $C1$ and $C3$ have about them a speculative and hypothetical character. These doctrines as well as those about presumed members of other religious communities like $C4$–6 are affirmed in much of Christian literature after late antiquity as implications of central doctrines. Given circumstances of limited religious interaction, such doctrines would possess a certain plausibility as referring to comparatively small numbers of human beings and a narrow range of religious traditions.

The ages of exploration and colonialism marked the beginning of a decisive shift in the circumstances of religious interaction to which the Christian community had become accustomed over the course of more than a thousand years. The discovery of new worlds brought with it a growing realization of the great variety of distinctive religious beliefs and practices and of previously unimagined numbers of human beings beyond the reach of Christian proclamation. In part this realization served as a stimulus to the Christian missionary enterprise. Another important long-range effect was to bring Christian doctrines about other religions into new prominence. Specifically, Christian theologians were now being called upon to develop the traditional doctrines about other religions in such a way as to make them suitable in circumstances vastly more complex than any experienced by the Christian community in previous periods, late antiquity included.

Thus the contemporary Christian community is heir to formulations of doctrines about other religions originally proposed to account for particular religious traditions but subsequently developed mainly for internal purposes or in endorsement of evangelization policies. The Christian community may be understood to suppose that these doctrines can continue to be propounded for standard internal purposes and in the other ways they have customarily been used. But in circumstances of religious interaction decisively influenced by a determination to pursue a policy of dialogue in its relations with other religious communities, the Christian community can further be understood to suppose that these traditional doctrines about other religions could be invoked anew in ways that would do justice to the distinctive doctrinal claims put forward by other religious communities. Numerous theologians in the Christian community are advancing proposals along these lines, in connection with distinctive orderings and explications of the doctrines of the Christian scheme.

V

In this essay I have offered an account of some features of the logic of doctrines about other religions. I have not meant to be exhaustive. The account presented here is intended primarily to point the way towards a fuller inquiry concerning the logic of doctrines which arise in religious communities in the course of interaction between them. I understand it to be an important aspect of cross-cultural philosophy of religion to advance the philosophical analysis of this range of doctrines. An obvious weakness of my presentation here is that it draws its illustrations of the logic of such doctrines almost exclusively from the Christian scheme of doctrines. But studies of the doctrines of communities other than Christianity suggest that in its main lines the account of the logic of doctrines about other religions proposed here can contribute to the study of such doctrines in these communities as well.[5] It remains to be seen whether this point could be sustained by detailed study of such doctrines in the schemes of Muslim, Buddhist, Jewish, Hindu or other religious communities.

9

The Logic of Interreligious Dialogue

◻

Norbert M. Samuelson

In recent years scholars of religion have taken part in a number of interreligious dialogues. On one such occcasion I was engaged in a forum on the question, "What is a gentile in Judaism and Christianity?" Each of the participants gave brief statements about the history of this term in these two religions and indicated problems connected with the various positions without attempting either to condemn or justify those positions. Following the presentations, two colleagues from diametrically opposed perspectives condemned our failure to be more judgmental. One objected to the fact that we were so relativistic, by which he meant that we failed to assert with appropriate certainty the truth of our respective religious commitments. The other objected to our dogmatism, by which he meant that we failed to be critical in judgment of the religious claims we had presented. In both cases my personal judgment was that my learned colleagues were naive, by which I meant that they failed to recognize the distinctive character of an interreligious dialogue. Both saw interreligious dialogue as structurally alike to an academic philosophical debate. They assumed that since both contexts in theory are committed to discovering some truth, the rules for judgment in one setting are the same as the rules in the other setting. Hence my observation that their critique betrayed naiveté. However, on subsequent introspection, I decided not that my initial judgment was wrong, but that their naiveté was quite sophisticated in the sense that many if not most participants in interreligious dialogue will make the same uncritical associations that these otherwise highly critical scholars made.

Occasions on which individuals who in some way represent a given religious community meet to have a discussion in some formal way with individuals who in some way represent a different religious community generally are called *interreligious dialogues*. The term *dialogue* initially was used because of its association with the religious thought of Martin Buber, in which case the term minimally meant the following: If two or more people are involved in a dialogue, then their relation is such that their interaction will make them significantly different people than they would be without that interaction; and this state of affairs entails that the individuals related view each other as "ends in themselves," that is, no one individual in the relation has objectives in the relation that would in any way exploit or use another individual in the relation; one individual will relate to another solely for the sake of the relation, and that relation will be in no way viewed by the individuals involved as a means to some different end. However, Buber's use of the term has little application to the ordinary use of the term in the context of actual interreligious discussions. I am not concerned here with whether or not an interreligious dialogue should be *dialogue* in Buber's sense of the term. Rather, my attention is confined to the logic implicit in these dialogues as they in fact occur and not as they may or may not occur ideally. (As will become clear, in my view Buber's kind of dialogue is a valid objective for a dialogue, but it is not the only valid objective. Different people meeting in different contexts will and should have different goals. In some contexts Buber's kind of dialogue would be either inappropriate or undesirable.)

I. Truth in Interreligious Dialogue

There are all kinds of motives behind a dialogue. Some of them are social, some are psychological and some are political. However, whatever the motives are of the people who meet, when they do come together their meeting usually involves the utterance of declarative sentences. To at least this extent all dialogue is concerned with truth. Speakers assume that what they say is true or else there would be no legitimate reason for making the claim, and if other participants do not accept the truth of a speaker's claim and that claim is considered relevant to the meeting, they will object to what is said. Thus, truth is at least one objective in an interreligious dialogue. Some people will claim more than this. They will say that there are special interreligious truths, that is, truth-claims that are unique to this context. It is this claim that I now want to examine.

It is important to distinguish between propositions and speech acts. While there may be very special rules for judging the truth or falsity of different kinds of speech acts, if a proposition is true, it is true. It is not just true sometimes. For example, the proposition "Descartes exists" is a contingent truth. Even though Descartes' utterance "I exist" is necessarily true, the proposition "Descartes exists" remains contingent even if Descartes says it. "Descartes exists" is true because Descartes exists. It is not the truth of Descartes or anyone else; it simply happens to be true. Thus it is not the case that "Descartes exists" is Spinoza's contingent truth, Descartes' necessary truth, and someone else's falsehood. In this sense, then, when speaking of propositions, there are no special kinds of truth. There is no Jewish or Muslim or Christian truth; there is only truth.

Although the truth of propositions cannot be qualified in this way, speech acts can. A speech act differs from a proposition in that it consists of the proposition within its context where context includes such factors as who utters the proposition, to whom it is uttered, as well as when and where it is uttered. Depending on the kind of claim being made, in some contexts the religious community with which a speaker or a listener is connected may affect the truth value of what is said even if the proposition entailed by what is said absolutely is true or false. Thus, while with respect to propositions there are no Jewish, Muslim or Christian truths but only truths, with respect to speech acts there are such things as Jewish, Muslim and Christian truth-claims.

I want to claim that in interreligious dialogue the concern is primarily with speech acts and only secondarily with propositions even when truth is a major objective of the dialogue. Interreligious dialogue is not simply a discussion between people. To be an interreligious dialogue it is necessary that some of the people in some way represent one religious community and that others of the people in some way represent a different religious community. Otherwise neither Jews nor Christians need be present at a Jewish-Christian dialogue. Such a condition would be irrelevant if dialogue dealt primarily with propositions rather than speech acts. If a group of Christians met where some of them were experts in Islam and others were experts in Judaism, the meeting could be a discussion of Islam and Judaism, but that discussion could not be a Muslim-Jewish dialogue.

Hence, people who say in interreligious dialogue that "their concern is solely with what is true" and mean by this assertion that they dismiss the relevance of religious identity in either making a claim themselves or judging someone else's truth claim mistake the setting. The error is logical and not just political. They confuse a setting in which propositions are primary with a setting in which speech utterances are primary. What is distinctive about interreligious dialogue is that the important statements made are religious claims, that is, speech acts in which the identity of the speaker with a religious community affects the truth of the claim made.

Both Islam and Judaism emphasized that tradition as well as reason is a means to gaining truth. Claims based on reason were judged on the basis of propositional logic either as self-evident, necessary propositions or necessary inferences from self-evident, necessary propositions, or as accurate descriptions of direct experience or necessary inferences from accurate descriptions of direct experience. In contrast, claims based on tradition, which involve propositions that are contingent rather than necessary, incorrigible or impossible, were judged on the basis of the intellectual and moral character of the persons reporting the claims and the context in which the reports were given. The same procedure was involved when Roman Catholics judged certain religious claims on an appeal to past religious authority.

It is interesting to note that the modern logicians who initially limited logic solely to propositions on a mathematical model also tended to be Protestants who as Protestants rejected the validity of argument from tradition. Thus, for example, a Christian was encouraged to go directly to his/her own religious experience or to scripture, and not to rely on "mere" traditions about scripture in order to determine religious belief. Scripture in this context was a valid source of truth solely because as a purported direct report of revelation it had the logical status of an incorrigible claim in the same way that any report of direct experience was considered incorrigible.

(For the above reasons I would like to call the error of limiting truth claims solely to a consideration of propositions without considering speech acts "the Protestant Fallacy".)

II. Religious Claims

A religious claim is a truth-claim that is made in the name of a given religious community in which the association of the claim with the community is relevant to determining the truth-value of the claim. Any such claim can be interpreted and judged by any individual whether he/she is or is not a member of the relevant religious community.

Let us distinguish two ways in which such a claim can be both interpreted and judged, that is, evaluated. It can be evaluated *internally* and it can be evaluated *externally*. *Internal evaluation* means that the rules of judgment of the proposition entailed by the claim are set within the linguistic context in which the claim is made. In this context a religious claim is evaluated internally when the meaning of the claim is set within the special use that the language of the claim has within the relevant religious community. *External evaluation* involves evaluation based on factors other than the linguistic context, so that a religious claim is subject to external evaluation to the extent that what that claim means is independent of any special function for the terms that express the claim within the relevant religious community.

A baseball claim that is judged only internally is "You're out." *Out* is a technical baseball term whose meaning has little if any relation to the term as ordinarily used in spatial judgments, and the criteria for judging that the statement "You're out" is true or false are determined almost entirely by the rules of baseball. A comparable Roman Catholic claim is "John Newman is a saint," and a comparable Jewish claim is "Sturgeon is a kosher fish." In the former case the term *saint* is a technical term within Catholicism that need not have any relation to how this term functions in other contexts, and the truth or falsity of the claim for Newman is determined almost entirely by Church law. In the latter case *fish*, like *kosher*, is a technical rabbinic term that need not correspond to the use that this term has in other contexts. Thus whether or not sturgeon can or cannot be called kosher is to be determined almost entirely by the rules of rabbinic law.

A baseball claim that is judged externally is "Babe Ruth was a great athlete." To the extent that Ruth's excellence is determined by his ability to perform certain functions that have value solely because baseball judges those activities to be valuable, this sentence is internally evaluated. But *athlete* is a term that encompasses more than the term *baseball player*, and for this reason, since the claim involves a classification that transcends baseball and is common to other sports as well, to judge this claim requires an appeal to criteria that cannot solely be defined by baseball. The same can be said about the Christian claim that Paul was a rabbi, since as the term *rabbi* is used here an appeal to something other than Christianity, namely, Judaism, is required for the criteria of judgment. Similarly, the Jewish claim that Moses gave the Torah to the children of Israel on Mount Sinai makes a factual, historical claim. Given that the term *Moses* names a single individual, the expression *children of Israel* designates a definite class of individuals, the term *Mount Sinai* refers to a definite spatial location, and the term *Torah* means a given set of laws, the claim is true if and only if Moses in fact gave the Torah to the children of Israel at Mount Sinai. In other words, this is a factual, historical claim whose truth or falsity is to be determined independent of how this sentence functions in rabbinic tradition.

Some claims can only be judged internally and other claims can be judged externally as well as internally, but no claim can be judged only externally. To say that a claim is true or false presupposes that you know what that claim means, and to some extent the meaning of any claim is dependent on the linguistic context in which that claim is set. Hence the internal evaluation of a claim takes precedence over its external evaluation. For example, before we consider any general moral grounds for judging the claim that a Jew may or may not give blood to a blood bank, we ought to consider how this claim would be judged solely from the perspective of Jewish law (*halakhah*), since this internal consideration would establish a context for judgment that is relevant that makes this question significantly different from the question, ought a person give blood to a blood bank. Similarly, the claim that all people have salvation through Christ cannot fairly be judged until we first see what it means in an appropriate Christian context to speak about salvation and/or Christ. For example, if what it means for people to be saved is that they make no mistakes in moral judgment and/or that they enjoy a certain level of pleasure, we would judge this claim in a different way than we would if being saved meant, for example, to be set in a direction towards achieving better moral judgment and/or more pleasure in the future than in the past, or if salvation simply meant membership in a certain kind of community independent of individual moral excellence or prosperity.

What is important for religious dialogue about this priority rule that internal evaluation takes precedence over external judgment is that Jews and Christians share many terms in common that are critical to the discussion that seem to be the same and at one time may have been the same but now have little in common, while there are other terms that seem to have different meanings in the different religious contexts but do not. For example, many Jews and Christians think that they mean the same thing by the words *Christianity* and *religion*, but I suspect that this is not the case, while many Jews believe that when Christians speak of *God* they mean something different than what Jews mean by *God*, but I suspect that this also is not the case. Similarly, many Jews and Christians think that the term *Christ* expresses something totally central to Christianity and totally opposed to Judaism. I would contend that the term *Christ* functions differently in different Christian contexts, and that some of the senses of the term are as common to varieties of Judaism as they are to Christianity. For example, in classical theology (Jewish and Christian), *Christ* as God in God's aspect of love seems to me to be indistinguishable from the term *Adonai* as it is used by the early rabbis. Similarly, the Christian term *Holy Ghost* and the rabbinic term *Shekhinah* seem to me to be indistinguishable in many contexts.

Conversely, while Jews and Christians seem to share moral commitments in common, there are major ethical issues between them. For example, whereas many Christians would argue that all persons ought to be treated as equals, many Jews would object that it is morally wrong for a parent to treat his/her child in the same way that he/she treats someone else's child, that is, many Jews would understand the morality of parentage or family identity differently than many Christians. Some Jews and Christians might not be aware that some moral duties to family are not coherent with some moral duties to humanity, but given this recognition I suspect that more Jews will choose familial obligations over universal duties to humankind than will Christians, and that this difference has something to do with Jewish and Christian ethics. Similarly, as some Christians use the term *grace* it means something very different from the Hebrew term *hesed* as it is used by many classical rabbis even though one acceptable English translation for this term is "grace". The difference between these two words can be illustrated as follows: Suppose I tell my son that he cannot go to the movies until he cleans his room and then I discover that his room is such a mess that if he cleans it he will miss the movie. In this context "grace" means that I let him go to the movie even though he did not finish cleaning the room. In contrast, "hesed" means that I clean up some of the room for him so that he will be able to finish and go to the movies. In other words, sometimes divine grace means that God gives people what they do not deserve and sometimes *hesed* means that God helps people to achieve what otherwise they would not deserve, and these two concepts are very different.

At least in theory ethical issues are subject to objective evaluation, but the internal judgment of any religious ethical claim would take precedence. Thus, before Jews and Christians begin to pass judgments on each other's moral claims, they ought to be familiar with the religious context appropriate to those claims within their respective religious traditions. It is a mistake to assume that any such claims have the same meaning in the relevant two religions.

III. Rules of Judgment

Having determined adequately what a given religion or religious spokesperson in a religious dialogue means by a given claim, the question now is, is it legitimate for a participant from another religion to pass judgment on that claim? The obvious answer is yes, because dialogue is concerned with discovering truth, and without the right to judge that something is false there can be no way to decide that something else is true. But since dialogue deals with speech acts rather than propositions, and since the religious framework of the languge claims are essential to the evaluation of those claims, what constitutes a legitimate or illegitimate truth judgment in dialogue is no simple matter. The goal of this section of the essay is to spell out some of these complexities.

When a medieval Jewish philosopher such as Maimonides said that angels are the intelligences of the spheres, logically he was doing the following. The sentence p "Angels exist" is a claim in the language of rabbinic Judaism; the sentence q "Heavenly intelligences exist" is a claim in the language of the Aristotelian sciences. The two claims p and q are so related that one is true if and only if the other is true. In this case q can serve as an explanation of what p means. The context in which q will have this function will be when Maimonides explains the Jewish claim that angels exist to a learned Aristotelian with a minimum knowledge of and/or commitment to rabbinic Judaism. Similarly, p can serve as an explanation of what q means. The context in which p will have this function will be when Maimonides explains the claim that heavenly intelligences exist to a fellow rabbi. Logically there are no grounds for claiming that p or q are primary in such a way that one necessarily is an explanation of the other. Rather, what is involved is a translation between languages. P is no more primary to q than "Nihil videmus" in Latin is primary to "We see nothing" in English.

The same point can be made whenever any religious claim is said to correspond to any claim in a language other than the language of that religion, be it the language of another religion, a social or physical science or a human science such as sociology or history.

The fact that more often than not statements in the sciences and humanities are taken to explain religious claims rather than religious claims are taken to explain claims in academia only has to do with what most people today happen to be familiar with and personally affirm.

Assume a dialogue situation in which a Jew makes a claim that seems to be contrary to a claim made by a Christian. In such a case if the two claims in fact are contraries, then while both can be wrong, both cannot be true. Assume for example that the Jews says p "Jews ought to remain Jews," where this claim at least entails that Jews ought not to convert to any other religion, including Christianity, while the Christian partner says q "Christians have a mission to convert all of humankind," where this claim at least entails that Christians ought to try to convert Jews to Christianity. How is this conflict to be resolved?

One option is that Christians will decide to reject q altogether, or they may modify q in such a way that it no longer is contrary to p. For example, they may claim that while Christians have a mission to convert all of humankind, "convert" in this case does not mean to become a member of a Christian institution. Rather, it means to lead a God-centered, morally reponsible life, and someone can lead this kind of life without joining a church. Given this interpretation, the modified claim says "Christians have a mission to convert all of humankind to a God-centered, morally responsible life," and it does not conflict with p. Or our Christians may interpret "humankind" to mean "gentiles", which excludes the Jewish people, so that while the nations of the earth need salvation through Christ, both the new and the old "Israel" already have salvation. Given this interpretation, the modified claim says "Christians have a mission to convert all people who do not participate in God's covenant with the people of Israel," and it does not conflict with p. Let us label these two modifications of q or any other modifications of q that do not conflict with p by the name q^*.

Similarly, it is possible that Jews may decide to reject p altogether, or they may modify p in such a way that it is no longer contrary to q. For example, they may claims, as many "Jews for Jesus" do, that being Jewish is a matter of ethnic identity whereas becoming Christian is a matter of religion, so that by becoming Christian Jews may remain Jewish provided they continue to identify with the Jewish people and to participate in their cultural and communal institutions. Or they may claim that Jews believe that Christ came to save gentiles and that he was in some sense a manifestation of God rather than only human and that this belief does not entail a denial of Judaism on their part as long as they continue to be observant Jews who do not participate in the community of any Christian church. In other words, to remain a Jew involves the positive obligation to participate in Jewish religious and communal life, but it does not involve any negative obligations such as not in some sense to accept what Christians claim about Christ. Let us label these two modifications of p or any other modifications of p that do not conflict with q by the name p^*.

This option raises at least one important consideration that is distinctly relevant to interreligious dialogue and illustrates the difference between this context and an academic discussion between philosophers. It is legitimate to ask if Christians who either reject q or who modify their commitment so that they affirm q^* are really Christians. Similarly, it is legitimate to ask if Jews who either reject p or who modify their commitment so that they affirm p^* are really Jews.

"Legitimacy" in this case means not only that the question follows logically from the positions stated. If a Christian is not really a Christian or if a Jew is not really a Jew in a Jewish-Christian dialogue, then it is not really a Jewish-Christian dialogue even it continues to be a dialogue, and because the dialogue cannot be modified as "Jewish-Christian" the dialogue has failed. Conversely, if for example a liberal and conservative economist are having a debate and it turns out that the liberal is not really liberal or the conservative is not really conservative, it need not be the case that the debate has failed. Such debates are intended to be a context for people with apparently different views to exchange ideas. That the participants turn out not to be identified in the way that initially they were thought to be identified need not harm the debate if in fact an excellent exchange of ideas takes place. But no matter how good the exchange of ideas in a Jewish-Christian debate turns out to be, if no Jews or no Christians were involved in the debate, the dialogue has failed. In this sense interreligious dialogues are more like many political exchanges than they are like philosophical or scientific debate. In discussions between philosophers and scientists the goal is simply to discover some new insight into philosophy or science. How the conceptual commitments of the scholars involved differ is at best only of secondary importance. But if you are involved in a Russian-American discussion about human rights, for example, it is essential that both Russians and Americans be involved. Merely to have a group of individuals of whatever nationality discussing human rights is not the same thing. What is true or false about human rights is not the only concern. Rather, the goal is to reach some understanding about human rights as Russians and Americans. Similarly, in a Jewish-Christian dialogue the goal is not merely to reach some understanding about religious issues. Rather, the goal is reach some understanding about these issues as Jews and Christians.

Some people might object to this radical distinction between what philosophers or scientists do and what happens in religious dialogues on the grounds that all truth-claims are what I have called speech acts and that there are no such things as propositions. I do not wish here to enter into this discussion. However, even granting this point, I would want to set aside religious dialogues from other academic forums in this way. Suppose that I invite a Hegelian to a philosophy department forum to discuss universals with a linguistic analyst and it turns out that they do not disagree with each other. At this point I may decide that the Hegelian is not really a Hegelian or that the analyst is not really a linguistic analyst. While I have promotional grounds to be disappointed, in terms of philosophy the interchange was not primarily a confrontation of two kinds of philosophers. Rather, the primary concern was a search for some truth in which it was considered desirable, but not necessary, to bring together these two kinds of philosophers. But this is not the case in a religious dialogue. If in a Jewish-Christian dialogue the Jew turns out not to be a Jew or the Christian turns out not to be a Christian, then in a primary sense the dialogue has failed. In other words, in the one case the discussion is between philosophers who happen to be Hegelians and linguistic analysts, but in our case the discussion is between Jews and Christians rather than practitioners or scholars of religion who happen to be Jewish or Christian.

Let me state this issue again in a more formal way. The statement p is one statement in a set of statements and rules of inference that constitutes a language of Judaism. I say "a" rather than "the" because different interpretations of Judaism involve a different list. For example, while all interpretations of Judaism will involve p, only an Orthodox language would include the claim that the Torah was directly given by God to Moses and the Jewish people at Sinai. Similarly, while the rules of inference in many Jewish languages, secular as well as religious, will grant to biblical statements a special status of authority, only conservative religious Jewish languages will use the specific rules of rabbinic logic in *halakhah* to draw inferences from biblical claims. Hence, while many Jewish languages will include the claim that a Jew ought not to eat meat and milk together, only a conservative religious Jewish language would infer this claim from the statement that one ought not to boil a kid in its mother's milk (Ex. 23:19; 34:26; Dt. 14:21).

If two languages are identical in every respect except one, that is, if one contains a claim that the other does not or if one uses a rule of inference that is not used by the other, the two languages are not the same. Thus, there are many languages of Judaism. By "language of Judaism" I mean any language through which individuals can express themselves as Jews. Similarly, the statement q is one statement in a set of statements and rules of inference that constitutes a language of Christianity, and there are many languages of Christianity.

Now the question is, how are we to decide that a given language should or should not be included in the list of languages of any given religious community? To a certain extent the answer is based on tradition. For example, the claim that the Torah was given to Moses at Sinai is a claim in a language of Judaism because throughout the history of the Jewish people those who have identified themselves as Jews, insofar as they have identified themselves as Jews, have made this claim. In this sense there is no question that the claims of Orthodoxy are Jewish even if there is considerable doubt that its claims are true. The claim that Christ came and died for our sins is clearly a claim in a language of Christianity for the same reason whether or not the claim is true. The problem comes when such a traditional claim is either rejected or modified. The question is, at what point of modification or rejection does a language cease to a language of the relevant religion, and how are we to decide these matters? In other words, let L stand for any religious language that consists solely of claims and rules of inference that traditionally express that religion, let L stand for any religious language of which L is an instance, and let L* stand for the language L that includes a claim that in some way rejects or modifies a claim in L. The problem is, when does L* cease to be an L?

There is no easy answer to this question, and I doubt that there is a single set of rules that will fit all cases. Sometimes the judgment can be made externally as well as internally, but at other times the judgment can be made purely internally. An example of a question whose determination is purely internal is whether the Sabbath ought to be on Sunday or Saturday. Here the issue is, if a Jewish community observes the Sabbath on any day other than Saturday, does it remain a Jewish community? I cannot see how any data external to the life of the Jewish people could be relevant in answering this question. The issue is not, for example, what Jews should do on Saturday and on Sunday. The answer to this question could involve considerable external data. Rather, the question is, can we call Sunday or any day other than Saturday the Sabbath, even if, for example, most Jews must work on Saturday and most Jews attend worship services on Sunday? The answer to this question is entirely a matter of internal interpretation. I suspect that requirements for mission in Christianity have a similar logical status within Christianity; that is, I suspect that while Christians can differ about what Christian mission ought to be, any Christian position that rejects the claim that Christians as Christians have a mission ceases to be a Christian position, and that this judgment is to be determined solely by reference to the life and thought of Christians.

An example of another judgment where external considerations are relevant is the set of questions that center around the status of women in Judaism. Whether or not, for example, women can be witnesses in a Jewish court or counted in a *minyan* (i.e., the number of adult Jews needed to conduct a communal worship service) or be ordained as rabbis cannot be settled solely on the grounds of Jewish law. In this case no matter what the commitment to *halakhah*, general moral sensitivity will affect how the *halakhah* is interpreted. I suspect that the same can be said for women's issues in Christianity. Similarly, the claim that the universe was created 5,737 years ago, as one reading of the beginning of the book of Genesis would seem to suggest, is subject to external criteria of judgment. No matter if this claim is Christian and/or Jewish or not, the claim states a fact and if the fact is false, a Christian and/or a Jew ought to reject it. Now a Jew and a Christian might choose to affirm this claim if there is no clear way to settle its truth. But if the veracity or lack of veracity of the claim is evident, then an appeal to religious tradition is irrelevant. Rarely do religious claims fall subject to such challenges, but when they do either they must be rejected from or modified in the religious language or that language forfeits any claim to be concerned with truth.

Consider a case of interreligious dialogue in which p in L which is an L is contrary to q in language M which is an M religious language. The first option considered above involves the participant adopting p^* in L*, which may or may not be an L, where p^* is not contrary to q, or the participant adopting q^* in M, which may or may not be an M, where q^* is not contrary to p. In this context it is legitimate to ask, do Jews who understand the commitment to being Jewish not to entail rejecting belief in Christ continue to be Jews, that is, is their language of commitment a language of Judaism, or do Christians who understand Christian mission to exclude attempting to convert Jews to Christianity continue to be Christian, that is, is their language of commitment a language of Christianity? In either case if the answer is negative, the dialogue has ceased to be Jewish-Christian, and for that reason the dialogue has failed.

Advocates of one language may dialogue with advocates of another language without an appeal to a third language. In such cases statements such as p in L will be translated into a statement q in M so that the participants will be able to determine if what they believe is or is not the same. In such an enterprise several things can be learned.

1. We might discover that there is no way to translate p into M, which might suggest that p is the kind of statement that can only be internally judged within L, whereas otherwise we might have thought that p is objective in the sense that we have used this term.

2. The translation might lead advocates of M either to reject something else that they claimed or claim something that they never claimed before or modify something that they otherwise would have claimed, because the process of translation itself led the advocates of M to have a different perspective on their claims. The same thing could happen to the advocates of L as a result of observing what happens to their claim when it is expressed in a different language framework.

3. Or the translation process itself could (on rare occasions) result in either advocate abandoning his/her advocacy, which will be bad for future dialogue but may not be bad for the individual who undergoes this conversion. (For example, liberal Jews or Christians could becomes conservative Jews or Christians.)

4. Or the participants may become convinced that there is no way in which they can speak to each other, whereas previously they thought that there were grounds for communication. In most cases the suspicion would be that this is a negative consequence. But there is no reason why every language should be communicable in another language, and there is no necessity to the claim that no matter what one believes all people can communicate with each other. In a case where two languages are not communicable or compatible, the discovery that in terms of commitment to these particular languages

communication or agreement is not possible is a positive one, since it is valuable to discover that an experiment that cannot work does not work.

What is more usual in interreligious dialogue is that the participants either communicate in a third language or agree to appeal to a third language in passing judgment on claims in the other two languages that they represent. The former alternative is most characteristic of discussions of medieval Muslim, Jewish and Christian philosophy. An Aristotelian theologian who follows Averroes will communicate with an Aristotelian theologian who follows Maimonides and with an Aristotelian theologian who follows Thomas Aquinas in the language of the Aristotelian sciences and not in the language of Islam, Judaism or Christianity. Formally what is happening in this context is the following. Whereas there may be a conflict over p in L and q in M, these participants opt for p^* in L^* over p in L and q^* in M^* over q in M, and at this level they may find that they have no areas of disagreement except about claims that from their religious traditions cannot be so modified. Hence these Aristotelian participants will have little disagreement if any about God, God's relation to the world, and the ideal form of a political state, but they may decide, for example, that there is no way for a Maimonidean to speak of "faith, hope and charity" to a Thomist. (However, I doubt that there would be anything that the Jewish and Muslim Aristotelians could not communicate to each other.)

The example introduces another problem. Conflict in a dialogue may not be due to differences in religious language. Rather, the conflict may be due to different commitments by the participants to nonreligious languages. For example, a medieval Christian may be in conflict with a medieval Jew not so much because one is a Christian and the other is a Jew but because one is an Aristotelian and the other is a Platonist or an Atomist. Conflicts about what it means to say that God created the world were like this. Similarly, conflicts between a Jew and a Christian in modern terms might arise from the Jew being politically and culturally liberal whereas the Christian is politically and culturally conservative, or vice versa. Jews such as Arthur Goldberg and Norman Podhoretz would have very different kinds of dialogues with "born-again" Christians such as Harold Hughes and Charles Colson. Both participants and observers must be careful to distinguish between differences based on religion and differences based on ethical and political values whose direct sources are not the religious languages.

The problem is that a participant may believe that what he/she claims is a p in L when in fact it is a p^* in L* and that, while there is a conflict over p^* and q^*, there is no conflict over p and q or p^* and q or p and q^*. Hence one rabbi or minister might believe that his/her politics have more to do with his/her religion than with other factors when in fact that is not the case. This is particularly a problem in terms of Judaism in which religious claims are so often tied to general values in a community whose sources lie as much in the community's gentile environment as they do in the Jewish past. Hence Jews in the 1930s might see their political universalism as a distinctly Jewish value, whereas their counterparts in the 1970s might hold the same belief about Jewish nationalism. (There is the same problem when mystics and so-called rationalists or religious humanists from different religions enter into dialogue.)

In some cases all of the participants in the dialogue are more committed to a shared third language than they are to either of their religious languages. I believe that this situation characterized much of the so-called Jewish-Christian dialogues in America prior to the mid-1960s. The real faith of all of the participants was a positivistic or pragmatic American variation of democracy and humanism into which the participants already had translated their religious language. In other words, both the liberal Jews and the liberal Christians who had participated in these dialogues advocated religious languages that included only those claims from their traditions that were compatible with their commitment to the thought of intellectuals such as James, Freud and Durkheim. In this context it is not surprising that they discovered they shared a great deal in common. This in itself is not objectionable, but it can become boring. Hence you used to find Jewish-Christian dialogues in which liberal rabbis would verbalize traditional Jewish attitudes about Jewish law so that they would have something to discuss with their liberal Christian counterparts, even though everyone agreed that the traditional view of Jewish law was intellectually indefensible. Such contexts may sometimes be good role-playing, but they are not dialogue. What seemed to be a Jewish-Christian dialogue was in fact a liberal seminar on conservative religion. On the other hand, given the presence of conservative Jews or Christians, there probably would not have occurred a Jewish-Christian dialogue, although there may have occurred a Liberal-Conservative dialogue.

In general, a dialogue presupposes that the participants share something in common and disagree about something else. If nothing or everything is shared in common, dialogue is not possible. Dialogue only occurs when what is shared can serve as a basis for dealing with differences. Whether or not such a dialogue is religious or not depends upon what it is that the participants share and do not share. Ideally, even where the participants speak in a third language, they will discover that some claims in one language complement claims in the other language, and that prima facie other claims in the one language conflict with claims in the other language. Minimally the participants in such a dialogue will learn something that otherwise they did not know about themselves and/or about their counterparts.

Let me add that this learning need not be limited to the cognitive realm, although in dialogues involving religious academics we ought not to feel our time was wasted if only cognitive learning takes place. Contexts in which academics learn from other academics in this day and age are sufficiently rare that even this meagre level of achievement should be cherished.

10

Gadamer's Hermeneutics as a Model for Cross-Cultural Understanding and Truth in Religion

◻

Mary Ann Stenger

Recent awareness of the cross-cultural dimension of philosophy of religion has intensified the urgency of dealing with questions of religious knowledge and truth. On one level this involves understanding and interpreting diverse religious phenomena and persons. But on another level it involves the normative question of developing and applying criteria of knowledge and truth. Clearly such a process is dependent on an adequate hermeneutics of the religious phenomena of diverse cultures. In this essay I shall analyze insights from Gadamer's hermeneutics and their applicability to specific questions involved in developing criteria of cross-cultural religious knowledge and truth. The focus will be on the process of developing such criteria rather than the proposal of specific criteria.

I. Gadamer's Hermeneutics—Insights and Applications

Gadamer sees an integral connection between hermeneutics and the experience of truth. In the introduction to *Truth and Method* he suggests that it is part of the basic experience of philosophy that the attempt to understand the philosophical classics involves a consideration of their claims to truth, which cannot be immediately rejected or affirmed (p. xii).[1] Similarly, when studying and interpreting religious traditions, we cannot simply dismiss the truth-claims of religious traditions different from our own. Their claims to truth ask us to consider them openly and fully.

The "Fusion of Horizons" in the Hermeneutical Process.

Gadamer uses the concept of *horizon* to explain the initial relationship of openness and difference between the interpreter and the phenomena to be interpreted. "Horizon" means "the range of vision that includes everything that can be seen from a particular vantage point" (p. 269). The interpreter's horizon includes his/her own immediate situation but also the roots in the past and openness to the future. Because of these outward directions that form part of one's horizon, the phenomena to be interpreted are not totally alien.[2] To acquire such a horizon involves the effort to look and think beyond our immediate situation, which then gives us a wider perspective for considering and understanding our own situation.

Our present horizon includes our present prejudices and foremeanings for the phenomena, but is it not fixed by such preunderstanding. These meanings and preconceptions are continually tested in relation to the phenomena themselves. Sometimes, before interpreting, in an effort to be "objective" we try to reject all of our prejudices—or at least those prejudices which would arbitrarily determine the meaning and understanding of the phenomena. But Gadamer suggests that we cannot reject all of our prejudices and foremeanings before we try to interpret; some stay with us whether we recognize them or not. But in the encounter with the phenomena we can be open to varying possibilities of meaning, allowing our foremeanings to be open to evaluation and change.

In the process of understanding a text, we are aware of a temporal distance between the author and the interpreter. Gadamer does not then suggest that, as a means to achieve objectivity and lose unproductive prejudices, we focus on the historical situation of the author and ignore the historical situation of the interpreter. Rather, he argues that the meaning of a text is partly determined by the historical situation of the interpreter (p. 263).

The temporal distance between author and interpreter includes the continuity of tradition and a productive process of interpretation of the text. The tradition influences the interpreter as to what objects are worth interpreting and investigating and what questions are important. In the process of interpretation errors and meanings that obscure the meaning of the text are "filtered out" at the same time that new insights can open up new dimensions of meaning. As historical beings our self-reflection is limited by and based in our historical situation, which includes the effect of past history and tradition on us and our present situation. Thus, when we try to place ourselves in the situation of the past, it is not a totally alien situation because our horizon has been formed in part by this other situation. When we recognize that our present horizon is not really isolated from the past, our understanding involves the "fusion of these horizons which we imagine to exist by themselves" (p. 273). In any tradition this fusion is an ongoing process of the old and new which together form present understandings.

When understanding because a "scientific" task in the hermeneutic situation of interpreting a text, we experience "the tension between the text and the present". To deal with this tension we "project an historical horizon that is different from the horizon of the present" (p. 273). But in this process of acquiring a more universal vision which includes our relation to the past our present horizon also changes and there results a fusion of horizons which eliminates the historical horizon as a separate horizon.[3]

In this act of fusion our understanding includes application to the particular situation (p. 275). Application, for Gadamer, is not applying a given or discovered universal to a particular case. Rather, it is "the actual understanding of the universal itself that the given text constitutes for us" (p. 305). The interpreter is not "over" the text through some kind of superior knowledge but rather stands "under" the *text's* claim to knowledge and truth (p. 278). For example, the interpreter of law or scripture does not take a position superior to the text but rather tests understanding and application against the text. Application is part of the understanding that results from the fusion of the horizon of the particular text and the horizon of the particular interpreter.

Let us now apply these ideas to the situation of cross-cultural religious claims of truth. We have suggested that these claims ask us to consider them openly and fully. Our first task, following Gadamer, would be the effort to develop a historical horizon broad enough to include the religious phenomena from these traditions as well as the historical situations in which these traditions have arisen. Gadamer has suggested that in dealing with texts from one's tradition the person has roots in that past history and tradition. But in relation to cross-cultural claims of truth it would appear false to suggest that our present horizon has any roots in those *other* traditions. Yet in another sense our interest in interpreting and understanding these religious traditions suggests that we have some relation to them, that their claims to truth bring us into relationship with them.

Even on the so-called descriptive level of understanding we are involved in a fusion of horizons that includes testing of our prejudices and foremeanings concerning those other religious traditions. For example, when I read and interpret the *Bhagavad Gita* I come with some (however inaccurate or accurate) foremeanings of what I expect to find. I concern myself with searching for passages that would support my foremeanings and prejudices. But even in such a questionable procedure the words in the text hold some claim against my foremeanings and prejudices. I cannot simply invent words to support my foremeanings and prejudices because I have the text before me and in some sense over me. Most of us prefer and attempt to follow a much more open process of interpreting the text, but in either case the process of interpretation involves the testing and adapting of our foremeanings, that is, a fusion of our present horizon and the historical horizon that includes the text. The failure to recognize that fusion does not mean it is not occurring.

If we consider the normative issue of religious truth and not just the adequacy of our interpretations and representations of other religious traditions, we are perhaps just opening our present horizon more fully as we attempt to achieve an even more universal horizon which can encompass a diversity of religious meanings and truths. The questions raised here are part of the effort to be open to the historical situations and meanings of diverse religious traditions. As such they are part of the effort to achieve a more universal horizon in relation to cross-cultural meanings and truths. Most of these questions have arisen from earlier efforts to understand diverse religious phenomena. This suggests that our present horizon is really a result of earlier fused horizons, each of which attempts to achieve a more universal vision of religious truth, a goal which defines our present effort. Such a view suggests that the difference between the descriptive and normative levels of interpretation is one of degree rather than a distinction of objectivity versus subjectivity.[4]

The "Experience" Structure of the Hermenetical Process

Gadamer describes the hermeneutical process as having the structure of an experience, involving a dialectical process of discovering and learning through negation (p. 310). We approach "experiences" open to what will occur but also with some expectations (foremeanings, prejudices). Through the experience our expectations are often negated or at least refined, and thus we are part of a "new" experience. Experience involves insight developed through the negation of expectations along with awareness of our human limits. "Thus true experience is that of one's own historicality" (p. 320), involving the awareness of one's finitude and historical limitations.[5]

Gadamer relates the openness required in understanding and interpreting to openness to another person that may involve some claims of that person against oneself. In the hermeneutical experience real openness to the tradition may even call into question one's own criteria of knowledge (p. 325). Gadamer contrasts this to the type of historical consciousness which claims to read the texts (phenomena) objectively and free of prejudices, when in reality the person is operating with prejudices about the nature and criteria of knowledge and truth, prejudices that unconsciously dominate the procedure and approaches (pp. 324–25).

This discussion of openness to the other seems particularly applicable to work with religious phenomena from diverse traditions. Following Gadamer's model of openness in developing this type of historical consciousness means being asked to listen to the claim of the other religious person openly enough to allow that claim to affect one's own understanding not only of that person but also, more broadly, of religious knowledge and truth. This does not mean becoming a slave to the other, blindly acknowledging the other's claims. Rather, it involves enough openness to take the other's claim seriously, to consider one's own prejudices about religious knowledge and truth in relation to the other's claim, and to adapt and adjust one's own prejudices and fore-meanings in terms of the claim of the other (cf. p. 324). Such openness involves a recognition of our own limitations, and more generally of human finitude, in relation to questions of religious knowledge and truth.

The "Conversation" Structure of the Hermeneutical Process

Gadamer relates the dialectical character of this openness of experience to the structure of a question. In asking a question one is aware of what one does not know as well as of one's interest in the other. The question may show doubts about a preconception, a prejudice, an opinion, or previous knowledge. Asking a question shows that one is able to think and free enough to ask (cf. p. 330).[6] The role of this questioning in the dialectical process of hermeneutics leads Gadamer to describe the interpretation of a text "as a conversation with the text" (p. 331).

This conversation not only includes the interpreter asking a question of the text but also a questioning of the interpreter by the text (p. 333). To understand historical events or texts one must try to reconstruct the question they were answering (p. 334). But the reconstruction is only part of the hermeneutical process, since the understanding and questioning of the interpreter is also included

(p. 337). "To understand a question means to ask it" (p. 338). Thus, this question is raised for the interpreter and not just for the text.[7]

If understanding a text is comparable to involvement in a conversation, then the question of the text and the question of the interpreter interact in a dialectical process of question and answer. The interpreter recognizes a claim of truth in the text and thus a question to the interpreter. The recognition of this overriding relationship to the text involves a fusion of horizons and provides the common basis for mediating between the text and the interpreter (p. 340).

Similarly, when we approach religious phenomena from diverse traditions, even if only to achieve "scholarly understanding and description," we approach with certain questions for the material. Those questions show that the material raises a question of religious knowledge and truth for us. (Even the Christian who approaches non-Christian religious traditions to support his/her own views and to undermine non-Christian truth-claims is showing that those truth-claims have raised a question of religious truth which must be dealt with.) The interpreter will be aware that others have understood the phenomena differently in the past and will in the future as well (cf.p. 336).

Questions by philosophers and religious thinkers concerning the possibility of cross-cultural religious knowledge and truth, including cross-culturally valid criteria of truth, indicate an openness to the truth claims of various religious traditions. Those truth-claims and indeed those religious traditions raise questions for us. Perhaps Gadamer would suggest that what we find philosophically interesting in our analysis of religious truth cannot help but pass over into our own personal thinking. The analogy of conversation fits well with descriptions of cross-cultural interreligious dialogue in which both the interpreter and the other religious persons refine their understandings in an ongoing process of questioning and answering.

(Gadamer notes that sometimes such understanding occurs and sometimes it does not. We cannot make it happen just by wanting it or trying to achieve it. But when it happens, as in the middle of a conversation that is going well, we perhaps feel more led by it than leading it [p. 345].)

The "Universality" of Language in the Hermeneutical Process

Gadamer sees significance in the fact that language is the medium of conversation and also of understanding. Just as in a conversation we assume that we are speaking the same language as the other person, so also the process of interpretation presupposes that it is possible to be understood through language (p. 347). It is part of human experience to try to put our experiences into words. We search for the right word to express the experience so that the word can bring it forth, but this does not mean that the experience can be separated from the word. Rather, the linguistic expression of our experience is part of the experience itself. In conversation and interpretation each person tries to open oneself to the other person so that each can understand what the other is saying. When we try to penetrate another's thinking our objective is to understand the other's views on a particular subject, which we can then relate to our own views.

Thus, Gadamer suggests that we could describe the hermeneutical process as a hermeneutical conversation which depends on a common language (p. 349). The text that the interpreter works with puts an object into language, but it is the interpreter who brings it forth through the dialectic of question and answer and the resulting fusion of horizons. Both the tradition of which the text is a part and the interpretation are expressed through language which makes them available to each other across the gaps of time (and cultures).

Gadamer suggests that written tradition has a unique relationship to time in that the tradition is "simultaneous with any present time" and "involves a unique co-existence of past and present" (p. 351). Through language the written tradition is detached in part from the original author(s) and audience and is "free" for our present understanding and interpretation.[8] The interpreter approaches what is said as possible truth, not just as an artifact of the past to be reconstructed.

The role of language in understanding has several important implications for our understanding of the hermeneutical process. First, we recognize the diversity of languages and therefore must touch on the problem of translation for understanding. We become aware of the difficulty of transmitting the spirit and truth of the words, and not just the words. Gadamer speaks of "the gap between the spirit of the original words and that of their reproduction" as part of the situation of translation (p. 346).

In studying diverse religious traditions many of us are often dependent on another's translation of materials. We have to recognize that the translation may carry the spirit of the original in varying degrees if it is able to carry it at all. The translation is already a product of a hermeneutical process, including the translator's understanding and interpretation of the original along with some application of that in presenting his/her translation. In the situation of cross-cultural interreligious dialogue, we are often painfully aware of the difficulties of different languages and the inadequacy of translation. Gadamer points out that "there is nothing more difficult than dialogue in two different languages in which one person speaks one and the other person the other, each understanding the other's language, but not speaking it" (p. 346).

Second, the linguistic character of understanding has implications for the so-called objective historical understanding of texts. Gadamer points out that the concepts that the historian uses to describe the material reflect that particular historian's interest in the material and that historian's conceptual frame of reference (and, I would add, horizon) (p. 357). The concepts used to describe the material may in fact hinder true understanding of the material. For example, when some of us look back at some of the nineteenth-century descriptions of Indian religions, we find prejudicial understandings influencing the descriptions. We criticize those in relation to our own approaches today, which we see as more objective. But Gadamer's point suggests that we fail to recognize the preconceptions and prejudices that influence our own understandings as well as our views of those past descriptions. Gadamer is not saying that the historian has failed in not being objective enough or in not separating him/herself sufficiently from the historical task. Rather, he is saying that thinking historically and interpreting always involve forming a relationship between the ideas of the text and one's own ideas (p. 358). Only in that way does any understanding of the meaning of the text take place.

Third, our view of the truth of interpretations is affected by the relation of the language of the interpreter to the language of the text. Gadamer says that "there cannot, therefore, be any one interpretation that is correct 'in itself'" (p. 358). Each interpreter interacts with the text and adapts to the particular hermeneutical situation in which he/she is involved (p. 358). This does not mean that every interpretation is isolated. Rather, the linguistic character of all interpretations allows interrelationship of interpretations (p. 359). Also, the fact that the text being interpreted is still the same text linguistically provides a point of continuity in the interpretations.

Gadamer points to the linguistic character of interpretations as the basis of his claim that the truth-claim of every interpretation is "not in the least relativised" (p. 359). This suggests that language is a universal underlying all understanding and interpretation. Gadamer relates the universal character of language to the universality of reason. Both have an infinite dimension transcending all bounds in the linguistic forms, including the particular text and hermeneutical situation. This implies that the particular languages of particular cultures can also be transcended through reason, which continues to be expressed linguistically (p. 363). Put differently, there is an intimate and indissoluble unity of thought and language that is experienced as the unity of understanding and interpretation in the hermeneutical process (p. 364). This unity underlies the diversity of languages and words and enables words to be meaningful. Because language and thinking are bound together, word and meaning are tied together (see p. 377).

Gadamer moves from this view of the universality of language and reason and the unity of thought and language to suggest that there is an ultimate harmony between the words of one language and those of every other language, because "all languages are an unfolding of the one unity of the mind" (p. 395). Gadamer realizes that such a view contrasts sharply with some modern views of the diversity of languages that emphasize a relativism resulting from that diversity (p. 397). He does see a relationship between the diversity of languages and the diversity of worldviews, but he does not see that as ultimately relativistic because of their basis in the one unity of the mind that makes intercommunication and understanding possible.

In language, in speech, in naming things, we bring forth our world into language (p. 402–3). This ability to name and speak relates to human freedom in relation to one's habitat or environment. Because humans are able to rise above their environments, they are "free for variety" in their linguistic use and expression (p. 403). This also means that they are free to expand their worldviews through linguistic interaction with other worldviews. The differences are there, but underlying those is the fact that each person expresses a human (and linguistically formed) world. Gadamer sees each such world as open to every possible insight and therefore to expansion of its own worldview, and consequently each world as open to others (p. 405). For Gadamer, within each language there is "a direct relationship to the infinite extent of what exists," and thus the possibility of the expansion of one's worldview through knowing another language and worldview (p. 411). In learning another lanuage, we do not shift worldviews but rather expand our present worldview.

This connection of language, experience and worldview provides the basis for interacting with other worlds. It does not entail an exclusive perspective but rather shows our historical contingency. We bring our linguistically formed world to our encounters and involvements with "foreign" worlds, and we retain our past worldview even as we expand our horizons. But our own experience and linguistic expression of our world gives us a common basis for entering other worlds and worldviews, which are also based on human experience and expressed linguistically. In such encounters, we become aware of our historical contingency, but our awareness of historical contingency does not eliminate it (p. 406).[9]

Gadamer expands on this understanding of historical contingency by saying that "language is the record of finitude" (p. 415). Each language is constantly being formed and transformed as it continues to express human experience of the world.[10] Gadamer sees each word as interrelated with the rest of the language and also with the worldview in such a way that when each word is spoken, it "causes the whole of the language to which it belongs to resonate and the whole of the view of the world which lies behind it to appear" (p. 415–16). Each word is related to the whole, to a totality of meaning, even though it does not express that totality of meaning completely. The words of a tradition encounter the interpreter; but also, through the interpreter, the tradition is expressed anew in language. The interpretation is something new that did not exist before but exists now and extends the tradition (see p. 419).

Similarly, in expressing understandings of various religious traditions, we put forth something new which is not the same as earlier expressions of the traditions but which is related to it and can be said to expand that tradition. One might consider here the effect of some Western interpretations of Indian religious ideas and practices in the nineteenth century on later Indian development and expansion of the tradition. Could we perhaps say that the "foreign" interpretations were yet part of the tradition itself? For the interpreter, the encounter with these traditions includes the expansion of his/her horizon and worldview through the dialectic of the question that affects the questioner as well as what is questioned. One allows one's prejudices and foremeanings to be tested by the religious activities and texts themselves. Such a process involves some opening up of the totality of meaning, which is the goal of understanding (see p. 422).

Gadamer sees this understanding of humans, language, world and the totality of meaning as pointing to a "universal hermeneutics" that involves the general relationship of humans to their world. He sees the human relationship to the world as basically linguistic, and it is the linguistic character of the relation which makes the relationship and the world intelligible (p. 432–33).

When something is present to us it asserts its own truth, which disturbs and expands our own horizon as we encounter it (p. 422).

Gadamer suggests that in the hermeneutical process, there is a "play of language itself" which draws into it both the interpreter and the text (p. 466). The interpreter is attracted to the text or tradition and drawn into a process which can lead to understanding through the play of language involved. In such a process of understanding, one is drawn into an event of truth (p. 446). It is clear that this event of truth does not mean that the interpreter is free of all prejudices, but it does mean that the interpreter's own being is involved. This is a "limitation of 'method' " but not a limitation of knowledge for the human sciences, since knowledge in the human sciences concerns humane significance (p. 447). Gadamer sees the dialectic process of questioning and research as "a discipline that guarantees truth" (p. 477). This is not to say that the truth achieved is absolute truth as if from an absolute standpoint beyond historical contingency, but it is certainty and truth experienced as such. Yet the process described here is ongoing, which implies that present experience of truth can be expanded through future experience of truth. Such a view fits well with the ongoing interaction of various religious traditions through study and dialogue.

Gadamer's discussion of the relationship of languages and the process of learning and using a foreign language also seems applicable to the relationship of religious traditions and the process of learning a religious tradition other than one's own. Gadamer suggests that it is the use of a foreign language, in conversation or in studying texts, that brings one to a new standpoint in relation to one's former view of the world (p. 400). But this new standpoint is not a replacement of one's former view, as if one had forgotten one's earlier view. Rather, one experiences the new as different and somewhat strange but also as having some truth. This relationship between language and worldview is not merely accidental for Gadamer. Rather, human being-in-the-world and having a world depends on the use of language (p. 401). Gadamer acknowledges the variety of languages and accompanying worldviews, but he does not see these as a barrier to "knowledge of being in itself." Analogously, we can speak of our present religious worldview being expanded through study of and dialogue with other religious (and philosophical) traditions.

Similarly, we might be able to draw an analogy between the realtionship of the diversity of languages to the unity of thought and language, on the one hand, and the relationship of the diversity of religious traditions to some kind of ultimate unity or unity of the ultimate, on the other. Such a view would imply an ultimate unity of truth which transcends the particular religious traditions, but which also takes account of the diversity of traditions. The idea of cross-cultural religious truth seems to raise the possibility of such a unity, as does ongoing cross-cultural, interreligious dialogue, which assumes enough common ground to talk, interpret and understand.

Having presented several ideas from Gadamer's hermeneutics and applied them to the situation of cross-cultural, interreligious understanding, let us move to a discussion of the extent to which these ideas and applications can help us answer certain questions concerning the possibility of criteria for cross-cultural religious truth.

II. Gadamer's Hermeneutics and Cross-Cultural Religious Truth

We now need to address the bearing of Gadamer's hermeneutics on questions of conflicting truth claims; developing criteria for cross-cultural understanding and truth; the relationship of unity and diversity to the ultimate, on the one hand, and to the particularity of religious persons and traditions, on the other, without ending in pure relativism; and, finally, various concepts of the ultimate.

Let me begin by comparing Gadamer's approach to hermeneutics with some assumptions about cross-cultural religious knowledge.

1. Reality and Knowledge and Truth of Reality Are Dynamic

If this is true, present norms of knowledge are subject to future correction and development. Gadamer's view of historical reality corresponds to this assumption, since he speaks of changing historical traditions and the diversity of languages and world-views. Moreover, his understanding of how present prejudices and foremeanings are challenged and developed through the fusion of horizons corresponds to concern for the future correction and development of cross-cultural norms of religious knowledge. Gadamer's description of the process of achieving the fusion of horizons offers an analysis of human interaction with reality that can account for such a dynamic approach.

2. Religious Truth Is Present in More Than One Tradition

An implication of this view is that criteria of cross-cultural religious truth should transcend particularistic religious criteria. Gadamer's understanding of the hermeneutical process includes the view that the interpreter is affected by the text and tradition interpreted. He sees that encounter as broadening the horizon of the interpreter, including the testing of some foremeanings and prejudices, and eventually leading to a fusion of horizons. In relation to truth, this would mean that the interpreter is open to truth within the text in relation to his/her historical situation. Such a view of the hermeneutical process, a process that is constantly repeated in the ongoing process of understanding, suggests a multiplicity and diversity of truths, each of which is developed and presented in the process of interpretation and understanding. Such a process could allow for truth in various texts, various traditions, and various languages and worldviews.

The issue of developing criteria of religious truth transcending particularistic criteria can be handled through Gadamer's description of the fusion of horizons. Through the encounter with the text and through the play of language, as the fusion of horizons takes place one achieves new understanding and meaning, related to earlier understanding and meanings and yet also different. The resulting new understanding is not just the imposition of the interpreter's prejudices on the text at hand (or else the fusion of horizons has not occurred). Rather, it is the result of interaction of the two horizons—the historical horizon of the text and the original horizon of the interpreter. As such, the new understanding would not be particular to one or the other. Analogously, in relation to cross-cultural criteria of religious truth, the interpreter of the traditions would be involved in the process of the fusing the horizons of two traditions—the horizon of the tradition reflected in the phenomena and texts studied, and the personal horizon of the interpreter, including the religious tradition out of which she/he operates. The resulting fused horizon would not be particular to either "original" horizon. If we assume that the intepreter would enter the encounter with the religious traditions openly and yet also with some understanding of how one judges religious truth, and that the traditions encountered include understandings of judging religious truth, then the fusion of horizons that could result from the encounter could also result in cross-cultural, interreligious criteria being brought forth through the encounter and hermeneutical process. Since we recognize the contingency of our knowledge, these criteria would be subject to further correction and development in future encounters.

3. Cross-cultural Religious Truth Includes the Importance of Religious Persons to Ideas and Practices

As Gadamer likens the hermeneutical process, particularly the dialectic of questioning, to conversation, one sees the importance of persons and human experiences to the linguistic expression of world-views. His description of the process of conversation includes the importance of each person and each person's horizon in the effort at understanding. But there is also a sense in which Gadamer's approach suggests that meaning and truth transcend the particular person, especially when one is involved in interpreting a text or tradition. He argues against attempting to present the text just as the original author understood or intended it. The text takes on a certain independence of the original author as the interpreter interacts with the meanings it contains in relation to his/her own present situation.

These three assumptions in turn point to several questions important for a discussion of cross-cultural religious truth.

How Is Cross-Cultural Religious Knowledge and Truth Possible?

As has been suggested, Gadamer's analysis of the hermeneutical process can be applied to developing cross-cultural religious knowledge and truth. Such knowledge and truth are the result of an ongoing hermeneutical process in relation to diverse religious traditions. The elements of foremeanings and prejudices, encounter, play and fusion of horizons are all applicable to our understanding of developing cross-cultural religious knowledge.

In relation to this question, however, it is also possible to ask what basis one could develop for making judgments if one did not want to take the position that all religious truth claims were equally true. If one follows Gadamer's analysis, it would be incorrect to see the interaction of the interpreter and religious traditions as resulting in a set of criteria distinct from the interpreter and the traditions which would then be applied to the traditions. Rather, the criteria would be developed through the fusion of horizons resulting from the encounter with the tradition. Accordingly, the application of these criteria and the resulting judgments would arise from this same process of encounter and fusion.

We can also ask whether Gadamer's analysis offers us a way to deal with conflicts between persons, cultures and historical situations. Rather than staying with whatever conflicts one has, Gadamer's approach would seem to suggest that we interact with the conflicts, taking in but also recognizing our own prejudices and foremeanings while being open to meaning and truth from the opposing view. As our horizons fuse through such encounter, we can better understand and sometimes transcend differences and conflicts with the development of meaning out of conflict.[11] Such an approach does not deny differences between various traditions or historical situations, or between persons or cultures in the present. Rather, the approach takes account of the differences while suggesting some resolution of conflicts through a new understanding or norm.

Can We Develop Intersubjective Criteria to Avoid Subjectivism and Cross-Cultural Criteria to Avoid Relativism?

The process of achieving fusion of horizons overcomes pure subjectivism because it involves interaction with another (text, person, worldview) and can result in cross-cultural criteria. In such a fusion one broadens one's original horizon and interacts with another tradition or culture in such a way that each is affected and something new is brought forward.

But if the event of truth occurs for the interpreter, is it possible for truth or criteria of truth to really transcend the interpreter and his/her situation? The answer appears to be both yes and no. Yes, the event of truth and any criteria developed in the process can transcend the interpreter and that particular situation if by that one means the interpreter prior to the hermeneutical process and the "original" situation. Both of those are transcended in the resulting fused horizon achieved through encounter with another. But the answer would be no, if one meant the interpreter and the particular situation when or after the fusion of horizons is achieved, since both are a part of that event of truth and fused horizon. Yet it can also be recognized that that fusion of horizons is not absolute or final, but rather can be the starting point, the new "original" horizon, for an ongoing hermeneutical interaction.

Thus the process does maintain a kind of relativism, but not a pure relativism in the sense of no absolute grounding. The totality of meaning could provide an absolute toward which understanding and interpretation are directed. But, as an integral part of our experience of understanding and truth, the relativity associated with our historicality is not to be totally transcended.

Can Religious Truth Include Diversity?

Again, Gadamer's approach suggests a means of understanding the diversity of religious truth while not giving up the concept of truth and judgment. His view of the diversity of languages offers insight into the relationship of persons and words and worldviews that suggests that all are directed toward a totality of meaning and express human experience of the world. This suggests an ultimate unity in relation to the many. If we take such an approach to the diversity of religious worldviews, however, that leads to the question of our understanding of the ultimate.

How Is the Concept of the Ultimate Related to Our Understanding of Religious Truth?

Involved in this question is the issue of how the diversity of religious truth affects our concept of the ultimate. This in turn raises the question whether the ultimate should be seen as one or many. If the ultimate is seen as a unity, how does it relate to the diversity? One possible approach would be to compare Gadamer's discussion of unity and multiplicity in languages to the unity of the ultimate and the diversity of religious truth. Perhaps one could draw an analogy between the idea that all languages are an unfolding of the one unity of the mind and religious traditions as the unfolding of one religious truth or ultimate.

But one could still raise the question whether the ultimate could be multiple and not unified. Where would this leave the discussion of cross-cultural religious truth? Is there not a sense in which truth implies unity? Are not all human efforts at knowledge attempts to express the totality of meaning? But is there not another sense in which our human concepts of truth are so pluralistic that we might be led to suggest that truth is multiple? We are often tempted to say that several truths are correct in relation to particular situations and persons. It would seem strange to deny the truth quality of a truth, once taken as universal but now no longer seen that way, seen rather as a product of its historical period, if yet it had relevance to our time. But if all such truths are relative, not absolute, can we posit an absolute truth, an ultimate unity of truth? Or must we see the ultimate as simply a formal goal, a formal limit, not a substantive truth or reality?

Let me now turn to a few concluding evaluations of Gadamer's hermeneutics as a model for cross-cultural understanding and interpretation of religious truth.

First, one possible objection to Gadamer is that we need to distinguish different degrees of "fusion of horizons." Certainly there are times when one finds ideas or practices from diverse religious traditions intellectually or spiritually appealing. In that case perhaps a great deal of one's own worldview is included in the new fused horizon which results. There are other times, however, when we come to understand another tradition to some extent and do not deny that that understanding affects our worldview, though to a lesser degree. But many times we do not in fact open up our worldview or integrate it with another sufficiently to speak of a truly fused horizon. At those times perhaps we like to distinguish between our approach as scholars or academicians and our own personal views.

Yet the very fact that we study those traditions and often teach them to others reflects our view that they contribute something to the totality of meaning, that they add something to our human understanding of religious truth. This does not invalidate the distinction between descriptive and normative knowledge, but it does point up a similarity of epistemological structure in each. Here Gadamer's analysis of the hermeneutical process provides helpful clarification.

A second possible objection to Gadamer's approach is that it is too slow. The process of achieving a fusion of horizons which involves play with language and encounter with another (text, person, worldview) certainly provides a way of understanding other religious persons and traditions which takes them seriously and treats both the interpreter and the other fairly. But to engage in such a process with just one religious tradition different from one's own would be demanding. To do so with several traditions or to consider cross-cultural religious truth in general seems a monumental task. Yet Gadamer's description of the hermeneutical process suggests that this process is going on, however small or large the other to be interpreted might be. Thus, whatever one's goal of understanding, whatever depth one goes to, the structure of the process remains the same. What is different is the depth and breadth of the fusion of horizons that occurs. Also, the truth and adequacy of the fused horizon can be further tested through ongoing hermeneutical interaction.

Moreover, in an attempt elsewhere to apply proposed cross-cultural criteria to specific examples of conflicting truth-claims, I have argued that historical, cultural, and personal factors are inescapable in people's evaluations of religious phenomena.[12] Even given seemingly more universal criteria such as reason, moral goodness and humanization, we still have to account for diverse understandings of these concepts and therefore of the application of any criteria based on them. Any application of cross-cultural criteria will depend upon ongoing cross-cultural discussion and dialogue on the meaning of the concepts used as criteria. It would seem, therefore, that there is no short-cut for the kind of ongoing hermeneutical process which Gadamer has described. Such a process, in which we do more than evaluate, in which we deepen our understanding as well, is inevitably slow but valuable.

A final objection to Gadamer might be that his discussion, like ours, focuses on the experience of truth rather than on criteria of truth. Gadamer focuses on understanding another (text, person, worldview, actions, etc.) and the effect of that understanding on each side in the hermeneutical process. But the hermeneutical process as he presents it seems to ignore the question of criteria of truth.

But, as we have argued, Gadamer's analysis of the process of interpretation can also be viewed as a model for the process of developing criteria of truth. One's initial criteria can be one's fore-meanings which are then tested in relation to other possible criteria presented in texts, persons or actions. Such encounter can result in a fused horizon which may involve adaptation of criteria from both sides of the process. The experience of truth in the hermeneutical encounter would suggest workable criteria of truth, on the one hand, and would negate those criteria that do not account for the experience of truth in such encounter.

In conclusion, we must not look at Gadamer's hermeneutics as though it has given us final answers to difficult issues in cross-cultural religious studies. (That would be very un-Gadamerian, to say the least!) But his analysis of the hermeneutical process involved in historical knowledge offers us a perspective for understanding our interaction with diverse religious traditions. As that interaction continues cross-culturally, our present horizon (however formed by Gadamer at the moment) is open to new approaches and understandings to help us develop cross-cultural religious knowledge and truth.

PART IV

Hermeneutics of Cross-Cultural Truth in Religion

11

Rethinking the Doctrine of Double-Truth: Ambiguity, Relativity and Universality

◻

Conrad Hyers

> Only the paradoxical comes anywhere near to comprehending the fullness of life. Non-ambiguity and non-contradiction are one-sided and thus unsuited to express the incomprehensible.
> —C. G. Jung[1]

When the Dalai Lama toured the United States some years ago, he was received at St. Patrick's Cathedral in New York by a very ecumenical gathering of Roman Catholic, Eastern Orthodox and Protestant clergy, Jewish rabbis, and sundry representatives of Hindu and Buddhist traditions. The Dalai Lama spoke magnanimously of the various religious persuasions represented there as different in approach but one in aspiration, all striving toward the same ends but employing different methods. The message, however, elicited an immediate disclaimer from Cardinal Cook, who insisted that Christianity was not to be placed in the same category or on the same level as other traditions. Not only was the method different, but the beliefs and goals were different as well.

One of the ironies in this type of confrontation is that both positions claim to be offering principles of unity and universality: the Dalai Lama in terms of belief in a common end that transcends the particulars of all religious traditions; Cardinal Cook in terms of a specifically Christian truth, revealed in a single stream of history, which is nevertheless true, not just for the inhabitants of that stream but for all humanity, and before which eventually "every knee shall bow and every tongue confess."

While my sympathies are with the inclusiveness to which the Dalai Lama aspires, and its generous acceptance of religious diversity, at the same time I am unable to find sufficient corroboration of the contention that, despite a diversity of methods, there is a commonality of goals or results. Religious diversity, in fact, exists at all levels, not just at the level of method. The difficulty is one that plagues most liberal theories of religious unity: they claim to be more inclusive than they actually succeed in being. The fault is not that they try to be inclusive, but that they fail to be inclusive enough.

Such a problem, however, is not peculiar to religious liberals. The various major religions themselves came into full flower offering universal truths and liberal visions of unity, relative to the more parochial understandings that preceded them. In the great era that begins in the early part of the first millenium B.C.E. a "unitarian universalist" vision was emerging in all the major basins of civilization. Yet none of the major religions, even those that have actively sought to become *world* religions (Buddhism, Christianity, Islam), have actually succeeded in achieving unity and universality. Each has remained but one among many competitors in the spiritual marketplace of contesting and often conflicting "unitive" visions and "universal" truths. And each tradition has, within itself, fragmented into a variety of competing interpretations of its own vision, thus subverting its own claims to the achievement of unity and universality. The principal reason for this failure of the major religions, whether singly or combined under some presumed common denominator, is that their visions are not in fact sufficiently unitive or universal. Always something that is a central truth or pivotal experience for one religious group is subordinated, or omitted, or denied as idolatrous or illusory.

I. Quasi-Inclusivisms

Ultimate Agreement

The simplest and most popular type of inclusivism is that which sees all religions as finally pointing to the same sublime experiences and teaching the same eternal truths. Despite the considerable differences from tradition to tradition, those differences are viewed as secondary rather than primary. Religious diversity is like so many variations on a single musical theme. What is of greatest importance is the underlying commonality, not the endless variety—those things that unite, not those things that divide. Absolute truth is to be found within this commonality; relative truth within the diversity. Thus, dialogue between traditions either is unnecessary, sustained by a vague and unexamined belief that somehow everything amounts to the same thing in the end, or it is for the purpose of clarifying and deepening those spiritual realizations on which all are presumably in final accord.

Such an attempted inclusiveness is certainly laudatory. In a sense it is implicit in the nature of religious experience itself which, by virtue of its sense of ultimacy, is inclined to see its own particular form of experience as proper to all, and its implications as universal and all-embracing in their validity. But in its impatience to establish a broader fellowship, or in its conviction that the profound realities which it apprehends must of necessity be those apprehended by all great religious seers, it moves too hastily to the conclusion that, finally, when all excrescences are stripped away, all historical and cultural and individual accidentals are set aside, and all differences in terminology and form are resolved, the common kernel of religious understanding will shine forth in all its purity.

There are, no doubt, many points at which two or more religious traditions may find themselves in concert. Unfortunately, however, when the great variety of religious experiences and their expressions are more carefully examined, they do not all coincide, nor converge, nor even approach one another. And in some cases they appear to be moving in quite opposite directions. The actual result is that this type of liberalism achieves its inclusiveness by means of exclusion: ignoring or denying or distorting or downplaying those phenomena that are not in final conformity.

In fact, even the variety of people giving credence to the theme of ultimate oneness have never been able to agree on what that common denominator is. At most, it seems, one can speak in a very formal way, as does Wilfred Cantwell Smith, about the structure of faith as distinguished from belief,[2] or as did Paul Tillich about "ultimate concern." But when the effort is made to state, in a material way, the actual locus and content of this "state of being ultimately concerned," commonality becomes a very elusive thing.

Like Meeting Like

A second type of inclusivist approach is that which directly seeks out those forms of religion which have some affinity with one's own. Thus Christian or Jewish or Muslim mystics may discover areas of common cause with Hindu or Buddhist or Taoist mystics. And Eastern mystics, in turn, may find the teachings of certain select Western mystics more or less congenial. In this way a Zen scholar like D. T. Suzuki, who was critical of many aspects of Christian teaching, especially its dualism and its emphasis on sin and atonement, could become very open and sympathetic in his treatment of Meister Eckhardt who, located on the edge of the Catholic mystical tradition and under suspicion of heresy, might be seen as coming the closest to Suzuki's own position.[3]

At best this type of approach builds bridges of understanding where bridges are least needed. If, to take the case of Suzuki, Eckhardt is actually this close to Mahayana Buddhism, so that one can readily jump from one to the other, then the gulf that persists in yawning before us is that between Eckhardt and a large part of the rest of the Christian community. It is difficult to see how this can be anything more than establishing channels of communication between two islands of like religious phenomena, leaving the vast array of unlike phenomena to flounder among the flotsam and jetsam in a surrounding sea of lesser and greater darkness. One should also not be oblivious to the possibility that this may be but an indirect way of fortifying one's own perspective by finding further confirmation elsewhere. Such an easy unity may only solidify rather than soften the more stubborn differences between traditions by discounting their integrity and by fostering the illusion that the differences have been so simply transcended. The approach succeeds in being inclusive by being resolutely exclusive of those positions which fail to conform with the avowed principles of inclusion.

Fulfillment Theories

A methodologically more ambitious approach to interreligious dialogue has been that which systematically attempts to work out a relationship between different religious traditions on the grounds of a theory of lesser and greater truth. Basically these theories are of two types: *mystical* theories which operate in terms of a hierarchy of levels of religious insight, with the insight of the particular mystic offering the theory being the culmination of the process of deepening religious understanding; and *prophetic* theories which operate more historically in terms of a hierarchy of stages of divine revelation whose fulfillment is embodied in the tradition which the theorist represents. (There are no known cases in which the claimant offers his/her own religious persuasion as the lesser truth in relation to the greater truth of others.)

It is immediately apparent that these schemata are already to a large extent explicit in the great religions themselves, and that the problem of interreligious dialogue eventually is confronted with the fact that all the traditions have used much the same type of argument in relation to their own religious backgrounds, and in relation to one another—though with, to say the least, differing results.

A common variant of this type of argument, especially among mystics of both East and West, is the exoteric-esoteric thesis, with its ranking in terms of lower levels of perception available to the many and higher levels available to the initiated few. The lower levels only receive their true meaning and fulifllment at the higher levels. On the interreligious scene the exoteric-esoteric thesis has become a familiar argument advanced to show that mysticism in its various forms stands at the esoteric level, whereas both priestly and prophetic traditions belong to the exoteric level. Notable exponents of this approach have been Joseph Campbell, Mircea Eliade and Frithjof Schuon,[4] who in this way achieve a kind of religious unity in the sense in which mature parents and immature children may be said to constitute a single family. The irony, of course, is that in a similar manner, but with very different results, prophetic religion can argue that mysticism has, at best, a provisional value as one species of natural religion, groping its way toward those truths given definitive articulation by revelation.

The distinct merit of such schematizations is that they at least make some effort to accomodate religious pluralism, and to recognize and legitimate other types of religious phenomena, if only as lesser and dimly prefigurative forms of religious perception. Yet even the most liberal and charitable attempts to work out the relationships among religious traditions on a hierarchical model finally result in leaving the situation essentially as it has been all along. Each tradition in the end reiterates its claim to be in possession of, or possessed by, certain experiences and truths which are ultimate, and which define the telos of the religious history of the race. And the obvious difficulty is that the same types of stepped-pyramids not only can be, but have been built by those of different, even opposite, persuasions.

The attempt, then, to avoid the extremes of exclusivism and relativism by claiming universality for certain beliefs or experiences is an attractive but often misleading trail. One may find some commonality at a very formal level—Tillich's "ultimate concern," Smith's "faith," Eliade's *axis mundi*—or among certain psychological traits—peace of mind, joy, sense of integration, compassion for others, and so on. But these levels are intimately related to context and content.

It is always faith *in*, ultimate concern *about*, peace *because*, hope *toward*, joy *over*. And the actual locations of the *axis mundi* have been, to put it mildly, in a large number of very diverse places.

At the level of concrete content, not only do so-called universal truths and insights prove, on close examination, not to be fully universal, but what turn out to be equally "universal" are in fact opposing points of view on any fundamental religious or philosophical issue, along with the variety of gradations in between. If a certain archetype (Jung, Eliade, Campbell), for example, is declared to be universal, one either finds it to be quite ambiguous, or one can find a counter-archetype with its own claim to universality—as in the case of the opposite readings of the Greek myth of Prometheus as hero/villain, savior/tempter, or the case of Buddhist art where the "archetypal" symmetry of the mandala is to be juxtaposed with the preference for asymmetry in Zen art.[5] Not only do the understandings and value-judgments appear to be relative to a variety of factors: cultural, historical, psychological, sociological. They are also relative to their opposite logical possibilities, and have meaning in relation to those opposites.

II. Beyond Commonality

Given the problems in envisioning religious unity on the basis of commonality, what is needed is a perspective which is capable of showing the unity of positions which are unlike, rather than like, even those positions which are so unlike as to appear to be logically incompatible and mutually exclusive. The major flaw in the liberal approaches which have been noted is that they think of unity in terms of likeness and agreement, while the real issue and true test is whether one can find unity in the context of unlikeness and disagreement. Unity implies difference, not mere uniformity. Genuine union comes in the juxtaposition and joining of opposite forms, and in such a way that one side is not subordinated to the other as unequal and inferior. To be sure, union also implies some commonality as well; male and female share a common humanity. Yet, as has been suggested, the discovery of commonalities gives no basis upon which to accomodate differences, let alone oppositions. These must be dealt with *as* differences and oppositions, not as something reducible to a common denominator.

To illustrate and test such a view I will address one of the more stubborn divisions in the history of religions, the division between *prophetic* and *mystical* spirituality. By prophetic I mean the kind of religious experience and belief which sees a radical separation between the divine and the human, an otherness which is bridged by divine grace and revelation, but cannot be overcome—the very attempt at doing so being an act of transgression and idolatry. By mystical I mean the kind of religious experience and belief which sees, beneath all the multiplicities and divisions of phenomenal perception, a fundamental unity which is understood as the ultimate truth and reality of all—the failure to perceive and rest in this being the mark of ignorance and illusion. Prophetic religion experiences separateness (whether of the divine from the human, or the human order from the natural order, or one human being from another) as basically good—created distinctions to be maintained and protected. Mystical religion experiences separateness as fragmentation and alienation of one thing from another, and from the totality, and strives toward a recovery of oneness or emptiness. The mystic begins with a pressing sense of a disunity that must be overcome, not a discrimination that must be fortified.

Mohammad, for example, is a clear instance of the prophetic type in his insistence that the truths which he delivers are given to him from *without* (revelation), and therefore that he is "naught but a messenger" of the will and word of Allah. Though Mohammad received these divine messages in a trance state, and though interpreters such as A. J. Arberry have therefore referred to Mohammad's "mystical experiences," the structure and implication of these experiences are characteristically prophetic. They are decisively different from experiences in Socratic/Platonic, Upanishadic, yogic, or Buddhist contexts where the truth is that which wells up from *within* from an innermost point of union or identity, or at least concert, with the ultimate reality.

This broad distinction has been variously expressed. Friedrich Heiler's *Das Gebet* used the same terms in distinguishing between prophetic and mystical forms of prayer. Paul Tillich spoke of "cosmological" and "ontological" types of religion. Ninian Smart contrasts the sense of a "dynamic external presence" with the approach of "inner contemplation." Similarly Frederick Streng differentiates between the way of "personal apprehension of the holy" and that of "freedom through spiritual insight." Each designation selects certain features from a range of possibilities, none of which are adequately descriptive.

While there are many varieties of each type, as well as combinations of both, the question still stands whether even the most extreme instances of the prophetic and mystical types can be accommodated without excluding or subordinating the other. Is it possible, for example, to imagine affirming both the radical dualism of a Karl Barth and the equally radical nondualism of Advaita Vedanta or Madhyamika Buddhism? Such a position would be capable of accommodating the widest variety by virtue of affirming the mutual validity of apparently contradictory positions.

The theme of the unity of opposites in some final *coincidentia oppositorum* is a familiar one in the literature of mysticism, East and West. And to suggest it at this point would seem to be agreeing with the mystical view and its criticism of the prophetic view. But though the thesis I am arguing has certain affinities with such a vision, and some indebtedness to it, it is being applied in a very different way to the opposition *between* mysticism and prophetism. Implicit in it is the refusal to subordinate either prophetism to mysticism or mysticism to prophetism. If one were to use the term "perennial" for either vision, it would have to be used for both, since both visions reach full flower almost simultaneously in the ancient world, and have had equally sophisticated developments.

This prophetic/mystic polarity in religious experience and expression is at first glance a problem of West versus East. Beyond the priestly level of religion, and to some degree in tension with it, the four major religions that develop to the West of the Himalayan divide (Zoroastrianism, Judaism, Christianity, Islam) are dominated by the figure of the prophet and his/her revelations, while the major religions of India and Asia (Hinduism, Buddhism and, with qualifications, classical Taoism) are dominated by the figure of the mystic and his/her enlightenments. Yet this is not simply a matter of "East is East and West is West, and never the twain shall meet." The prophetic traditions also produce strong mystical minorities (Gnosticism, Neo-Platonism, Sufism, Kabbalism, Hasidism and a variety of Catholic and Orthodox contemplatives). And the mystical traditions contain influential movements emphasizing grace and faith (most notably the *bhakti* movement in Vaishnavism and the Pure Land movement in Buddhism). Such developments only further press the issue. For even in a context that is primarily shaped by either the prophetic or the mystical perspective, its counterpart arises as if out of an inevitable impulse to fill in the other side. The problem of conflicting truth-claims *between* religions becomes, therefore, remarkably similar to the problem of conflicting truth-claims *within* each religious tradition.

The issue may be stated very succinctly by saying that if a religion is given enough time and space, whatever its initial and prevailing orientation, it will eventually take up almost all, if not all, possible positions on any of the fundamental religious questions. This is the doctrinal history of all the major religions. Thus a Buddhism which begins with the enlightenment of Gautama and his instruction to his disciples that they, too, should "work out their own salvation" and "walk lonely as a rhinoceros," eventually develops the Pure Land movement which, in its most extreme form in Japan under Shinran, insists that one's only hope in this life is to have faith in the vow of Amida Buddha who will, by his grace, take all who call upon him to his Western Paradise. The ecumenical problem, then, or the problem of religious unity-in-diversity, is essentially the same problem whether one is concerned with ecumenicity between or within religions.

The reason for this state of affairs, the evidence would seem to suggest, is that human experience, relative to the various conflicting religious and philosophical truth-claims, is *ambiguous*. If experience (of the sacred, the self, the world, etc.) is fundamentally ambiguous, then it would be quite natural that experience would give rise to differing and even opposing interpretations, with each being able to make a convincing appeal to experience.

III. The Paradox of Sacrality

It is the nature of religious experience itself—the experience of the sacred—that is ambiguous, paradoxical; it moves outward, centrifugally as it were, in two opposite directions. At the simplest, most elemental level of the experience of a sacred reality, a holy object or holy place is untouchable—because it is sacred; at the same time it is that which everyone seeks to touch—because it is sacred. Both the impulse to dissociate anything sacred from other objects and places which might profane it and the impulse to be in immediate contact with it, if not one with it, are natural responses to something identified as sacred.

The paradox posed by such experiences of sacrality, then, is this: that which is sacred posits a radical distance between itself and the profane sphere, and the attempt to deny or overcome this distance is an act of transgression and trespass upon holy ground; yet at the same time that which is sacred extends an invitation to cross that distance and be connected to the very springs of meaning, being and power. If on the one side lies a sense of distance to be maintained, on the other side lies a sense of a bond to be realized.

This ambiguity in the experience of the holy was analyzed by Rudolf Otto in his classic distinction between *mysterium tremendum* and *mysterium fascinans*: the awesome dreadful mystery from which one recoils in fear and trembling as from an alien Other, and the wondrous, alluring mystery to which one is drawn as toward one's own true origin and home.

> These two qualities, the daunting and the fascinating ... combine in a strange harmony of contrasts, and the resultant dual character of the numinous consciousness to which the entire religious development bears witness ... is at once the strangest and most noteworthy phenomenon in the whole history of religion.[6]

Otto had been attempting to define certain universal elements in religious experience, the common denominator of which was understood as being the experience of the holy. Yet what proved to be universal was not a single, one-directional experience, but an ambiguous one which elicited opposite interpretations and responses.

The question remains whether Otto drew the most important conclusions from this. For Otto this ambiguity in the experience of the holy is articulated in terms of the "ideograms" of divine jealousy, wrath, judgment and righteousness (*tremendum*) and of divine love, mercy, forgiveness and grace (*fascinans*). Such an interpretation is quite understandable inasmuch as the paradox of divine wrath and love, justice and mercy, law and gospel, is a central problem in Christian theology, and one to which Otto's Lutheran tradition is especially sensitive. This was also one of the more pressing theological questions at the turn of the century, with the efforts of liberal Protestant theology to accent the theme of divine love and de-emphasize that of divine wrath. But while the ambiguity of *tremendum* and *fascinans* may express itself in these theological motifs, this is a definition of issues in terms especially suited to the *prophetic* tradition. A case may also be made for reading the ambiguity in a more inclusive way, applying it to both the prophetic and mystical contexts.

If one looks at the ambiguity of the sacred from the standpoint of the prophetic/mystical polarity, rather than the specific issue of divine love and wrath, some interesting observations come to light. The structure of prophetic religion corresponds closely to what one might expect from a religious experience that is centered primarily in the experience of *tremendum*, while the structure of mystical religion corresponds closely to what one might expect from a religious experience that is centered primarily in the experience of *fascinans*. In prophetic religion one kneels or prostrates oneself in humility and prayer before the holy Other; in mystical religion one sits in meditation, seeking within oneself to close those distances between the divine and the human, self and other, or nirvana and samsara, in a vision of ultimate oneness, identity, or emptiness. Thus, prophetic religion tends to ritualize and cultivate its centering in *tremendum*, while mystical religion tends to ritualize and cultivate its centering in *fascinans*.

Out of the sense of *tremendum* arises the suggestion of a great distance from and dependence upon a sacred reality, in relation to which the individual appears as nothing, empty and unholy, and totally dependent for worth, meaning and being (Schleiermacher's "feeling of absolute dependence"). The corresponding modes of religious expression are thus fear and trembling, repentance and sacrifice, humility and faith, trust and obedience, praise and thanksgiving. Out of the sense of *fascinans* arises the suggestion of an inner bond of unity with the sacred, such that notions of dependence or independence are seen as belonging to the illusions of separateness that must be dispelled. Here the corresponding modes of religious expression are those meditative techniques of inner awakening to a truth that is already in one's possession and to a reality which is the true center of one's being.

Paul Tillich expressed the differences quite succinctly in his contrast between "the way of overcoming estrangement" and "the way of meeting a stranger":

> In the (former) way man discovers something that is identical with himself when he discovers God; he discovers something that is identical with himself although it transcends himself infinitely, something from which he is estranged, but from which he never has been and never can be separated. In the (latter) way man meets a stranger when he meets God. Essentially (i.e., in essence) they do not belong to each other.[7]

The isolation of this particular area of ambiguity in the experience of the sacred is hardly, of course, a point from which the whole cloth of any of the prophetic and mystical traditions can be interpreted, or from which the rich variety of types within each can be understood. Religious experience and interpretation is the crossroads of a great many lines of ambiguity: cosmos and chaos, freedom and determinism, faith and works, the symmetrical and the asymmetrical, substance and emptiness, primitivism and progressivism, and so on. The various arenas of conflict in the history of religion, or the history of any particular religion, may be understood as arising out of, and therefore as reflections of, certain fundamental ambiguities in experience. What is needed is a method for defining these ambiguities and identifying the opposite possibilities that may arise out of them. To discuss, then, any particular religious position one would need to note where it is located along a great many lines of ambiguity. The influence of these various locations on each other, as well as the various other factors—psychological, historical, cultural, sociological—would need to be taken into account in order to interpret any specific case. This is why it is so difficult to generalize, and impossible to find any "single symphony of the soul." In this kaleidoscope of intersecting lines of ambiguity, however, this particular line of ambiguity—the sacred as *tremendum* and *fascinans*—is of crucial significance in interpreting the broad divergences between the prophetic and mystical traditions. That it *is* crucial may be demonstrated by observing the high degree of coincidence between this polarity and the entire pattern of opposing motifs and structures, respectively, of the various prophetic and mystical traditions.

IV. Beyond *Tremendum* and *Fascinans*

Whereas Otto viewed the ambiguity of the holy as expressing itself in the themes of divine wrath and love, the prophetic and mystical traditions understand such themes—if they appear at all—quite differently, a difference in fact which may be attributed to their respective focusing upon *tremendum* or *fascinans*. For the prophet the divine wrath is directed toward any human attempt to violate or annul the distance between Creator and creature, and a failure to fulfill the requirements that attend this distance, while the divine love is the bridging of this distance, but from the divine side and without abrogating it. This connecting link between the divine and the human through the Word of God or the Word-made-flesh is distinctively different from that presupposed by the mystic, which is an inner link, a divine spark or intuitive capacity within the depths of one's being and accessible to the depths of one's consciousness. The radical conclusion drawn from this in the Advaitist position, in fact, is that ultimately this distance and its bridging cannot properly be said even to exist except by virtue of an illusion. Divine wrath, at best, symbolizes the awareness of a distance that is to be surmounted or denied, the suffering of separation from the ultimate ground of one's being, or the pain of forgetfulness of one's true identity. Divine love, if meaningful at all, symbolizes the invitation to overcome this estrangement, to return through meditation to the Womb of all Being, or to reunion with God, a return or reunion in which all separations and all "bridges" are finally dissolved and, insofar as the terms may even be used at all, lover and beloved, object and subject, self and other are one.

In the prophetic context divine wrath is the dark side of divine love. It is the gracious attempt on the part of the Creator to preserve precisely those distances and obligations ordained as proper to the creature, apart from which both the existence of the creature and the sovereignty of the Creator are threatened. The divine love therefore not only spans the distance but reinforces it, and through the gracious acts of creation and redemption the creature is granted, at most, a relationship-of-being (*analogia entis*), if not, as Karl Barth insisted, simply a being-in-relationship (*analogia relationis*). In the mystical context, on the other hand, divine love and wrath, if meaningful at all, are seen as aspects of a divine bi-unity whose oppositions are finally transcended, as in the mythologies of Lord Shiva and Mother Kali/Durga. For all distinctions, which are distances (i.e., between love and wrath, good and evil, creation and destruction, etc.) disappear in the Totality or Void which lies behind them.

As these distinctions suggest, in the prophetic traditions the *mysterium* as *fascinans* is subordinated to, and read in terms of, the *mysterium* as *tremendum*. The aspect of the divine approach does not abolish the aspect of divine distance, it presupposes and confirms it. In the mystical tradition the reverse is the case: the *mysterium* as *tremendum* is subordinated to, and read in terms of, the *mysterium* as *fascinans*. The experience of otherness does not abolish the aspect of oneness; otherness is, rather, the alienating illusion that is to be overcome. Given the ambiguity of the sacred, the prophetic and mystical traditions resolve this ambiguity in opposite ways by giving priority to one side and reconciling the other side to it. In this manner one arrives at a vision of transcendent otherness, the other of transcendent unity or vacuity.

One reason that Otto does not follow up on the implications of these distinctions is that for him both the *tremendum* and the *fascinans* reach their zenith of development in mystical experience. This, in large part, is because for Otto the *non-rational* is the core of religion, a "unique original feeling-response," and on his definition mysticism is that form of spirituality with its focus in the nonrational. "Essentially mysticism is the stressing to a very high degree, indeed the overstressing of the non-rational and supra-rational elements in religion; and it is only intelligible when so understood."[8] Since for Otto ineffability is a distinguishing mark of the mystical experience, mysticism is implicit in all religious experience, and in its finest expressions has cultivated that at its center which is central to all religion. But prophetic religion also has its nonrational and suprarational dimensions, as well as its vivid, primary, direct and self-authenticating experiences. Thus a clarification of the differences between the two encounters and readings of the sacred is not advanced, but impeded, by arguing that prophetic religion, as well, has its "mystical" (i.e., nonrational, ineffable, experiential) moments.

The same may be said for the distinction often made between "conventional awareness" and "mystical awareness." Conventional awareness is usually understood as that of an "ordinary consciousness" which is analytical, dualistic and pluralistic, and which expresses itself in "ordinary language" of subjects, predicates and objects. The distinction, however, has pitfalls, and is loaded in favor of mysticism. The tendency is either to treat prophetic religious experience as mystical, or to classify the prophetic along with the conventional. Actually, prophetic experience is different from both mystical and conventional awareness. Now, if by conventional awareness one means subject-object consciousness, then, yes, prophetic experience is closer to *that*, in fact gives positive support to it. Yet this observation is misleading, for there is also a kind of conventional awareness which is unitive and intuitive, as in certain kinds of creative activity, poetic vision, scientific endeavor, even scholarly insight. Thus, at the level of conventional knowledge too we find both what Freeman Dyson has called "unifiers" and "diversifiers."

In fact, it is these two types of conventional awareness that provide a good deal of analogical experience upon which the more transcendent and ineffable religious experiences of both prophets and mystics can draw in attempting to articulate their understandings. The difference is that prophets draw their analogies from one kind of conventional awareness (subject-object, linear, discriminating) and mystics from another (unitive, intuitive, wholistic). This is quite apparent in their contrasting vocabularies, images, examples and arguments. One type of religious experience is not necessarily more or less transcendent or ineffable than the other, and both employ elements from common experience to point toward and attempt to persuade others to approach the ultimate realities and verities which they have perceived.

Though the "Word of God" is stressed in prophetic religions, mysticism proves no less wordy. And though silence is stressed in mysticism, the prophetic traditions acknowledge that the truth is finally inexpressible and unknowable. The same divine Word that commands the prophet to speak also commands him/her on occasion to shut up, to "be still and know," to "keep silence before him." It is at this point, in fact, that the two traditions intersect: in that *mysterium* beyond the ambiguity of *tremendum* and *fascinans*, beyond all imaging and mythmaking. They arrive at this intersection in part on the basis of similar realizations of the problematic of words and concepts in dealing with religious experience, and especially in dealing with ultimate reality. But they also arrive at this point on the basis of their own contrasting perspectives.

Prophetic religion speaks of the inadequacies of words out of the context of *tremendum* and therefore in terms of the problem of *idolatry*: the confusion of the radical distinction between the finite and the infinite, and the misguided elevation of any finite form (image, myth, symbol, concept) to the status of the infinite. The Word of God, given through the prophet in revelation, is both revealed and hidden, delivered in words but never fully exhausted by them. Mysticism on the other hand speaks of the inadequacy of words out of the context of *fascinans* and therefore in terms of the problem of *dualism*: the making of alienating distinctions between subject-object, I-it, self-other. Words and images (*nama* and *rupa*, name and form) are part of that illusory world of *maya*-consciousness. They are products of the discriminating mind which separates things from one another, isolating and abstracting from what is an indivisible whole.

The problem is that, though both prophets and mystics agree that the final truth can never be spoken or conceptualized, they tend to insist that particular sorts of words, and a particular set of images and myths, are the best way of expressing what cannot be expressed. Thus both traditions persist in favoring their contrasting vocabularies, mythologies, metaphors, rituals and practices. Yet these contrasting expressions proceed from the same ambiguities and, like the earthen vessels that they are, are broken before that Mystery of Mysteries out of which all things come, and to which all things are returned. What Paul Klee has said of art is equally true of religion: "Art in the highest sense deals with an ultimate mystery that lies behind the ambiguity which the light of the intellect fails miserably to penetrate."

The prophetic word and the mystical word have a common origin both in the ambiguities with which they wrestle and the mysteries about which they would speak. Like brother and sister they can never quite escape their common bond. Each belongs to the other, needs the other, and is incomplete apart from the other. If pressed to their logical conclusions on the basis of their respective perceptions, they become mutually exclusive visions, like the Barthian Christian and the Advaita Vedantist. Having abstracted intellectual positions which are rigorously coherent and self-consistent, and having walked off in opposite directions, dueling pistols in hand, they eventually reach the point where each affirms what the other denies and denies what the other affirms. Nevertheless, inasmuch as they are defending opposite sides of a fundamental ambiguity, they are necessarily complementary visions. Their cumulative religious wisdom is correct: they are to be affirmed and denied—affirmed in that both are appropriate responses to the Mystery of Mysteries, denied insofar as they insist that they are to be taken as absolute, final, exclusive, or literal articulations of the truth. In Martin Buber's words:

> Of course God is the "wholly Other"; but He is also the wholly Same, the wholly Present. Of course He is the *Mysterium Tremendum* that appears and overthrows; but He is also the mystery of the self-evident, nearer to me than my I.[9]

Though the notion of a *coincidentia oppositorum* is usually understood as the special possession of the mystic, the term has an even broader application to the contrasting visions of the prophet and mystic. In this context it represents an affirmation of both visions without subordinating one to the other. This affirmation is also a negation insofar as, in the name of purity and finality, they not only set themselves up in contradiction to their opposite, but they become themselves self-contradictory.

The radical nondualist, for example, still must contend with the existence of dualistic consciousness and the dualistic distinction between those who see the truth of *advaita* and those who do not, as well as the difficulty of explaining the origin and existence of dualism if all is in fact one, without differentiation or agents of differentiation. The radical dualist, on the other hand, for all of the impassioned concern to insist upon the otherness of the divine, and salvation through divine revelation and grace alone, has difficulty in locating any point of contact to which this revelation and grace could address itself. The dualist thus manifests a distinct tendency to annihilate the integrity and freedom of the creature to the point that God becomes All in All and the creature nothing.

Huizinga's dictum seems to hold true in both cases: "All consistent thinking out of the dogmas of faith leads to absurdity."[10] Radical nondualism affirms dualism in the act of denying it, and conversely radical dualism affirms nondualism in the act of denying it. Both keenly observe the contradictions in the positions of each other, but not in their own. These absurdities are themselves a reflection of the ambiguities of experience which, despite all efforts to avoid them and to achieve consistency, faithfulness and clarity, persist in troubling the waters of rational coherence. In the very extremity of their apparent exclusion of one another, the radical dualist and the radical nondualist are returned to the *mysterium* to which they have responded, and the ambiguity of *tremendum* and *fascinans* out of which they have arisen.

If one may speak of a synthesis of these perspectives, it cannot be a synthesis which can be put into words and images, just as a synthesis of wave and particle models ("wavicles") cannot be given conceptual or picturable form. It is a synthesis that is seen as through a glass darkly, beyond both *tremendum* and *fascinans*, in the *mysterium* itself. It is a "synthesis" that is both revealed and hidden, a unity which nevertheless remains a duality and plurality, for the duality and plurality are also a part of its manifestation. In the words of van der Leeuw:

> The religious significance of things . . . is that one which no wider or deeper meaning can follow. It is the meaning of the whole; it is the last word. But this meaning is never understood, this last word is never spoken; always they remain superior, the ultimate meaning being a secret which reveals itself repeatedly, only nevertheless to remain eternally concealed. It implies an advance to the farthest boundary, where only one sole fact is understood: that all comprehension is "beyond."[11]

Such an interpretation, though differing in application from that of Otto, is nevertheless in accord with the universality of his vision. As he wrote on the related issue of personal and suprapersonal designations for the *numinous*:

> Each of the two, the personal and the mystical, belongs to the other, and the language of devotion uses very naturally the phrases and expressions of both commingled. They are not different forms of religion, still less different stages in religion, the one higher and better than the other, but the two

essentially united poles of a single fundamental attitude, the religious attitude.[12]

V. Concluding Summary

The thesis being proposed may be summarized in six propositions:

1. Wherever there emerges a fundamental conflict in religious or philosophical interpretation, this conflict is traceable to an ambiguity in experience which makes possible such a conflict and of which it is a reflection.

2. Central to the difference between prophetic and mystical understandings is a basic axis of potential ambiguity in the experience of what is perceived as ultimate reality and truth.

3. The major differences between the prophetic and mystical traditions may be understood as in part the consequence of their respective emphases upon one or the other side of this ambiguity.

4. A recognition of this ambiguity inherent in the religious situation provides a basis for an acceptance of both types of tradition as appropriate, meaningful and valid responses, yet as partial and incomplete apart from the other. This recognition also provides a basis upon which the historian of religion may serve the contemporary scene as an arbiter of historic conflicts.

5. The ambiguities within the religious situation and the double-truths that arise from them are what are universal, not some common experience, archetype, belief or aspiration. Religious unity is to be found within those ambiguities from which disunity has arisen and in that inexpressible truth that lies beyond all experience and its formulations.

6. If criteria for the justification of truth-claims cross-culturally were to be developed along these lines, the result would be that truth-claims could neither be absolutized nor reduced to cultural and psychological relativities. Absolute truth lies beyond conceptualization and cannot be contained or exhausted by any image, name or form. Relative truth on the other hand is not only relative to cultural and psychological factors, but also relative to contrasting possibilities within the ambiguousness of experience.

12

Mystical Experience as a Bridge for Cross-Cultural Philosophy of Religion: A Critique

◗

John Y. Fenton

I. The "Essence" of Mystical Experience

The Common Argument

The belief that mystical experience is both ineffable and essentially the same in all religious traditions has become fairly common in the twentieth century. The use made of these two alleged facts about mystical experience by different authors varies, but in general putative ineffability has been used to discount all language and all differences in language about mystical experience as merely accidental and to characterize mystical experience as either trans- or sub-conceptual. Putative unanimity in the descriptions mystics have given of their experiences follows easily from the ineffability of the experiences. Since ineffability supposedly makes it impossible to make any distinctions between one ineffable experience and another, and since theological interpretations have nothing to do with mystical experience, all mystical experiences are therefore essentially the same.[1]

In the more extended forms of the claim that mystical experience is ineffable the experience becomes so different from other kinds of experience that ineffability becomes unique to mystical experience and even a part of its definition. A barrier is made to appear between mystical experience and its interpretation, so that nonmystics cannot really know anything about mystical experience. Mystical experience is sometimes characterized as sub-conceptual—as primarily emotive, aesthetic, or consisting in a certain sort of attitude or special awareness.[2] Other authors understand mystical intuition to be trans-conceptual—a special kind of truth or wisdom that far transcends ordinary conceptual knowledge. It is only a small additional step to argue that mystical intuition is self-authenticating and indubitable. Truth then appears, implicitly or explicitly, at two levels, with ordinary *knowledge* confined to the level of mere conceptuality, below *wisdom* and incommensurate with it. Knowledge, scholarly or otherwise, is thus unable to get at mystical wisdom.

The claim that mystical intuition is trans-conceptual also gives additional support to the claim that mystical testimony is unanimous in essence. Since Truth must always be in agreement with itself, mystical truth, wherever it is found, must also be in essential agreement with itself. Specific traditional contexts in which mystical experience occurs can be abstracted and generalized without respect to context.[3] The truth as understood in one mystical tradition can also be used to understand the truth in any other mystical tradition. Extracted from its contexts mystical experience then appears to transcend linguistic, cultural, philosophical and theological differences as a sort of universal vision, and the unanimous testimony of mystics gives mysticism a kind of intersubjective verification that is in principle replicable.

Thesis: Mystical Experience Is Not Ineffable in the Strong Sense, and Mystical Experiences Vary Significantly from One Tradition to Another

The putative unanimity of mystical experience is based primarily upon its putative ineffability. It must first be shown that mystical experience is not ineffable in the strong sense discussed before it will be possible to treat differences in theological description and evaluation among different mystical traditions as significant.

While it is true that mystical experience is frequently not susceptible to straightforward literal description, and while the relationship of mystical experience to conceptuality is complex and somewhat peculiar, the language mystics use to talk about mystical experience does communicate meaningfully and gives specific directions to the aspiring student. Once this has been proved, it will be possible to marshal sufficient evidence to show that the language of mystics discriminates the right method and the right mystical experience from counterfeits and that different mystical traditions disagree with each other about which experiences are the right ones and which are counterfeit. Within specific mystical traditions theology has a constitutive role because the issue at stake is liberation or salvation.

The combination of ineffability with unanimity on this subject has, of course, a certain initial implausibility that strikes one immediately. If mystical experience were completely ineffable, it would have no intellectual content and no descriptive characteristics, and the claim to unanimity would be meaningless. Alternatively, if the claim to unanimous description of the mystical experience is meaningful, then the experience must in some sense be characterizable, and mystical experience is thus not entirely ineffable. Ineffability and unanimity cancel each other out.

Mystical Experience and Philosophy of Religion

If mystical experience were an objective intuition of Truth beyond all conceptual conditioning, if it were a cross-cultural common human emotion or attitude, and if mystical experience were everywhere the same as a sort of cross-cultural constant, the prospect for a Western philosophy of religion that is attempting to become cross-cultural would seem more feasible. If the argument of this essay is correct, however, we are not dealing with a cross-cultural fact but with the product of culturally specific assumptions by Asians and Westerners that for somewhat different reasons happen partially to converge.

For the Westerner the idea of the identity and objectivity of mystical experiences meets a continuing cultural need for a "natural religion" as "old as creation" that would serve as a bond of unity over against the institutional and theological conflicts of religious traditions and denominations. The idea also accords with the Western Romantic notion that raw experience precedes and is more fundamental than the ideological, social and political categories that divide us. Some Asians, especially Neo-Vedanta Hindus, concur with these Western orientations, partly because of Western cultural influence, but more importantly because (1) these notions have some affinity with the Advaita Vedanta belief that the nondual mystical experience is the highest and only truly liberating spirituality, and (2) because this idea seems to support the self-presentation of some Asian religious movements as scientific or objectively true rather than as something either theological or religious.[4] That such partial convergence of Western and Asian interests constitutes an adequate basis for a cross-cultural philosophy of religion is by no means evident. According to my argument such a claim would also be factually incorrect.

II. Ineffability and Mystical Experience

Consensual Experience, Analogues and Indescribable Experience

Ineffability as such is not sufficient either to set off one particular kind of experience from all others or to classify them all together as the same experience. We all have experiences that are difficult to describe. In many such cases, however, this causes little difficulty primarily because a consensual fund of experience makes up for the inadequacy of the words we use to talk about such experiences. The communication problem seems to be much more striking in the case of mystical ecstasy. If shared experience is absent it will be considerably more difficult to break through the words. But meditational experience, for example, is becoming much more common for a sizable minority of Americans, and it is at least comparable to mystical experience. Meditation may provide "foretastes" of what mystical experience is like. This sort of comparable experience make mystical ineffability less of a problem than it might have been formerly. If there are analogues to mystical experience in either common or meditational experience, mystical experience will also not be totally ineffable.

Some things that are initially indescribable may become describable when we have understood them better. Some cases resist clear understanding. But even for these a conventional language and vocabulary can be developed if talking about these matters is important to us. Special conventional languages of this sort have at times been developed within the mystical traditions. The inner experiential reality of mystical experience nevertheless seems to be at least partially lost in attempts to express this reality in direct, literal description even of a conventional sort. The mystical traditions also ascribe a certain sacred aura to mystical experience that makes direct description inappropriate if not taboo.[5] When conventional language gets too close to the mystical goal there is a tendency to increase the distance between conventions and the ultimate mystical culmination. But even at this level there are ways in which communication is possible.

A certain degree of indescribability or ineffability therefore seems characteristic of mystical experience. But if there are comparable experiences and if there are analogues to mystical experience in common human experience, then even for the nonmystic the ineffability of language about mystical experience cannot be absolute. Mystical ineffability is weak rather than strong.

By the *weak ineffability* of mystical experience I mean the following: (1) Mystical experience is not directly describable or conceptualizable and the intent of the language of mystics about mystical experience is not conceptual. (2) The language about mystical experience nevertheless "takes off" from or is oriented away from descriptive and conceptual language, frequently in negative or superlative fashion. (3) Language about mystical experiences does distinguish specifically among potential ineffable experiences, choosing some and avoiding others. (4) Mystical experience is therefore regarded in mystical traditions as something about which communication is possible such that the language conducts the aspirant through a specific mystic path in a specific way toward a specific goal.[6]

Mystical Wisdom and Knowledge Are Commensurate

Mystical experience is often discussed by mystics explicitly or implicitly in the context of two incommensurate levels of truth: wisdom and knowledge. True wisdom is nondual; subject and object are not-two. Ordinary knowledge (nescience or *avidya*), however, is completely pervaded by the subject-object dichotomy. From the standpoint of ordinary knowledge, therefore, mystical experience must appear ineffable.

In fact, however, the isolation of wisdom from knowledge and of knowledge from wisdom is not and cannot be maintained either in the Vedanta or in any of the other mystical traditions. An initial and official proclamation of *strong ineffability* is followed by an unofficial and unacknowledged shift to *weak ineffability*. The supposed hiatus between the two levels is continually bridged in both directions: knowledge must be used to obtain wisdom and wisdom is relied upon to provide new knowledge and to sanction it. In the theology of the great Shankaracharya, for example, ordinary knowledge not only conceals wisdom, it also reveals it. Philosophical and theological argumentation can lead to intuition of the nondual Reality.[7] The connection of knowledge to wisdom for Shankara is not merely theoretical. He also makes frequent appeal to a common element of human experience as a sort of "foretaste" or "inkling" of wisdom. This element is the "Witness of experience" (*saksin*), the ineluctable subject of all of our ordinary experience.[8] As the "knower" of knowing, the "hearer" of hearing, and so forth, the true Self (*atman*) is involved in and makes all ordinary experience possible. Both theoretically and experientially knowledge and common experience have a positive relation to wisdom.

In fact, mystical experience is not entirely different from "ordinary" kinds of experience. The Theravada Buddhist Nyanaponika Thera emphasizes, for example, that the development of mindfulness (*sati*) does not depend upon acquiring a new mental capacity.[9] Mindfulness consists in the development of the common human capacity to pay attention passively. Already in the beginning stages of the practice the student experiences "foretastes" of the goal of the path. As these experiences accumulate and as the techniques of meditation are increasingly mastered, both the instructions for how to practice and the kind of insight that is sought as the goal become increasingly comprehensible. Once the student begins to practice meditation she/he also realizes that there are any number of possible realms of consciousness available to explore. Both the techniques and the description of the desired state of consciousness are expressed clearly enough that the student is guided into the right kinds of consciousness and avoids those that lead away from the goal or that have no significance in relation to that goal.[10]

Mystical Traditions Communicate the Path and the Goal

If different kinds of meditation lead to different experiences, the unanimity that does obtain within a particular mystical tradition indicates that mystical experience cannot be entirely ineffable. The particular mystical traditions reject some methods and goals and indicate others. There are shared descriptions, direction and techniques. Within a particular tradition the mystical experience sought comes close to being a stereotype to be reduplicated. The Zen way of no-way is actually a particular way that leads to a particular type of insight. Further, the dharma-battles (question and answer contests) in which enlightened Zen Buddhists engage are intended to *test* the depth of the combatants' insight.

The language about mystical experience is difficult, complex, time-consuming and closely tied to experience, but it is not absolutely mysterious. In principle the jargon of mystical language may be no more esoteric than the jargon of nuclear physicists, although the specifics are obviously quite different. Mystical language is an esoteric jargon, but it is not ineffable in the strong sense.

How Mystical Language Communicates

1. Mystical language communicates and discriminates with sufficient precision to serve its peculiar transformative purposes. Of course, mystical writers can and do employ forms of communication that are also used by nonmystics. The kind of communication peculiar to mysticism occurs in the service of processes of spiritual therapy. It selects and develops certain ingredients of ordinary experience that are judged to be inklings of the human malady and its resolution. Other aspects of common experience are excluded as irrelevant or obstructive to the process of transformation. This selection and exclusion lead to experiential levels that may be quite peculiar to the path being followed. On the way some faculties are enhanced, others are repressed, so that the content of the experience itself is changed. Diagnosis, treatment and resolution are formed and informed by the theological language of the specific tradition, the language serving as a *model of* experience that, when internalized, becomes a *model for* experience.[11]

2. Straightforward description of the "advanced" stages of the mystical path is often not possible. Frequently literal description is not even desirable at this level because the student might confuse the meaning of the words with the intention of the path. Other means of communication have been devised to give instruction without describing. Some of these instruction devices are *superlative*: the intention of the words used is in the same direction as, but is more than, what is said. Many of the means of communication are *negative*, but even in negative cases the intention of the words is positive.

Shankara and Nagarjuna, the Indian mystical theologians, used philosophical or theological argumentation as their primary means of communication. Both follow the dialectical method of discrediting alternatives.[12] When all of the alternatives have been shown to be unreasonable, when the student no longer has any alternatives, the *siddhanta* or wisdom emerges.[13] Reasoning is used negatively to force the transfiguration of knowledge into wisdom. Negative argumentation thus enables the mystical philosopher to intend more than can be said.

Both Shankara and Nagarjuna taught by the method of closing alternatives, but the openings they left for the student to find are not the same. Despite the negative form of the words in which wisdom emerges for both authors, their meaning is clearly not the same. For Shankara reality is nondual (*advaita*). For Nagarjuna it is empty (*sunyata*). Thus negative language is used to direct toward specific but differing positive intentions.

Mystical language frequently has a positive meaning even when its form and force are negative. What a student is supposed to do may not be susceptible to direct statement. In addition to offering analogues, the teacher may indicate what to do indirectly by saying what the student should *not* do. Closing some doors, excluding some of the alternatives experientially indicates the way to go or at least the area for trial-and-error attempts until there is success. In addition, of course, some of the transitions to be made are abrupt and unprogrammable. A common transition of this sort for beginners would be that from active to passive meditation, that is, from a self-consciously controlled program of paying attention selectively, to spontaneous attention that no longer requires effort or direction. Once the transition has been made the words about it seem quite appropriate and meaningful. The instruction, "Empty your mind, but do not impede any thoughts," may initially sound self-contradictory. But after it has been learned, the instruction seems both sensible and appropriate.

The frequent use of negativities, contradictions, paradoxes, absurdities and even jokes in mystical traditions is also at an initial level of analysis not really self-contradictory or nonsensical. But at another level closer to the needs of transformation such negative linguistic forms are intended to break up and destroy ordinary expectations of the student's structured world in order to push him/her, not to another structural alternative, but to a liminal state beyond structure altogether.[14] Destroying reliance on these structures opens up access to the liminal states.

3. Symbolic language often maps out the path in ways that experientially are not so much to be deciphered as to be traversed. Mystical language with a narrative plot (such as dialogues, question and answer sequences, dramas, contests, progress stories, and multiple-stage visualizations) are certainly susceptible to conceptual analysis and translation. But they are also aimed at providing a means of participation and identification so that the student may move with the plot—from diagnosis through the path to resolution. The mystical path is thus a particular kind of rite of passage with many of the characteristics of performance, especially of drama, of transaction, of role transfer and of role playing. It thus involves being a certain kind

of character, walking (*acharya*, *marga*) or behaving in a certain way, playing a role within a plot as much as in completing the story and leaving the stage.

4. Finally, the mystical path is communicated by means of what might be called "tactile" meaning. The use of melody, of timing and rhythm structures, of movement or lack of it, of recitation and repetition, of light and color, of sensory bombardment or sensory deprivation to retune and transform, is not formless or ineffable but quite specific in its intent and method. The body, the senses and the consciousness are reshaped in specific ways even though it may not be at present practicable to demonstrate how such methods work. Mantras, for example, work as much because they are sounds in specific patterns, possibly with certain unrecognized references, as they do for any translatable conceptual meaning.[15] That is, the repetitious patterns of sound force the mind to break the patterns of repeated sounds and hear the unvoiced sounds at the limit of the voiced. But even so, what is heard is not ineffable in the strong sense. The unsounded sound is specific to the means of hearing it and relative to the specific mystical tradition.

How to Read Mystical Texts

The case I have made for the weak rather than the strong ineffability of mystical language makes it possible to state some elementary principles for the interpretation of mystical texts. The notion of weak mystical ineffability entails communicability, specifically mystical but nevertheless intelligible principles of interpretation, and discriminations that are specific rather than vague.

1. The scholar is not kept from the meaning of a mystical text by some sort of intrinsic impenetrable mystery. The meaning of the text is accessible and general rules of interpretation are applicable.

2. The intent of mystical texts in general is a specific one: therapy for the human malady and the path to resolution.

3. The intent of mystical texts belonging to a specific mystical tradition may be peculiar to that tradition or even to some extent to a particular text. The principles of interpretation have to be picked up from each particular mystical tradition. Mystical texts are to be read in their whole immediate and general traditional context unless there is good reason not to do so. Taking elements out of context to represent mysticism in general is a quite misleading procedure.

4. Mystical intent is to some extent individual and varies with the author and individual text of the author. But no rigid distinction is warranted between the author's theology and the author's experience.

5. From a descriptive-interpretive scholarly point of view, there is no general key to the meaning of all mystical texts, and there is no general ranking system for different types of mysticism. Nor is there a best, highest, purest or most complete type of mystical experience. Such judgments are not phenomenological, they are theological.[16]

III. Unanimity and Mystical Experience

Theological Differences Are Practical

When mystical texts are read broadly in the fashion recommended, the differences among the traditions become as striking as the similarities. Mystical writers from different mystical traditions do discriminate the right methods from the wrong methods and the right goals from the wrong ones. Authors from different traditions do not agree with those of other traditions about which experience resolves the human malady. Not only do some of the spokespersons for the traditions want to exclude possession, mental disorders and aridity from mystical experiences, they also want to exclude some of the illumination experiences favored by other mystical traditions. Sometimes the reasons for rejecting the efficacy of other putative liberation experiences appear to be merely verbal, technical, procedural or a matter of misunderstanding. But frequently fundamental differences emerge. The differences are theological, but they are at the same time practical, for they concern what constitutes true liberation.

Right Experience and Mystical Theology

HINDU VEDANTA. Each particular Hindu tradition tends to have its own specific criteria for what the ultimate mystical state is. Hindu theologians have entered into detailed and sometimes heated argument with their opponents to prove their adversaries' conceptions and experience inadequate. Hindu toleration generally is paternalistic: other religious orientations contain truth, but not enough truth for genuine liberation. Divergencies are particularly marked between Vedanta and the other Indian *darsanas*, but there are also significant differences among the subdivisions within Vedanta.

Thus for Shankara nonduality is the theological norm of true Being and therefore of liberation. All other views and experiences are inferior and nonliberating. Sankhya and Yoga doctrine is pluralistic. In Shankara's judgment yogic meditative practice leads only to unusual states of consciousness that do not bring liberation.[17] At the most, yogic trance leads only to knowledge of the quality-free character of the self.[18] Shankara thought no better of Jains and most Buddhists.[19] Theistic orientations such as the *Bhagavata* were seen as inferior accommodations to weaker human beings who cannot get along without symbolic supports.[20]

Shankara's negative language about Being (*sat*) has a positive, discriminating function. It clearly delineates and demarcates the particular kind of mystical experience that is sought and differentiates it from other kinds of ineffable experiences that are possible (such as yogic trance). The ontological reality of undifferentiated pure Being is presupposed by the teacher as the seeker's target, so that negative description is thus contextually meaningful. *Brahmavid* is, so to speak, "what is left over" after all of the wrong alternatives have been blocked. "What is left over" is quite specific.[21]

Perhaps nowhere is it clearer that preferences in mystical experience depend upon the theological norms of the mystic than in the fundamental disputes between Ramanuja and Shankara. Ramanuja doubted that the kind of nondual experience described by Shankara was even possible, since perception of all kinds is always of objects.[22] The true resolution was not beyond the subject-object dichotomy nor was it in any sort of trance. The highest, right and only sufficient resolution experience is the steady remembrance of the constant, unbroken love of God.[23]

BUDDHISM. Although Shankara's norm for the liberating mystical experience has some affinities with Buddhist emptiness (*sunyata*) and shows Buddhist influence, nondual Being (*sat*) and Emptiness are specifically different, both metaphysically and experientially. Mahayana emptiness and Advaita *brahmavid* are both ineffable, in the weak sense, but it is nevertheless practicable to distinguish between the two experiences. The difference between nondual Being and Emptiness is expressed very emphatically in the *Heart Sutra*:

> [F]orm is emptiness and the very emptiness is form; emptiness does not differ from form, nor does form differ from emptiness; whatever is form, that is emptiness, whatever is emptiness, that is form.[24]

The same point is made repeatedly and unmistakeably in paired oppositions with each half of the pair intended to qualify the other. If the student took only the first half of each pair, she/he might well seek a seamless, undifferentiated trance experience. But the second half of each pair indicates that there is another possibility within the realm of the ineffable. No separate trance state that cuts off sense experience is to be accepted as the resolution. *Satori* is not the experience of the void. The void is another possibility within the nonconceptual and it is not sufficient for the resolution of the human problem. Emptiness without form, trance without insight, is mere withdrawal.[25] It is a "dead void."

This "dead void" corresponds to Buddhist *samatha* (calming) without its balancing and fulfilling *vipassana* (insight),[26] but it also corresponds phenomenologically with Advaita Vedanta's distinctionless intuition. Hui-Neng, the famous Chinese Sixth Ch'an Patriarch, makes the same point with great clarity:

> The deluded man clings to the characteristics of things, adheres to the *samadhi* of oneness, thinks that straightforward mind is sitting without moving and casting aside delusions without letting things arise in his mind. This he considers to be the *samadhi* of oneness. This kind of practice is the same as insentiency and the cause of an obstruction to the Tao. Tao must be something that circulates freely; why should he impede it? If the mind does not abide in things the Tao circulates freely; if the mind abides in things, it becomes entangled.[27]

Within Buddhism itself, the goal of the Zen tradition may be seen as different from that of the Theravada tradition. Hakuin, the eighteenth-century exponent of Rinzai Zen, expresses a general Mahayana view:

> The Hinayanists were inferior in methods of discipline and were fond of quietude; they simply had no knowledge of the noble activities of a bodhisattva.[28]

Hakuin's first criticism is directed against quietude as the goal of meditation. The quietude in question corresponds to the Theravada *samatha*, the calming of the senses by cultivating trance (*jnana*). Since *samatha* is paired with and completed by the practice of insight (*vipassana*) in the Theravada tradition generally, Hakuin's first criticism is possibly based upon misinformation and traditional prejudice. Hakuin's second criticism compares that *arhat* ideal unfavorably with that of the *bodhisattva*. This doctrinal difference is real and significant.

Zen meditation and Zen resolution experience are in strict alignment with each other. Zen meditation is not focused upon any one object of attention and it does not proceed from one object of attention to another. The form of Zen meditation conforms to the resolution sought: an empty mind full of what is being experienced now without any restraints, conceptions or attachments. The empty mind that has no conceptions or desires corresponds to *nirvana* while the flowing, unimpeded experience with which it is filled corresponds to *samsara*. The empty mind that is full is *nirvana* in *samsara*; the present experience in an empty mind is *samsara* in *nirvana*.

If there is the same sort of correspondence between method and resolution in the Theravada tradition as there is in Ch'an and Zen, then it is plausible that the difference of the *bodhisattva* doctrine from the *arhat* doctrine in the two Buddhist traditions indicates a significant difference in resolution experiences as well.[29] As Ramanuja and Shankara disagree with each other within the Hindu Vedanta, so also there would be disagreement between the Theravada and Mahayana mystical traditions within Buddhism.

PHYSIOLOGICAL DIFFERENCES CORRELATE WITH RESOLUTION DIFFERENCES. The possible correlations of brain waves to specific mystic states of consciousness have been questioned and rightly so.[30] But when measurable physiological differences correspond to intentional theological differences between specific methods of meditation, the evidence is significant. Experimental results obtained from subjecting Zen monks and accomplished yogins to external stimuli during deep meditation show differences that do correlate with what we would expect on theological grounds.[31] Yogins doing an "objectless" meditation should be oblivious to external stimuli and experimental results showed that they were. External stimuli had no effect on the alpha waves of the yogins. Zen meditators should be "object-oriented" rather than "subject-oriented" (as the yogins were), so that external stimuli should be experienced with clarity and as though they were newly presented each time. Each presentation of the external stimuli consistently blocked alpha waves for the Zen meditators. The Zen meditators' nonattachment to stimuli should also allow rapid return to alpha waves after each stimulus, and because they do not habituate, they should be ready to respond to repetition of the stimulus with the same intensity each time it is repeated. These expectations were experimentally verified. Control persons in a "normal" state of consciousness habituate, that is, they recognize the repeated stimulus as the same one as was experienced before, they classify the stimulus as "the same," and thus they experience the stimulus with decreasing intensity with each repetition. For the control persons, the external stimulus in a short time no longer blocked alpha waves.

SOME PHENOMENOLOGICAL SIMILARITIES IN CROSS-TRADITIONAL MYSTICAL EXPERIENCES MAY BE INCIDENTAL. Similar experiential effects may accompany different kinds of mystical resolution experiences in different mystical traditions. These similarities may appear significant only when they are abstracted from their contexts. If peak experiences or "zero experiences" are not regarded as self-authenticating within the mystical traditions and are not the source by themselves of the authority of mystical experience, and if theological differences are constitutive of mystical experience rather than subsequently added accidental interpretations, then some of the experiential elements that are commonly said to form the essence of mystical experience may not be particularly significant. Possibly the experiential similarities are side-effects of resolution in general and its emotional accompaniments. If so we would expect to find them in other kinds of resolution besides the mystical. Within the mystical traditions intensity of emotions and dazzling trips do not guarantee resolution. A mystic judges which experiences count as resolution by reference to the tradition which provides guideposts, theory, criteria, guides, mentors, authority figures and experiential stereotypes.

The metaphysical structure of the specific mystical tradition sets up the mystical situation, but it does not necessarily *produce* the experience. In fact, failure to succeed is apparently quite common. That what is experienced is conditioned, focused, and evaluated by the structure of the tradition by no means excludes the possibility that the experience is also objectively based. Many mystical traditions have criteria for checking and evaluating to make sure that the sought-for experience has not been merely imagined or intentionally projected.

Right Method

Disagreement is also widespread concerning the right method to be employed by the mystic seeker. Not only is there controversy about whether or not there even are methods for attaining mystical experience, but even those who say that there are methods disagree about which procedures are right.

Some kind of renunciation is probably universal among the mystical traditions, but what must be renounced varies significantly. Full-time vocation? certain foods? sexual activity? There is no obvious consensus about what constitutes renunciation. Some form of concentration is also probably universal in the various mystical traditions, but how one should concentrate varies widely. Discursive meditation? visions? meditation? subject-oriented or object-oriented? focused or not focused?

Not only is it not possible to carry out all of these methods at once, but many are mutually exclusive. What the seeker is able to experience is heavily conditioned by the method which determines in large measure what can or cannot even cross the threshold of notice. The method limits the kind of experience that is possible and acceptable. Within the limits of the method mystical experience might or might not occur due to a wide range of variables. Some of the transitions are abrupt and mysterious. Mystery is part of the method. Even the method of no-method, of complete passivity, is also directed by method, for it excludes a whole range of possible activities, thereby directing consciousness elsewhere.

It has been questioned by some scholars whether method has anything to do with the mystical goal.[32] If the only aim of mystics were to have "peak experiences," the matter would be quite debatable. But insofar as the aim is resolution/liberation and being a certain kind of person of a traditional type specific to a mystical tradition, the specific mystical path is essential to the specific mystical goal.

IV. Conclusion

I have argued that the language of mystical traditions about mystical experience is characterized by weak rather than strong ineffability. Thus even when the explicit language of a tradition points beyond what it literally says, it does so in a way that is sufficiently explicit to discriminate the particular kind of experience that is sought from those that are regarded as counterfeit and to guide the aspirant toward that particular goal as opposed to others that might be sought. There is a plurality of possible kinds of mystical experience. Which kind of mystical experience is regarded as liberation or resolution is typically a value-judgment guided by the theology of the particular mystical tradition. Theological and other differences among the mystical traditions are therefore not accidental matters to be ignored. They are intrinsic to and constitutive of the mystical path and its goal.

The argument I have made for significant differences among the various mystical traditions is not intended to assert that there are no similarities among different mystical paths or to deny concrete cross-cultural and cross-traditional influences. Nor is it my intent to suggest that the basic character of particular mystical traditions is conditioned primarily by the general religious tradition to which they belong. This may or may not be the case. Possibly there is only a relatively small number of basic types of mysticism.

The term "mysticism" was originally a Christian and Western notion whose use was originally restricted to those traditions. However, a phenomenological use has developed for applying the term cross-culturally. This usage is quite defensible, but the specification of the term still seems quite vague except for those authors who want to restrict the term to "union" experiences. I regard the scope of the term as not yet fixed in usage and I am obviously proposing that the term "mystical experience" should be employed descriptively to include a wider variety of resolution experiences such as the ones I have discussed.

The study of mystical experiences is directly relevant to the development of a cross-cultural philosophy of religion, but not in an easy, monolithic, abstractly reassuring way through the "essence" of mystical experience. The attempt to bypass metaphysical and theological differences among the mystical traditions by treating mystical experiences as sub-conceptual feeling, emotion or attitude, or as trans-conceptual intuitions of the "same" ultimate reality, is both initially and ultimately to be false to the data. The divergences among the traditions are essential and real. Mystical experience does not sub- or trans-cend these differences. Cross-cultural bridges will have to be built upon clear recognition of the divergencies as well as upon the hope for some degree of mutuality. Cross-cultural philosophy of religion is by no means an impossible task, but the "bridge" will be plural and complex, not single and simple.

13

Structures of Ultimate Transformation and the Hermeneutics of Cross-Cultural Philosophy of Religion

◻

Frederick J. Streng

I. Ultimate Reality and Religious Transformation

One of the most complex issues in cross-cultural philosophical discussion is the expression of the "nature of things."[1] This is in part because anyone talking about "the nature of things," or ultimate reality, does not stand outside of that to which she/he refers, but stands within it. In this essay we will analyze three different expressions of ultimate reality according to the religious intention expressed in three different structures of religious transformation. Our concern with the religious intention is based on the assumption that the communication of the nature of things is not simply a matter of finding the right words or of logical clarity, it is a construction of a world of meaning. In this approach, every notion of ultimate reality has two connotations. One is that the notion of ultimate reality intends to account for all existence. The second is that it specifies a difference between a lesser and greater quality of life. Thus an understanding of the nature of things applies to all existence, but it also expresses an awareness that some moments and forms of existence are better than, not just different from, others.

In relating these ontological claims to religious intention we will use a broad functional definition of religion. Religion, as a generic term, is defined as any "means of ultimate transformation." A major element in any structure of ultimate transformation is an apprehension of the nature of ultimate reality. By relating the description of ultimate reality to the intention of the structure of ultimate transformation we can note how the structure molds the character of the experience of ultimate reality. This means that we will focus on different modes of valuing experienced existence in understanding claims about ultimate reality, rather than simply comparing the doctrines or formulations themselves. In this way we hope to show differences in the primary experience which people articulate by their claims of what is ultimately real. To understand the intention of religio-philosophical claims is central to the effort of interpretation in an intercultural dialogue. The labels given to ultimate reality are the "tip of the iceberg" exposing different mechanisms of apprehension.

In contrast to a philosophy of religion that defines all religious phenomena as a single type of inner experience, the approach used in this essay will be to regard "religion" as a complex, or family, of different and overlapping structures of ultimate transformation. These different structures express in part different processes of human valuing. Two aspects of any structure of ultimate transformation are the function of religious language and the mode of human consciousness whereby one apprehends the nature of ultimate reality. We hope to show that there are different ways that language communicates translinguistic apprehension of reality, and that these differences of language provide one indicator of the different ways that people are religious. Insofar as they reflect and constitute the very mechanism of the subjective side of the creation of selfhood, the articulations determine not only the terms for reality but the way in which the quality of existence can be known. Different formulations, together with the mechanisms of apprehension inherent in those formulations, serve as limitations for one's religious experience by providing an existential norm of the valuing process.

The understanding of a claim for ultimate reality is as much the development of a sensitivity for a context of meaning as it is learning specific representative or descriptive definitions of reality. A process of valuing selects many factors that constitute the context in which a person will recognize what is real or true. In sum, there are two assumptions which are found in the approach of this essay: first, that formulations of ultimate reality, that is, the nature of things, are best understood as part of a process which places valuing at the center of experiencing; and second, that there are different structures of ultimate transformation which require one to analyze the function of statements about ultimate reality if their religious intention is to be understood.

The religio-philosophical material that we will examine comes from three contemporary spokesmen for different ontological positions.

They reflect three different structures of religious transformation. (1) The first position is Paul Tillich's understanding of "being" and the dialectic relationship that nonbeing has to being.[2] (2) The second is Hellmut Wilhelm's interpretation of the philosophy of change in the ancient classic Chinese text *I Ching* (*Book of Changes*).[3] (3) The third is Keiji Nishitani's formulation of the Buddhist position that the fundamental ontological term is "emptiness."[4] We will focus on the interaction of positive and negative terms about the nature of things to expose the existential assumptions and axiological decisions in these three ontological formulations.

What is important is not just the use of different positive and negative terms or even the differences in meaning of these terms, but how each thinker uses these terms with a different assumption about their function in communicating the nature of things. This means that we are calling into question the assumption that at the most fundamental level everybody in different cultures experiences ultimate reality in fundamentally the same way. To do so, we suggest, misconstrues the intention that is found in the formulation of these statements as they express different processes of ultimate transformation. By reviewing the positive-negative ontological terms used by these three contemporary interpreters we hope to expose the dynamics of different human perceptions about life in relation to different worlds of meaning. This will lead to the conclusion that there are different processes of philosophizing at least so far as expressed in the formulation of ultimate reality. If this is a valid conclusion, it indicates that cross-cultural philosophy of religion requires deep sensitivity to a variety of processes for knowing and communicating the nature of things.

II. Structures of Ultimate Transformation

The search for structures of ultimate transformation comes from the effort during the last hundred years in the study of religion to find an "essence of religion." This effort derives from the attempt to understand religious life in terms of the claims made by adherents. This concern was expressed by the phenomenologists of religion during the current century when they tried to discover what was *sui generis* in religion. In the discussion of the phenomenologists of religion there has been a common assumption that there is one universal essence of religion, expressed by such notions as the experience of a mysterious and awesome mystery (Rudolf Otto) or the symbolic manifestation of the sacred (Mircea Eliade). In reviewing the wide range of religious phenomena in human history, however, scholars are having difficulty in interpreting the inner character of all religious life according to a single universal essence. The solution to the question about the nature of "religion" proposed here is that there are different structures of religious experience. The structures of religious experience express the fact that there are different types of religious life, each type defined by a particular structure. Each structure is recognized to be a type of ultimate transformation within the general definition of religion as a means of transformation.

These structures are models that are derived from various empirical examples of religious phenomena, but the structure is not identical with any specific historical-cultural reality. When religious data are compared we note the similarities of such things as the notions of ultimate reality, the basic problematic of life, and the different ways or means whereby the problematic is solved. When these elements are recognized and the relationship between them is understood, they specify the kind of intended meanings that provide an ideal type, or "way," of being religious. These structures of ultimate transformation also reflect different modes of valuing, different processes of value formation. By locating these structures we have a hermeneutical device to perceive variations between religious goals as related to a life-problematic and a process of ultimate transformation.

We will be looking at three ways or types of being religious, that is, three structures of ultimate transformation. Each one has a number of common concerns that we have already indicated by the phrases "a notion of ultimate reality," "a means of ultimate transformation," and "a problematic of human life." The point of designating the different structures, however, is to clarify in *what way* these different religious processes bring about the transformation claimed by the religious adherent. The three structures that we are going to use to interpret the claims regarding ultimate reality can be labelled as follows: (1) sacred action through myth and ritual; (2) living in harmony with the cosmic law; and (3) mystical insight through spiritual discipline.[5]

1. In the first type, "sacred action through myth and ritual," we note such elements as (*a*) the assumption that there is a radical difference between the sacred realm and the profane realm, (*b*) the belief that concrete but special symbols (including words) are the forms through which the sacred reality becomes manifest in everyday (profane) life, and (*c*) the experience of a sacred (or real) world as requiring the conscious act of identification and the designation of that reality as different from other experiences.

2. The second structure, "living in harmony with the cosmic law", has such elements as (*a*) the assumption that ultimate reality involves a continuity between the invisible principles of life and all concrete forms of life, (*b*) the recognition that human beings have an innate capacity to cultivate or perfect their deepest capacity through living harmoniously in relation to other human beings and to the physical world, and (*c*) cultivation of perfection as occuring naturally when people understand their own cultural tradition and follow the example of ancient seers who are models of virtue. This structure is epitomized in the Indian context of the *varnashrama dharma* and in the Chinese Confucian family religion that prescribes a set of obligations derived from the innate working, or principles, of nature.

3. The third structure of ultimate transformation, "mystical insight through spiritual discipline," includes such elements as (*a*) the recognition that ultimate reality is already within all human consciousness but is hidden by illusion, (*b*) the belief that the perfection that is available in life begins with a transformation of consciousness, so that there is a focus on the various states of consciousness, and (*c*) the view that the spiritual goals that are sought can be attained through one's own effort by becoming nonattached to the physical and social conditioning that most people take for granted as their self-identity. The prime examples of this structure are found in yoga and Zen.

While in all of these the transformation in general can be said to be from a state that is problematic (defined variously as sin, illusion, chaos or weakness) to an ideal goal of existence (expressed as worship of God, true humanity or perfect freedom), the specification of different structures of transformation focuses on the different ways that ultimate values come into play in human consciousness. When we look at the different formulations of the positive and negative terms in the expression of ultimate reality in the three contemporary spokesmen and relate them to these three different types of ultimate transformation, we hope to show how different ontological terms function differently in order to express what that ultimate reality is.

III. The Conscious Act of Knowing Being-Itself through Symbolic Formulation

For Paul Tillich, in his *Systematic Theology*, "being-itself" is the ground of all existence, and finitude is the expression of the interaction between nonbeing and being. The dialectical relationship between nonbeing and being is inescapable for anyone or anything in existence. Tillich points out that within Christian understanding there are two ways that nonbeing is related to being. First, nonbeing is expressed through the Greek phrase *ouk on*. This is the recognition that humanity is created out of nothing and must return to nothing. He states, "The *nihil* out of which God creates is *ouk on*, the undialectical negation of being."[6] This leads human beings to a sense of radical negation, a sense of "being not."

The other understanding of nonbeing integrated into Christian theology is one that is called "the dialectical form of nonbeing" in relation to being. This is expressed in the Greek phrase *me on*. The dialectical form of nonbeing is experienced existentially in anxiety about the transitoriness of life. For Tillich this anxiety is rooted in the very structure of being and is not a distortion of this structure. The direct experience of nonbeing is the anxiety that every person has in having to die. It is an automatic direct experience that every person has of the dialectical relationship between nonbeing and being.

Similarly, the notion of causality is also an expression of the abyss of nonbeing in everything. It shows the inability of anything to rest on itself and its need for other things as a condition for its own survival. This is a very important assumption that Tillich expresses in his understanding of how the reality of being is related to change, since change is here understood to result automatically in anxiety over the threat of nonbeing. Any change assumes two things: that there should be an unchanging being, and that change is a threat to that basic reality. Thus the essential condition of existence is that there is finitude, anxiety and the threat of nonbeing.

Nonbeing, according to this position, is entirely dependent on being for any ontological value. Unlike the subsequent examples we are going to consider, Tillich insists that "nonbeing is literally nothing except in relation to being." Even in the direct experience of human finitude people must look at themselves and experience nonbeing from the viewpoint of "a potential infinity". The power of being as being-itself cannot have a beginning or end; it is simply the basic presupposition for anything to be. This power of being as experienced in the individual is the power of infinite self-transcendence. We should note, however, that the infinity is not being-itself, because being-itself lies beyond "the polarity of finitude and infinite self-transcendence." The power of infinite self-transcendence as related to being-itself is a very important notion in that one's reality is manifested by an *activity of self-transcendence*. Infinite self-transcendence is a negation of the finitude experienced in life. Thus while being-itself precedes both finitude and infinite self-transcendence, infinite self-transcendence is the expression of being-itself within finitude.

It is an act of consciousness whereby human beings manifest infinite self-transcendence that expresses the ontological negation of nonbeing. This makes the highest quality of human life an act which depends on being-itself, and which at the same time is a positive action within finite experience. While Tillich holds that "Being is essentially related to nonbeing," being-itself is not essentially in a state of disruption or chaos. (By contrast, as we shall see, the position of the philosophy of change assumes that chaos is the source and end of all creative action.) This means that there is no bipolar view between being and nonbeing. Being-itself is the primal a priori. Continuity in life is therefore credited to the presence of "being," and any change is understood to be real where it is identified substantially as a causal force that arises from being or "what is" from one moment to another. The "courage to be" is an act of finite self-transcendence through dependence on being-itself manifested in the infinite drive to seek self-transcendence.

The act of self-transcendence as related to being-itself is also an expression of another ontological aspect of human experience. This is that humanity is seen by Tillich as a kind of being who is immediately aware of a subject-object bipolarity in the structure of being. To ask the question about being presupposes two actualities: an asking subject and an object about which the question is asked. The experience of self-centeredness in an objective world is the basic dialectical ontological structure of life. This structure is something which, says Tillich, cannot be derived; it must be accepted. While "self" and "the environment in which the self exists" determine each other, Tillich insists that selfhood "is an original phenomenon which logically precedes all questions of existence." Human beings have an immediate experience of the polar structure of vitality and intentionality. Human vitality requires intentionality in order to relate meaningful structures to the dynamic that is inherent in the nature of being. This becomes crucial in the expression of human selfhood since it is through the shaping of reality in meaningful structures that human beings can formulate their sense of selfhood.

It is, as a matter of fact, the aspect of self in relation to the world as expressed in subjective reason and objective reason which makes the self and the world a structured whole. As Tillich says, "Without reason, without the *logos* of being, being would be chaos, that is, it would not be being but only the possiblity of it (*me on*)." The experienced world is regarded as having "reality" when it is looked on by the mind. And a segment of this reality is used as a symbol when one wants to express the notion of God. When God is seen as the ground of being, God transcends the subject-object bipolar sensibility. If God is brought into this subject-object structure of being, God ceases to be the ground of being and becomes one being among others. Any concrete assertion about God must be symbolic. Nevertheless, Tillich says, the statement that God is being-itself is a nonsymbolic statement. This is in part because the very act of thinking must start with being. Thought, he says, "cannot go behind it as the form of the question itself shows. If one asks why there *is* not nothing, one attributes being even to nothing."

In sum, we see that for Tillich symbolic formulation is an expression of the very structure of being-in-existence. This being-in-existence is dependent on the structure of reality which is being-itself. To know this being-itself, if only to a limited degree, is to experience the infinite self-transcendence of finitude. This requires the continual act of distinguishing one thing from another, such as the self from external environment. Among the intellectually sophisticated it leads to the conceptual formulation, in as precise and specific images as possible, of the basic realities of human experience. Symbolizing is an act of consciousness that constructs the world by identifying what is real.

IV. The Intuition of Rhythmic Forces in Change: The Firm and the Yielding

In the *Book of Changes* (*I Ching*) the meaning of appearance and events, according to Hellmut Wilhelm, "is not grasped in stasis but in movement. The meaning consists of the Way (*Tao*) of change and it can be understood only by treading the way."[7] According to the ancient Chinese view expressed in the *Book of Changes* we note that change is not defined predominantly as an expression of finitude, as it was by Tillich. Change is not a negative principle within the Tao. Rather, change includes both positive and negative, high and low, principle and particular, creation and disappearance. In contrast to Tillich's view, the changing phenomena of everyday existence are not seen as the threat of nonbeing to being-itself regarded as an eternal unchanging nature of essential reality. According to the *Book of Changes*, change is a movement of natural growth and development that takes place within a regularity. Nevertheless, it also includes irrational surprises and a deep mystery. In this view differences in particular forms of existence are expressions of a meaningful complex of change.

The opposite of the Tao of change is not cessation of movement or rest. Quietness is just an aspect of change. The opposite of the Tao of change is the dissolution of the change-process, or an inappropriate change such as growth taking place where decrease should prevail, as in a cancerous growth. This is because the Tao of change includes regularity within it. It is not a determinism imposed from the outside. However, there is recognition of spontaneous and natural development, an inner tendency that brings about abundance and renewal. Ultimately there is no escape from the regularity within change. Whatever is inappropriate activity or evil will be rectified eventually by the eternal laws.

The two great bipolar principles, the firm and the yielding, work in relationship to each other. Even when they are in opposition they relate to each other through an inner relationship of correspondence. Thus they do not interact in a dialectical movement of external and hostile forces. Rather, they are part of a system of corresponding and collaborating forces which work within a context, within a particular relative position. As Wilhelm points out, the bipolar concepts "did not constitute an over-riding dialectical principle. To be sure the yin and yang as a rule work in relationship to each other, but they always work within and from a given position."[8]

The two fundamental principles of the "firm" and "yielding," sometimes defined as the "above" and "below" or *yang* and *yin*, represent a relationship to each other in an overall state of harmony. Even where there is tension between the two or where there is a dominant role of one over the other, there is the principle of coordination and eventual reversal. The role of each of these principles is not given once and for all. Each must be understood not in terms of a fixed and exclusive nature but in relation to their manifestation in a particular situation. Since the two principles of firm and yielding, or creative and receptive, are not seen as mutually exclusive but as bipolar elements within a continuous rhythm of process and change, it is important to note that some characteristics of each will be those which might be considered to belong to its opposite. Therefore, in a lecture entitled "The Creative Principle," Professor Wilhelm states that the "creative" includes the characteristic of nonbeing while the "receptive," its opposite, is credited with the characteristic of being as the mother of all things. The creative principle is often associated with firmness, decisiveness and strength, yet it also has the notion of creative insight which is identified with the characteristic of nonbeing. The receptive, on the other hand, is identified with actual creation as the mother of all being. These two principles must be in relation to each other and must cooperate with each other as a complete resource. Wilhelm states, "Only the tension between them is strong enough to call forth from chaos creative changes and thereby to produce our world."

The inner workings of the bipolarity of the firm and the yielding are an important aspect of understanding "the way things are" in this ancient Chinese view of the world. The nature of reality is not seen as being-itself of which existence is then a derivative and only partial expression of being mixed with nonbeing. Rather, both being and nonbeing are part of the regulated change of life. To affirm that anxiety is a natural experience of nonbeing, as Tillich suggests, is to misunderstand the very nature of things. Such anxiety about nonbeing is found only where change is regarded as a partial return to a nonreal state, an essentially different state of reality from being. The close inner working of being and nonbeing depicted in the *Book of Changes* is the principle of reversal. This is the notion that inherent in any positive or firm aspect of life there is a force that pushes toward the negative or yielding. Similarly, the yielding principle becomes eventually an expression of the firm. Again, we must call attention to the view found in the *Book of Changes* that the particular movement from firm to yielding and from yielding to firm is not based on an abstract eternal principle but is seen within the context of a particular situation.[9] The basic rhythm, however, is that the firm and yielding transform each other.

The process of the creative act is seen to begin with what is hidden. The basic imagery is of a hidden dragon and the advice in this book of divination is *not* to act. The imagery is that beneath the surface, submerged and concealed, is the original element which must be recognized or perceived. This is done by an organism plunging downward into its own depths in uncertainty and inactivity. At a certain point, however, there is a changeover from the (inactive) perceptive to the active aspect, and the situation requires one to bring up from the depths the force and shape of what will become manifest. The completed creation of a thing, however, does not stop the process; inevitably whatever has taken form will again disappear. The creative force culminates in a self-sacrifice: as it continues to extend itself, the creative force transforms itself into the yielding aspect.

The principle of reversal of the two poles of reality has a twofold significance according to Wilhelm: (1) A strong and firm manifestation of the creative force already implies its own death. (2) Any cultivation of excellence is possible only if a person asserts a positive countervailing aspect where a situation is unclear or confused. What we see in this understanding of life is that human beings have the capacity to cultivate and perfect their true humanity through participation in a cosmic rhythm. The necessity for every person to actualize the harmony in concrete action is an important element within the structure of "living harmoniously within the cosmic law." Without this sense that one participates in the forces of life through one's own intuitive sensitivity and overt action, there would be no need to make a positive, assertive effort to manifest the cosmic harmony. By reviewing specifically these two aspects in the principle of reversal within the Tao we can highlight the differences between this structure of ultimate transformation and that expressed in Tillich's concern with being-itself and the formulation of symbolic expressions for knowing that being.

1. In contrast to the notion that death represents the prime and absolute confrontation that human beings have with their own tragic characteristic of nonbeing, the *Book of Changes* indicates that death itself means a return to the source. The creative process begins with the chaos of what is hidden in life. The significance of this, says Wilhelm, is that the movement's return to its starting point prevents it from dispersing.[10] Nothingness or chaos is the infernal darkness that prevails at the root of the creative process and it is the point of return after form has completed its existence. Chaos and darkness, then, are part of the creative principle. Wilhelm points out that while the imagery of chaos is understood in two ways, either as a stage from which creation proceeded or as the product of the first stage of creation, most frequently "the chaos is perceived in the shape of an egg out of which, through some development or creative act, the world differentiated." Nothingness as the unformed chaos and in reciprocal relation to the "receptive," that is, the manifest form of life, is real only in its relationship within the created unity of life. Similarly, any manifestation, any creation, has its roots in the vital force which has its dark and chaotic character. The negative aspects within this rhythm of bipolarity are not seen as realities that engage essential being as a confrontation with nonbeing, as in Tillich. Nor is this negative aspect seen as the root or basic reality that is the realization of a quality of nonattachment to things, as we shall see in Nishitani's understanding of "emptiness." Rather, nothingness is a

negative principle experienced *within* all particular forms. Likewise, it is not a principle of limitation; it is the principle of the possibility of actualizing concrete existence.

2. The second feature of the principle of reversal is the need for a person to confront everyday events with an awareness about life. Wilhelm points out, "Cosmic forces that shape fate are open to the insight, though not necessarily the influence, of man. Humility is imposed on man as he seeks to find his place within the interplay of these forces." The insight that human beings can have which is effective for the cultivation of one's true self is not the experience of an essence or a being. Rather it is perception, within the fermentation of change and multiple experience, of a harmonious order that is already presupposed within the immediately experienced world. What one sees is a relationship, a situation known through certain images as described, for example, in the sixty-four hexagrams used in the *Book of Changes* for divination purposes. Change, therefore, is not only the recognition of the appearance of new forms. It is also what is stable, what is secure and constant.

To perceive the nature of things through an image that exposes the interaction of forces in a given life situation is the goal of the *Book of Changes*. To see this there is no necessity for a complete systematic understanding of the being of life, nor is there a need to acquire special wisdom through meditative techniques or spiritual training. As Wilhelm points out, "All that is needed is integrity, a willingness to see things as they are, the attitude of one who does not fool himself or others and does not hide behind the conventional or sophisticated rationalizations." How do human beings perceive the nature of things and life? A passage from "The Great Treatise," a commentary in the *Book of Changes*, states: "In heaven primal images take form, on earth shapes take form. This is the way change and transformation are revealed."

By contemplating the images which are exposed in the *Book of Changes* through an intuitive attitude, one can perceive the meaning of one's participatory relationship to the cosmic rhythm disclosed in the image. Grasping these images is an organic, gestalt form of grasping the meaning of things rather than an objective analysis of the essence of something. Each of these images is seen in relation to a situation, and the intuition is a process of consciousness in which one perceives the nature and movement of life. The intuitive grasp is what Wilhelm calls a "contemplating attitude" which is full of inner truths. After one has perceived the image one makes a judgment about how to apply this organic grasp to one's situation in life. Then a person can make a decision to act one way or the other. Only after one has perceived the constellation of interacting forces can one understand the meaning of a situation. The result of this intuition is not a formulation that places a concept in a precise relation to an experience or a verbal system. Rather, the result is that a person makes a decision to act one way or another that arises out of an intuitive grasp of the forces at work in that situation. The expression of the philosophy of change, as Wilhelm interprets the *Book of Changes*, epitomizes the experience of "the nature of things" within the structure of living harmoniously in the cosmic law. It is assumed that one can intuit the reality that one already is living in, and that one will affect the actual situation by making the right decision as it relates to a whole cosmic order, a cosmic order that includes both principles of the "firm" and the "yielding."

V. Becoming Fully Conscious as a Mode of Being in the Field of Emptiness

The last expression of "the nature of things" we will examine is the affirmation by Keiji Nishitani that the most comprehensive understanding of "being" in relation to the experience of change and disappearance is found in the standpoint of "emptiness." He summarizes his position by saying, "It is only in a field where the 'being' of all things is a being at one with emptiness that it is possible for all things to gather into One, even while each is a reality as an absolutely unique being."[11] This notion of emptiness is not the negative principle that calls into question the reality of life, nor is it the dimension of chaos or anarchy as a necessary pole in the bipolar rhythm of change. Rather it is the root or basic field in which the affirmative and negative are possible at all.

At the same time it is not a substantive reality but rather a state of consciousness which gives a certain quality or character to the arising and dissipation of existence. The emptiness of which Nishitani speaks is not a *nihilum* as in the notion of nihilism. Rather it is a continual emptying of the self-centered grasp of personality and attachment to things.[12] The interplay between the affirmative and negative aspects in emptiness, however, is perceived only when one realizes that it requires a complete negation of any abstraction of emptiness or being-itself. Thus, this is a radical kind of negativity which seeks to plumb the very depths of a notion of emptiness by negating even "emptiness" as a notion. Only by negating the particular forms of one's experience can one get beyond the negation itself to a sense that there is an intrinsic relatedness between all things. One must pass through the nihilism of nihilistic existentialism which indeed undercuts the assumption of our absolute universal essence. Once one passes through the claim of absolute negativity as the opposite to a universal essence (being-itself), one does not perceive life as absurd, nor need one develop one's ego strength as a superman or wonder woman. Rather, there is a new mode of being, nonattachment to being-itself, that one perceives as one moves through nihilism.

The implication of this ontological experience of negativity is that a thing is "itself" when it is not-itself without ceasing to be itself. When one perceives "emptiness" one recognizes that the character of a particular form is intrinsically related to other forms, and thus there is no need to preserve its own identity independently. This perspective contrasts with a definition of reality as the substance of a thing, which assumes that there is something external to us, something which maintains itself in an unchanging way which is outside of our apprehension. The standpoint of emptiness requires that one penetrate directly to the precise point of what makes something what it is; otherwise it cannot really be known. In order to "penetrate directly" one has to let go of the assumption that the reality of what is perceived is composed of something other than what the perceiver is. The common reality in both, according to Nishitani, is that both are empty of any substantial essential being. No essence or anything else can stand ontologically independent of anything else. Nishitani summarizes this by saying, "That a thing is itself means that all other things, without ceasing to be in themselves, are in the home-ground of that thing; that precisely in the point where it is in its own home-ground all other things are present too and that all other things plunge their roots into its base." Whereas existential nihilism is a doubting mode of sensitivity that calls into question both substantial and subjective reality, the standpoint of emptiness of which Nishitani speaks is that one loses the substantial and subjective reality while at the same time affirming the close essential *interrelationship* among all things.

The deep subjective realization of the emptiness of everything makes it possible to penetrate the ontological reality of all particular things while at the same time affirming the relative reality of particular things in existence. Emptiness, as understood here, is not a reality as being-itself, nor is it a part of the rhythm of all changes. There is no reality outside the language system that correlates with the notion of emptiness. This is affirmed not because there is nothing outside the language system, but because words are seen to be powerful but inaccurate constructors of experienced reality. Ontological terms should not be seen primarily as indicators of some thing that is assumed to be outside the language system. Thus, to perceive the nature of emptiness, in distinction to the notion of "emptiness," is to avoid identifying this term with some presumed substance or principle. As soon as emptiness is taken as a reality either in the subject or outside the self, it is no longer the root source for both subjective and objective experience.

The effort to avoid both absolute nihilism and a simply negative form of some absolute essentialism is matched only by the intensity with which Nishitani affirms that one must perceive the relationships among particular things while at the same time maintaining their particularity. From the standpoint of emptiness,

> each thing is itself while not being itself, is not itself while being itself; its "being" is unreal in its truth and true in its unreality. This may sound queer at first, but, in fact, through such a view, we are enabled for the first time to conceive a "force" by virtue of which all things are gathered and brought into relationship to one another—a "force" which, since ancient times, has been called nature (*physis, natura*).

If one were not to assume this intrinsic relatedness through the "ground of emptiness," Nishitani is ready to admit, something would exist "in-itself," namely, when it is separate from everything outside of itself. In the everyday conventional subject-object awareness, the identification of something-in-itself is significant because it excludes what is not-itself. This results in a total lack of being able to perceive the nature of anything outside of oneself, and finally ends up in a chaotic awareness. As Nishitani states, "Only on the field of emptiness, where being is being-nothingness as well as nothingness-being, is it possible that each being is itself in the face of all the others, and thus, at the same time, is not itself to all the others."

The result of perceiving the world from this standpoint is that the uniqueness of a thing requires that it is situated as the root center of all other things. The relationship that particular unique things have with each other as essentially interrelated Nishitani terms "circuminsessional." When a particular thing recognizes its basic character as "no-self nature" it recognizes that its being is one with emptiness. By letting go of its own "self" it becomes a participant in the center of all other unique particulars. From the standpoint of emptiness, then, a thing "is" in terms of its own "selfhood" when it is subordinate to all things and at the same time becomes the center for all other things.

Since the field of emptiness is also identified as the field of the "circuminsessional relationship," all things manifest their own reality when they have let go of grasping after some unique essence of themselves and found their own absolute selfhood in complete interrelatedness. The mode of being which is the genuine "suchness" of a thing is inaccessible to identification simply with either the subject or the object. Rather, something really "is" when it is identical with itself and at the same time with other things. All things in the world, then, are seen to be interrelated. To be interrelated means being both the center and the supportive aspect of, or subordinate to, another thing at the same time. The absolute interdependency that one thing has with another for its own unique selfhood is expressed by the term "circuminsessional" in which "all things in their 'being' thus enter into another home-ground, are not themselves and, nevertheless precisely as such (i.e., on the field of emptiness) are themselves to the very end." This web of circuminsessional interpenetration Nishitani calls a "mode of being": it is "the thing's in-itself mode of being, its non-objective mode of being as 'middle,' its selfness."

The mode of being called "emptiness" is also regarded by Nishitani as a standpoint or perspective. To perceive emptiness requires converting one's consciousness to the place of emptiness, and thereby stopping ego-identification with the particular forms of things as if they had independent essential being. It means shifting one's conceptual focus from attempting to locate an essential stratum in things. Rather, it is to accept that while one is thinking, perceiving and feeling, one recognizes the lack of selfhood in oneself and in all other things. To let go of either absolute subjectivity or absolute objectivity is to transcend the conventional standpoint. In emptiness, therefore, nonbeing is not the threat-producing anxiety of an ego-centered consciousness. Nor is it a threat to a person trying to transcend the limitations of a finite self.

In converting to the standpoint of emptiness there is a release from the assumption that self-transcendence is a particular act or a series of acts, as suggested by Tillich. It is the recognition that one already is a particular entity while at the same time transcending that particularity. The shift to a process of knowing designated as the standpoint of emptiness is a shift from a mode of constructive consciousness that is fundamentally an act of designation—designating or separating one thing from one another—to one that is the negation of substantiation and specification of one thing over against another. This is to know that the true selfness of fire, for example, is non-fire, or that the selfness of a tree is "no tree." What we perceive, then, is that the selfhood of any particular thing is known by its context, and that there is no self-identifying essence that separates it from all other things.

The immediate realization of emptiness as a mode of being is also becoming conscious of the field of emptiness in a certain way. Nishitani states this explicitly: the field of emptiness "opens up, as it were, still nearer to ourselves than the ourselves we are ordinarily thinking of. In other words by converting from what is ordinarily called 'self' to the field of emptiness, we become truly ourselves." In the field of emptiness the experience is not as in other fields of experience where the mind is reflective or the awareness is an intellectual intuition. Nishitani makes this clear when he says,

> Ordinarily, our self is conceived as something knowing itself, being conscious of itself or intellectually intuiting itself. But what I term self-awareness here does not mean a field where in any sense the self knows itself. On the contrary this is just where such a "self" and such "knowledge" are emptied.

For the same reason, the base of all consciousness in the standpoint of emptiness is not the unconscious or subconscious. The original self-awareness is not-being-a-self while being-a-self. This means, says Nishitani, that

> our self-in-itself, on the field of emptiness, stays at the home of all other things. On the field of emptiness, the center is everywhere: all things—each in its non-objective and "middle" in-itself-ness—are an absolute center. On that field, therefore, it is impossible for our self to be self-centered like the "self" as ego or subject. Rather, it is precisely in the absolute negation of that self-centeredness that the field of emptiness can ever open up.

The field of emptiness ultimately appears as a field of wisdom which is called the "knowing of unknowing."[13] When the self has a field of emptiness as its home ground, it is free from the attachment to things-in-themselves or to abstract principles. Then "selves" can truly be.

VI. Concluding Remarks

In this review of statements about ultimate reality by three spokesmen from different cultures we have tried to focus not only on the meaning of the words but also on their context of usage for attaining that which they assert to be true. This is to say that our concern has been to focus on how meaning is available at all, and we have suggested that in each of the three cases there is a different process whereby language is used in relation to transforming one's life in the deepest value-context. By placing these different expressions of ultimate reality within the structures of ultimate transformation we can see how different formulations function in order to expose and evolve what is real. Rather than identifying any of these formulations of reality as systems of thought such as idealism, realism, nominalism or materialism, we have focused on the question of how both positive and negative notions of ultimate reality play a role in manifesting the nature of things.

The differences can be summarized by recalling that in the first type of ontological assertion, by Paul Tillich, ultimate reality was seen as being-itself and nonbeing was regarded as expressing the finitude that human beings experience as a threat to the very nature of things. To know the nature of things requires an act of consciousness whereby a person transcends the interaction of being and nonbeing. In second formulation, by Hellmut Wilhelm, ultimate reality was defined as a rhythm of change that required two interacting forces, the firm and the yielding, in relation to particular situations. In this case the positive and negative were seen to apply to the interaction of principles perceived by intuition in concrete situations. In the final formulation, by Keiji Nishitani, ultimate reality was seen as the field of emptiness, a mode of consciousness, rather than an act of consciousness (symbolizing and specifying the being-itself of things) or an intuition of interaction between two ultimate principles manifested in a particular form or situation. In Tillich's concern to "be," in the philosophy of change, and in the standpoint of emptiness, the reality of life is not found in categories of substance or subjective ego-centered consciousness. Rather, the very concept of reality requires a shift in the person who uses a philosophy to a mode of becoming informed by that world of meaning and the mode of consciousness that is necessary to be aware of it.

To communicate a sense of reality, then, requires a sensitivity to the mode of valuing in which that reality is known. In the first case we saw that the sense of reality assumed the expectation of essences whereby life is given value. Life has a reason and meaning through the categorization of what "is." The sense of reality in the second case focused on a holistic grasp of principles which themselves were not abstractions of essences but intuitions of moving forces within a concrete situation where a person lived. In the final expression, regarding the field of emptiness, the sense of reality is much more a state of consciousness or an attitude whose chief quality is found in the paradoxical expression that one knows "selfhood" when one is aware of the nonself. These formulations of ultimate reality, then, are not seen as "mere speculation" or systems of verbal abstraction. Rather, the formulations themselves become ontological activities whereby a person's sense of value and reality are given form and content.

We may conclude, therefore, that the nature of reality is manifested as much in the process of knowing and valuing it as in the formulations that specify it. In this sense, a cross-cultural philosophy of religion will be well served by looking beyond the labels of systems of ideas to the existential importance that they have in disclosing the truth about life.

14

The Hermeneutics of Comparative Ontology and Comparative Theology

◻

Ashok K. Gangadean

This paper is an exploration in the hermeneutics of comparative theology. The fundamental concerns of religious thought, indeed of religious life itself, emerge in a new light within the context of the hermeneutics of comparative theology. In this sense the hermeneutical question is the essential and substantive concern of religious experience.

I. The Challenge of Comparative Theology

The challenge of comparative theology emerges whenever we are concerned with radical transformations between different religious worlds: for example, in accounting for the nature of discourse between religious languages, or in the religious experience of conversion, or in the situation of interreligious dialogue. However, the notion of comparative theology is inherently problematic, for theology across actual (and possible) religious worlds finds itself faced with an apparently unresolvable paradox.

On the one hand, we are faced with a plurality and diversity of actual religious worlds. These worlds are radically different religious ontologies or languages or forms of relogous life. Once we reflect upon the nature of the differences between religious worlds, it becomes clear that the sense and reference of religious terms are relative to the religious world in which they are used. The relativity of meaning to a religious world implies radical and systematic ambiguity in the sense of terms between different religious languages. What makes sense in one religious world (e.g., the Christian world) is not intelligible in another (e.g., the Hindu or Buddhist worlds). In other words, the ontological structures of religious worlds define what makes sense, what is rational, what is possible, and so on, in logically incommensurable ways. If there appear to be common terms between different religious worlds, ontological analysis reveals radical ambiguity in sense. Thus, there can be no neutral terms, no common sense or reference between religious languages or worlds. This radical incommensurability of plural and diverse religious worlds appears to undermine the very possibilty of comparative theology. It seems to render rational discourse between religious worlds impossible. For it is natural to suppose that a formal condition of meaningful dialogue is that there be common ground or shared univocal terms. So one challenge for comparative theology is to show how there can be common ground, univocity or genuine unity when faced with the radical diversity of religious worlds.

On the other hand, and at the same time, we are presented with the primitive intuition that there is one and only one world, one ultimate reality, truth, infinite being, and so forth. This intuition appears to be incompatible with the radical diversity and differences of religious worlds. Indeed, we find a movement toward unity or the absolute in any given religious language, for any religious ontology, by its very form, universalizes itself and takes itself to be exhaustive of reality.

The theological articulation of this intuition of ultimate and absolute unity has been perennial in the history of thought, East and West. For example, the theme of the universal Logos is prominent in Hindu scripture in the form of AUM ("All is AUM"), in Plato's movement to the absolute Good (the form of all forms, beyond being and truth), in the thinking of certain Islamic theologians (Allah), in the teaching of the universal significance of the Christ, or in the theology of Spinoza where it is demonstrated there can be only one infinite being.

This theme of absolute unity is equally a threat to the possibility of comparative theology or interreligious dialogue. It implies that the differences between different religious languages are secondary, not fundamental, since ultimately there is one Word, one Absolute, one Logos. Different religious languages are diverse manifestations of the one Word. In effect, this rejects the complementary intuition of the radical diversity of religious worlds and dramatically alters the situation of transformations between religious worlds. The univocity of the Absolute Word denies the radical ambiguity between religious worlds. Interreligious dialogue threatens to degenerate into a monologue.

Thus, the combination of a radical plurality of actual religious worlds and the intuition of a radical unity of ultimate religious truth and being appears to call the possibility of comparative theology into question. Both univocity and equivocity seem to be formal conditions of the possibility of interreligious dialogue or any other transformation between religious worlds. The challenge to comparative theology is how to respect the primitiveness and irreducibility of both radical diversity (systematic ambiguity) and radical unity (inter-systematic univocity). The problem is, how is this to be done? How is intelligible discourse between different religious worlds, different ontological languages, possible? What is the nature of rational transformations between religious worlds (translation, dialogue, communication, conversion, etc.)?

In addressing these transcendental questions I shall argue that the either/or ("categorial" or propositional) logic of a dualistic hermeneutic is itself the source of the paradox of comparative theology. Instead I shall suggest that the nondual ("trans-categorial") logic of meditative reason is the hermeneutic which makes comparative theology possible.

The challenge of theology across actual worlds calls the rationality of a categorial hermeneutic into question. The categorial mentality thrives on the logic of predication, the logic of the dualizing and essentializing mentality. The nature of a religious world or language is revealed in a determinate ontological or categorial structure, a structure which is shaped by the formal logic of identity and difference: the propositional rationality of predication.

It is the particularity of a given religious language as an ontological or categorial structure which eclipses the truly universal power of the universal Logos or infinite Word. The universalization of the universal Word (infinite Logos) has usually been approached within the semantic framework of a particular religious world. The challenge here is to apprehend the universal significance of absolute Being as it is presented (named, referred to, characterized) in the particularity of a given religious ontology. The avenue of theological universalization through the particularity of a given religious language inevitably leads to a form of ontological reduction called "semantic imperialism."

This categorial rationality reaches a crisis in the hermeneutic of comparative theology. The striving for categorial unity between different worlds necessarily leads to reductionism either in the form of semantic/ontological imperialism or of abstract synthesism. The former reduces the diversity of religious languages to the particularity of a given religious world, the latter denies the particularity of any given religious world in the synthetic unity of the universal Logos.

It becomes clear that a deeper rationality is required to meet the challenge of comparative theology. A hermeneutic is needed which acknowledges at once the radical particularity of religious worlds (diversity) and the radical unity of the infinite Word (unity). How is it possible to acknowledge at once the universality and particularity of the infinite Word? The central aim of this essay is to address this challenge of comparative theology. I shall attempt to show that a transformation in rationality itself is required to resolve the paradox of diversity and unity in comparative theology. Only a trans-categorial logic can make room for a universal Logos for all possible religious worlds without denying the uniqueness and particularity of the diversity of actual religious worlds. Only trans-categorial unity can open the way to radical unity with radical diversity.

II. The Nature of Comparative Ontology

The concept of comparative theology becomes accessible against the background of comparative ontology. Ontology investigates the form, formation and transformation of worlds. A world is a reality which is constituted by a particular categorial structure, a configuration of categories which defines a system of possible experience. A world system is therefore at the same time a system of meaning which determines what is intelligible and prescribes a realm of meaningful experience. Thus, for example, the Hindu world is a reality which manifests itself in a particular categorial form, defines a language of meaningful experience, prescribes a realm of possible facts and delimits the bounds of human understanding. By contrast, the Christian world arises in a different categorial form with a different reality, a unique language of experience, a different system of meaning, and so on. What makes sense to the Hindu fails to make sense in the Christian world, and what is a possible fact for the Christian is not within the realm of possibility in the Hindu world. The diverse possible and actual worlds, ontologies or languages of experience involve such radically distinct structures of consciousness and being that different worlds appear to be incommensurable realities.

The history of thought, being precisely the articulation of diverse ontological languages, provides abundant examples of different worlds. Within the so-called Western tradition, for example, we encounter the emergence of different realities in the teachings of Plato, Aquinas, Descartes, Spinoza, Leibniz, Hume, Hegel, Wittgenstein and so on. These creative ontologists led the way in forging new languages of experience. In Indian tradition as well we encounter a rich diversity of ontologies, the Hindu and Buddhist worlds being two obvious examples.

While ontology is concerned with the structure of a given world, comparative ontology focuses on the transformation or reformation of a given world as well as on the intelligible transformations between different worlds. Comparative ontology is typically concerned with the following sorts of questions: How is intelligible discourse between different worlds possible? What is the logic of ontological revolutions? How is communication or ontological transition between different worlds possible? Can there be common meaning and cross-reference between different ontological languages? Are there any absolute terms for all possible worlds?

These typical transcendental concerns of comparative ontology help us to appreciate the fundamental problematic of such an endeavor. For, on the one hand, comparative ontology recognizes the diversity of radically different worlds, which in turn inevitably leads to realities or languages which are incommensurable. This means that the terms of reference and the reference of terms are relative to a given ontology, so no terms are "neutral," common, or absolute for all possible worlds. The incommensurability of worlds is synonymous with the relativity of sense and reference. This disclosure of comparative ontology leads to scepticism concerning the possibility of intelligible transformations between different worlds.

On the other hand, comparative ontology also recognizes the primitive intuition that there is one world, one unified reality. This intuition of course collides with and challenges the converse intuition of radical diversity. The intuition of radical ontological unity offers a solution to the problem of intelligible transformations between worlds, for if, indeed, there is ultimately one world, one unified, universal ontological language, then incommensurability evaporates, and the alleged transformations between different worlds turn out to be internal changes within the one common world.

Both voices of comparative ontology—the voice of radical diversity and the voice of radical unity—appear to be primitively true and irreducible. It is here that we find the antinomy of comparative ontology: each thesis appears to be axiomatic, and one contradicts the other. It is in this dialectic that the challenge of comparative ontology emerges.

The concern of comparative ontology has been alive throughout the history of thought. Stated simply, perhaps simplistically, it is the concern of negotiating the dual intuitions of radical diversity and radical unity. How is it possible at once to acknowledge that there is a diversity of realities and that there is one reality? I wish to suggest that this is the generic perennial concern of philosophy; it is the concern of the nature of rationality itself.

Comparative ontology is not another ontology among others. It is not a separate and distinct philosophical language which "ties" the diverse philosophical languages together. Rather, it is a rational mentality or hermeneutic which accommodates a diversity of worlds in "one" consciousness. The hermeneutic of comparative ontology must be rich enough to recognize the irreducible differences between realities or ontological languages, yet powerful enough to enter into discourse between possible and actual worlds. The perennial challenge for philosophy is first to recognize this and to explain how it is possible. The Western philosophical tradition, for example, has been exemplary in the articulation of diverse ontological languages and philosophical forms. But it has been deficient in the articulation of the possibility of common discourse between these diverse languages. Clearly it has assumed that rational discourse between ontological languages is possible, yet characteristically it has been negligent in exploring the logic of discourse between language forms. By being typically preoccupied with the excavation and articulation of particular ontological languages it has tended to overlook the form of rational consciousness which comes to the fore when attention is focused on a universe of diverse actual worlds.[1]

The recognition of a plurality of actual worlds seems to strain our ordinary rational sense. The rational heritage which emerged since ancient Greek thought has generally given the benefit of the doubt to the hermeneutic of duality, which assumes a differentiation between consciousness and its object, as well as an irreducible differentiation between determinate objects. This hermeneutic of either/or requires the thinker to maintain that there can be only one true actual world, all other purported possible worlds being hypothetical or fictional. Thus, either the Cartesian world is correct and actual or else the Humean world is real, but not both. Either the Christian world is true or the Hindu world, both cannot be equally acceptable and actualized on rational grounds. In this hermeneutical mentality there can be one and only one true world, one reality, and all else is at best merely possible and at worst impossible. For this reason the either/or hermeneutic of the categorial mind is not suitable for the rationality of a comparative ontology.

On the other hand, the classical Indian tradition has tended to stress the meditative hermeneutical attitude, an attitude which insists that there can be no duality between consciousness and its object. The meditative mentality characteristically takes the duality of categorial reason to be the essence of attachment, ignorance, bondage and suffering, and strives to overcome this in a transformation of consciousness which liberates reason and enlightens understanding in the wisdom of detachment and non-duality. This hermeneutic is quite vocal in its celebration of silence, a silence which is the highest achievement of a deeper rational consciousness which emerges only when particularity in all of its forms is finally defeated.

The meditative transformation of rational consciousness beyond the bondage of particularity seems at first to offer an intriguing alternative for the hermeneutic of comparative ontology. The wisdom of nondual consciousness appears to readily accommodate a plurality of actual worlds in the unity of one cosmic consciousness. The meditative posture takes reason to its highest regions where it witnesses the particularity of differentiated forms in "silence." But if meditative reason supports one primitive intuition of comparative ontology—that there is one world, one reality, one consciousness—it seems to do so at the expense of eclipsing the other primitive intuition of our dialectic. For the typical challenge for the "silence" of nondual discourse is precisely the recognition of the irreducibility of differentiation and the particularization of forms. Meditative reason celebrates unity by reducing diversity to some form of appearance. The particularity of a given world is a function of ignorance, and alternative actual worlds simply compound and multiply the intrinsic illusion of dualized reason. If the meditative hermeneutic reveals one world, one reality, it is some transcendent nonworldly world which escapes the particularity of determinate names and forms. If meditative reason achieves a "universal" unified consciousness, it is a peculiar form of cosmic universality beyond a plurality of determinate worlds. For this reason the "neither/nor" hermeneutic of the nondual meditative mentality is not suitable for the rationality of comparative ontology.

It appears that both the categorial hermeneutic and the meditative hermeneutic are necessary ingredients in the hermeneutic of comparative ontology. For we have seen that comparative ontology is required to listen to both voices in this rational antinomy. Categorial reason is essentially dualized and stresses diversity and differentiation, while meditative reason is nondual and accentuates radical unity and non-differentiation. The challenge for the hermeneutic of comparative ontology is to find a way to keep both voices alive, to negotiate dual and nondual reason. The future evolution of comparative ontology essentially depends upon its success in mediating these two forms of reason.

Needless to say various attempts to uncover a universal hermeneutic for comparative ontology have been made in the past. But any successful attempt must find a way to honor the particularity and uniqueness of a given world, and at the same time to celebrate the universality of cosmic unified consciousness or being. The depth of this challenge should now be clear. It is nothing less than negotiating the infinite ontological space between finite dualized reality and infinite nondual being. How is it possible to acknowledge both at once?

We now begin to discern a pattern. On one side we find particularity, differentiation, duality and finitude. On the other we find universality, non-differentiation, nonduality and infinitude. But in the context of comparative ontology it is clear that the polarity of particular/universal, finite/infinite, must not be confused with the distinction as it is typically drawn within the hermeneutic of dual reason. For example, in the context of a particular ontological language or world, the polarity of particular/universal remains relative to the particularity of that world. Thus, if with respect to a particular categorial world (and all worlds are categorial) the referent of "I" is some particular entity, then the universal relative to that particular is "personhood" or "humanity" or some such universal. A categorial universal[2] is therefore always relative and determinate in content (i.e., differentiated and dualized). Such a universal is relative to the meaning system of a particular world. For instance, the general term "person" would have one sense in a given world and a different sense in another. By contrast, universality in the context of comparative ontology must be absolute and valid for all possible or actual worlds; it must be a trans-world or trans-categorial universal.

Such a universal is nondual and transparent or indeterminate in form—the form of all possible forms. So the polarity of particular/universal in the context of comparative ontology must be the radical one between categorial particular and trans-categorial universal. A successful comparative hermeneutic must hold both together in a healthy dialectic.

It is here that we locate the future explorations of comparative philosophy. The categorial tradition is challenged to broaden its horizons in dialogue with nondual rationality, and the meditative tradition is challenged to expand its hermeneutic in a dialectical encounter with the rationality of categorial thought. The articulation of trans-categorial reason is the inevitable challenge for natural reason in its evolution toward comparative ontology. The most pressing philosophical concern of our age, or of any age, is this challenge of comparative ontology. It should be clear that this hermeneutical concern is precisely the question of bondage and liberation, sin and salvation, ignorance and wisdom. Thus, comparative ontology will lead us back to comparative theology.

In the next two sections I shall attempt to sketch the outlines of a trans-categorial heremeneutic. This requires, first, the articulation of the logical form of categorial thought. Next, I shall turn to the explication of the meditative rationality of nondual discourse. We will then be in a better position, in a final section, to comment on some implications of comparative ontology for comparative, trans-categorial theology.

III. The Logic of Categorial (Dualistic) Rationality

Categorial thought is dual and dualistic in every way. It works from oppositional principles which at once structure consciousness (thought, meaning, discourse) and being. The primary opposition or differentiation is that between thought and object of thought, between consciousness (the thinker) and the object of consciousness (what is thought). This is the formal structure of categorial reason. But this oppositional structure is inherent in the objects of consciousness as well, for to be an object is precisely to be differentiated from other entities. Such differentiation provides at the same time internal identity. So to be an object is to conform to the logic of identity and difference. Similarly, otherness is inherent in categorial meaning as well, and this is revealed in the isomorphism or "mirroring" between objects of thought and objects of being: meaning (sense, reference) is a matter of semantic representation: a name or referring expression is other than that which is named or designated. This is representational or dual meaning.

The rationality of identity and difference emerges in the form of predication. To be an object is to be constituted in a predicative structure: an object (of thought) is a logical subject constituted by predicates. Stated ontologically, an object is a thing which is constituted by attributes. Apart from attributes a thing can have no differentiating marks, hence can have no internal identity (essence). Thus, categorial thought manifests itself in the logical form of predication.

But predication, too, is oppositional through and through. First, the logical subject S is differentiated from logical predicates P. This reveals the dual structure of predication. And the formal principle of differentiation (otherness) applies to any possible object of thought, subject or predicate. To be a unique subject is to be differentiated, and the same holds for any possible predicate. In general, then, the essence of dual reason is the formal principle of difference (or identity):

> To be S is to be other than, differentiated from, non-S.
> To be P is to be differentiated from non-P.

This formal principle of dual thought has been codified in the principles of thought (and being) articulated in classical Greek (Aristotelian) logic in the form of the principles of non-contradiction, excluded middle, and identity. In more familiar form, the principle of intelligible rational thought is:

> A given subject S cannot be both P and not-P (at the same time and in the same respect); or
> A given subject S must be either P or not-P (etc.).

Let us review how this formal principle of opposition and duality defines categorial rationality. Any given term, subject or predicate, call it X, formally stands in opposition to its logical contrary, un-X. The meaning of X is a function of its opposition to un-X. Logical contraries, taken together, constitute the unit of meaning, and we bracket such a polar term in slashes: /X/ (= "X-or-un-X"). For example, in ordinary English the term "wise" stands in opposition to its contrary "un-wise," "colored" stands in contrary opposition to "colorless," "married" is bound in sense to its polar opposite "un-married," and so on. A polar term is called a *category*, and a category specifies some domain of the world, it exhausts some range of meaning and being. For example, while "red" is a property term, the polar or category term "/red/" (= "red-or-un-red") picks out a feature of the world. It must be stressed that polar terms are the units of meaning. Any property term takes its meaning from its polar or category term. Thus "wise" makes no sense apart from its contrary "un-wise", so the sense of "wise" derives from the sense of "/wise/."[3]

It is crucial to distinguish between the contrary opposition of polar terms and another form of opposition called *complements*. The complement of "wise" is "non-wise," the complement of "colored" is "non-colored," and so on. Contraries are internal opposites, while complements are external opposites. While contraries or polar terms specify some determinate feature of the world, some specific type of thing, complements designate the universal domain. For example, the polar term "/colored/" specifies the feature of color (i.e., all things that are or could be colored or colorless), but the complements "colored or non-colored" exhaust the domain of all possible things in the world.

Another way to grasp the difference between these two forms of primitive opposition is to recognize that contraries are logical privatives: one contrary pole is the privation of the other. For example, that which is wise fails to be unwise, hence it is potentially unwise (lacking something presupposes that it could be acquired). Again, that which is unwise lacks wisdom, hence is potentially wise. Privation and potentiality mutually entail each other, and this is the key to the definition of a category. Only the things which are potentially wise can become wise, only the sort of thing that is potentially married can become married. This means that not all things are /wise/. For example, stones are neither wise nor unwise, for they are not of the appropriate category; nevertheless, they are either wise or non-wise. Again, numbers are neither married nor un-married, though they are either married or non-married. So complementary opposites apply to any and all things regardless of their type or category, while polar contrary opposites apply only to the sort or type of thing which is of the appropriate category.

This logical feature of polar terms is the key to the formation of categorial meaning, for only terms of the appropriate categories may be meaningfully joined in predication. If inappropriate terms in a given language are joined, then nonsense (category mistakes) results. For example, to say that "stones are wise" or "stones are unwise" is nonsense, or to say that "numbers are married" or "numbers are un-married" is unintelligible. This is another way of making the point that the unit of meaning is the category-term, hence, categorial thought.

Remembering that the logical features of categorial thought have their ontological analogues, it is timely to notice that the category constraints on the formation of meaning at the same time set the bounds of rational understanding. We can only understand what is category-correct. This is why a particular category structure determines a system of meaning and thereby sets the bounds of human understanding for the ontology which it constitutes. Similarly, the intelligibility of process, change, becoming, and so on, is also determined by the structure of polar terms. Since polar terms define potentiality, it follows that all intelligible processes must unfold between the poles of contraries. We cannot in categorial thought understand an alleged process which unfolds between distinct and unrelated categories. Numbers can never become colored, stones can never become married. So reality itself, and all of its intelligible possibilities of transformation, are determined by category relations.

The appropriateness of terms for category-correct or meaningful predication is determined by the categorial structure of the terms which make up any language system. The categorial structure which constitutes a particular language is discerned when all of the polar terms of the language are taken together in their predicative possibilities. That is, if we take all of the possible predicative terms of a language simultaneously and "map" their predicative possibilities, we shall find that the categories of the language conform to a "pyramid" model, such that those terms which form a continuous line may be significantly joined, while those which do not would form a category-mistake if co-predicated. When the categorial structure of a language is discerned, we have a conceptual map of its meaning possibilities as well as of its possible facts. Meaning in a predicative language, therefore, is governed by its particular categorial structure. The categorial structure of the Christian world would be different from the categorial structure of the Buddhist world, and so on.[4]

The above procedure explains how the formation of meaning of a given language as a whole is determined by taking the totality of the polar terms together in their mutual configurability. The meaning of a term is defined by its "location" on the pyramid structure, and one sense (univocity) means one location. This formal requirement of univocity is an important characteristic of categorial meaning. A given term has a principle of identity which defines its unique meaning in the language. If a term of the language is ambiguous or equivocal, then it will have more than one location on the categorial map, and this means that they are really distinct terms. This logical feature of univocity is another form of the principle of identity and opposition which governs categorial thought.

The point to be stressed here is that what makes sense in one meaning system or categorial structure does not make sense in another. So, again, at the level of possible languages (taken as systematic wholes), we find the principle of identity and difference at work. Language systems are different categorial structures, different predicative possibilities, and since the meaning of any given term is a function of the meaning system as a whole, there can be no shared univocal terms between different languages. This logical feature of categorial reason is reflected in the principle of systematic ambiguity of terms of different languages. Thus, for example, if a given term appears in two different categorial systems, the principle requires that the term be judged systematically ambiguous, that is, it is not one term but two radically distinct and independent terms.[5]

These points may emerge with more clarity when we shift from the logical (meaning) import of categorial thought to the ontological (existential) import, for the categorial structure which defines a meaning-system thereby determines a world-system or ontology, as has been indicated earlier. Particular worlds are disclosed in determinate categorial configurations. Perhaps some further illustrations would be helpful. One world structure, the world of Cartesian dualism, holds that the two primary categories of being, thought and extension, are mutually exclusive and have no common terms. In the language system which displays this ontology we find that the sort of thing which /thinks/ is of a radically different nature or type from the kind of thing which is /extended/ (locatable in space). In this ontological language stones are /extended/ but non-thinking, while the ego or soul is /thinking/ but non-extended. It would be a category mistake to say that "the stone thinks" or to say "the soul is locatable." This ontology requires that the referent of the term "I" (the self or person) be a composite (dual) entity, for otherwise incoherence of meaning would result. This means that "I" is equivocal in reference. It refers either to the ego (a thinking thing which is non-extended) or to the body (a physical thing which is non-thinking). It cannot, without violating the sense structure of the language, refer to one unified thing which both /thinks/ and is /extended/. Strictly speaking, it is a category mistake to say in one utterance: "I am sitting in the chair and thinking about the future." For the term "I" here makes an equivocal reference. This shows that the meaning of the term I" is governed by the categorial configuration of the language as a whole.

By contrast, if we work with another possible ontological language, one in which the categories of /thought/ and /extension/ are mutually configurable (co-predicable), we enter a different world in which the meaning possibilities and factual possibilities are altered. For example, one configuration is the language of idealism (Leibniz or Berkeley) in which the primary unifying catgory is /thought/ and the category of matter or /extension/ falls within or under it. In this language the meaning of the categories themselves are radically revised from the Cartesian terms. In the idealist language anything which is /extended/ would also be /thinking/, since the former category is included within the latter. In fact, all things are potentially /thinking/ in the world of the idealist. In this categorial configuration it is possible for the term "I" to pick out one primitive individual entity which is both physical and conscious. In this language, then, the meaning of the term "I" is systematically different in sense from the term as used in the Cartesian language; and in general, what makes sense in the idealist world does not make sense in the world of Cartesian dualism.

These are just brief glimpses of how categorial rationality in its oppositional dual structure leads to the formation of different worlds or systems of meaning and experience. For our present purposes it needs to be stressed that this rational mentality, and the formal predicative principles which govern it, are constituted in duality, determinacy, particularity and essential identity. Any given term or object in this hermeneutic of duality and opposition has inner identity and fixity or univocity of meaning. The identity of an object, the self, for example, reveals its essence, which defines its nature and form. To be is to have determinate essence, to have identity, to be an individuated discriminated object. In general, the essence of a particularized entity, for any possible world, is revealed in its unique ontological feature or category. Thus, it is important to see the necessary connection between being a determinate individual entity and the dual structure of categorial reason. In this respect categorial logic is the logos of essence and particularity. This point is, of course, recognized by "existentialists" who insist that an entity (the self) may exist prior to having a determinate essence. For without determinate essence such an entity must be nothing. But this acknowedges its potentiality to become something. Such a "nothing" still has /essence/. And this clearly acknowledges the principle that to be is to be /something/.

This point is crucial for us here because it is precisely this formal feature of categorial reason which is the focal point of its critique by meditative reason. In general, categorial life is a life of individuated identity, a life of radical finitude, potentiality, becoming (existence in categorial time). By its very nature, ego-centered life is life of ontological /sin/ (i.e., alienation from infinite Being), /suffering/ and /mortality/. The Hindus call this form of existence *samsara*, the dualized life of particularity which is caught between the oppositional poles of contrariety and alienated from the infinite Being of the universal Atman. Categorial existence is the life of bondage, fixity and determinacy from which the life of meditation brings ontological liberation.

Finally, it should be mentioned that the categorial hermeneutic provides one model of rationality: the logic of premeditative understanding. This logic typically takes the form of a propositional (predicative) form of discourse which is concerned with facts and assertions which are true or false. This form of human understanding reaches its limits in literal discourse. Phenomena which are not factual in nature cannot be thought or spoken of in this hermeneutic. This mentality, which is governed by the either/or principle, necessitates a choice one way or the other. This is so with particular predications as well as with particular worlds. It requires that one world be true and the others false. In all of its forms it must conform to the principle of bi-valence: true or false. It is this commitment of categorial rationality which disqualifies it as an appropriate hermeneutic for comparative ontology.

IV. The Logic of Trans-Categorial (Nondual) Rationality

Having briefly outlined the logical form of premeditative or dualistic, categorial rationality, we have taken the first step towards the sketch of the logic of meditative, or nondual, trans-categorial rationality. For, as we have seen, the form of categorial (dual) reason is one of opposition, polarity, differentiation, univocity, and governed by laws of identity and difference. In striking contrast, nondual logos predictably flows in nonidentity, nondifference, bipolarity, relativity, nonfixity and multivocity (metaphor).

To appreciate this it would be helpful to characterize some features of meditative reason. First of all, meditation is a dynamic self-transformation of reason. This dynamic power expands the understanding beyond any form of fixity and any fixity of form. A key to entering this dynamic and organic reason is the expansion of time-consciousness. It is not possible to approach the logos of meditation from the fixity of categorial time. If we begin with catgorial time, the either/or logic of differentiation naturally follows. For within categorial time-consciousness nondual logos appears to be mere contradiction. There is a time element built into the formal principles of dual reason: "A given subject S cannot be both P and not-P at the same time." But what appears to be a contradiction to categorial time is revealed to be the literal truth in meditative time. With this in mind let us examine the "form" of nondual logos.

In meditative reason there is no differentiation (no logical space) between consciousness and object, no separation between sense and reference, no representative meaning, no differentiation between consciousness, word, idea, thought, name, object, meaning. Meaning is neither intensional nor extensional, and consciousness is not intentional. In meditative discourse there is only "self-reference" and predication is nondual, that is, there is non-difference between subject and predicate, and predication is non-representational or non-descriptive: it does not picture facts or anything else. The logical atomism of meaning which structures categorial thought in terms of fixed essence and identity as well as rigid designation melts in the light of fluid organic reason. The meaning of any term grows out of the meaning of every term. The identity of any entity reflects the identity of every other object. The significance of any predication recursively projects, reiterates and echoes the significance of any other possible utterance. In the logical space of meditative reason polar opposition and differentiation evaporates into a bipolarity (di-unity), and the fixity of essentialist univocal meaning flows into the multivocal unity of metaphor. This logical space turns upon itself in a virtuous circle in which the infinite distance is the point at which one begins: "here" is "everywhere," "now" is "everywhen," and "I" specifies everything and nothing. Process and development (becoming) moves in the stillness of nondual "becoming." In short, the categorial particular shines forth with the cosmic significance of the transcategorial universal. The space between the categorial finite and the trans-categorial infinite is "closed" as one flows into the other.[6]

But let us slow down this high energy logos and trace in slow motion the infinite expansion of logical time and space, meaning and existence. For the categorial mind is naturally sceptical and legitimately asks how it can be possible to question the principle of identity and difference, and how it can be intelligible to question univocal, essential meaning and being. Of course we are faced with a paradox of reason here. For what is coherent for categorial thought is incoherent for meditative logos, and vice versa. We must find a way for meditative reason to make itself intelligible to the categorial mentality.

A good device to show how rigid essentialistic meaning can begin to become fluid is metaphor. What appears metaphoric to categorial thought is literal in meditative awareness, a category mistake for categorial thought is very likely to find a creative use in the poetry of meditative speech. The logical form of metaphor is bipolar. In general a metaphor is a symbol (nondual) which unites opposites in a primitive unity, a special sort of unity which is foreign to the categorial mind.[7] For example, where categorial reason finds an irreconcilable opposition between polar terms (contraries), a metaphoric term reveals a di-unity. This is not an identification of opposites, but rather a preservation of the differences in a primitive unity. In the logos of meditation the categorial polar term /P/ takes on transcategorial signification. And the principle of di-unity recurs on all levels for all dual distinctions. One striking example of di-unity, already cited, is the Christ-being. The Christ is that primitive "unity" which is at once infinite and finite. /He/ negotiates the ultimate duality. From the point of view of the categorial hermeneutic we may say that the Christ is the paradigm of metaphor. The Christ is a paradox for categorial understanding, and a paradigm for meditative understanding. It is the bipolar principle of di-unity which heals the splits and suffering of categorial life.

Another meditative device which spans apparently unbridgeable dualities and distinctions of categorial thought is analogy. What appears to be a vague resemblance or similarity to dualized thought manifests itself as a unity and identity in meditation. Analogy is the wings of meaning. It helps to disclose the ultimate synonymy of all names.

Perhaps the most powerful instrument to aid categorial understanding in approaching the recursive fluidity of meaning is the principle of logical and ontological relativity. It is easiest to appreciate the power of this principle in the context of comparative ontology. We saw earlier that the sense of a term (in categorial reason) is relative to the categorial language or ontology which is its original context. The consequence of this is that any given term which occurs in different ontologies must be equivocal in meaning. For example, the term "I" as used in different world contexts is systematically ambiguous. Categorial thought is required by its either/or logical form to make bi-valent judgments as to the "true" meaning of such a term, as well as the true or best categorial language. But if it can suspend judgment for a moment and work with the assumption that there is a plurality of possible and actual worlds, and if it is capable of recognizing that natural reason is already capable of inhabiting a multiplicity of worlds (in its expanded meditative form), then the way is open to ontological relativity. For in the meditative attitude it becomes possible to expand the horizon of meaning of a term across possible/actual worlds. Expanded understanding is not required to fix itself in one ontological language at a (categorial) time. In meditative time and space the plurality of distinct senses of a given term across worlds, its trans-world significance, becomes manifest in some kind of "unity." For example, the meditative meaning of the term "I" is precisely its relativistic multivocal sense for all possible worlds: the sense of this term in the Cartesian world, in Hume's world, in the world of Spinoza, in the language of Leibniz, in the Christian world, the Buddhist world, the Hindu world, and so on, taken "simultaneously" (meditative time) constitutes its "true" meaning. Only when the fixity of essentialism, categorial identity and univocity is questioned is the way open for the relativity and multivocity of meaning. The relativity of meaning (sense and reference) opens the way to trans-categorial significance.

We have been seeking ways to make meditative logos accessible to the sceptical categorial mind. The general challenge in each case is the same: wherever the categorial semantic assumes or affirms any sort of ultimate or primitive distinction or duality it must be shown how meditative meaning melts the opposition in bipolar unity.

These illustrations of meditative discourse should help us to see that meditative utterances are not propositional assertions. Rather, they are ritual performances which function solely to transform rational understanding beyond the bounds of categorial sense. This is why the Indian yogic tradition, for example, stresses the use of mantras and concentration on sacred sounds in meditation.

Also, these illustrations should help us to understand the scriptural remark that in the beginning was the infinite Word. For the infinite Word (Logos) is non-different from infinite Being itself. And it may become more transparent that this Word may be incarnated in a (trans-categorial) living form.

In concluding this brief sketch of meditative discourse it is timely to return to the main theme of the hermeneutic of comparative ontology. It was indicated earlier that the suitable hermeneutic of comparative ontology must be capable of negotiating the logical space between finite (dualistic) and infinite (nondual) discourse. It should be powerful enough to mediate dialectically between the categorial particular and the trans-categorial universal. And it should be capable of acknowledging at once a plurality of actual worlds and that there is one and only one world. I wish to suggest that the rationality of meditative discourse meets this challenge. For the trans-categorial discourse of meditative reason explodes the myth of essentialism (absolutism) and liberates the categorial mind from the bondage of rigid designation. It rescues consciousness from the fixity of finite particularity and reveals determinacy and individuation in its transfinite form. The particularity that is shown in meditative discourse overcomes the alienation of categorial finitude and flows in the transparent presence of the infinite Word. Trans-categorial particularity is worthy of honor and is honored in meditative discourse. The distinctions and determinations of dual thought are transformed and celebrated in trans-categorial light. In meditative logical space the differentiations of diverse worlds are recognized, but now in a context of trans-categorial unity: there is, indeed, one world. But this unity is of a different nature from categorial unity: it is a unity beyond the category of quantity and number.

In this context we begin to see the power of the ancient ideal of the universal Logos. It is a trans-world (trans-categorial) universality. Meditative reason recognizes that natural consciousness (natural reason, natural language) is already trans-categorial: it remains perpetually ready for radical self-transformation. It becomes clear that the categorial mind is neither hermetically sealed nor hermeneutically bound. The self-transforming power of meditative discourse is designed to liberate reason from categorial bondage. Indeed, liberation, salvation, is essentially a hermeneutical concern.

V. Implications for Comparative (Trans-Categorial) Theology

I should like to conclude by returning to where we began and stating what I see as some of the implications of comparative ontology for comparative, that is, trans-categorial theology.

1. The hermeneutic for comparative theology must be trans-categorial. The meditative hermeneutic, as interpreted by categorial reason, turns out to stand in radical opposition to dual life. But when lived it is a dynamic dialogue between the polar voices of /reason/.

2. Once we have the distinction between properties (categorial predicates) and features (absolute predicates), we are in a better po-

sition to appreciate the ontological demonstration of infinite Being. The feature of /Being/ is itself equivocal between the categorial (dual) hermeneutic and the trans-categorial (nondual) hermeneutic. In its categorial sense /Being/ is inherently dual and comprises the opposition between existence and inexistence, hence formally carries the feature of /becoming/; these are ontologically synonymous. But in trans-categorial import /Being/ is nondual (which must not be confused with monistic) and no contrary opposition can be introduced. The latter is the /Being/ spoken of by Parmenides, the absolute being which has no otherness and hence is beyond the realm of becoming.

3. This distinction further shows why categorial theology must be incoherent. For categorial reason /Being/ must remain inherently dual in form. Only in trans-categorial reason can absolute /Being/ be discerned. In this respect Plato's instruction about /Goodness/, which is beyond /being/ and /truth/ ("far nobler"), is precisely the discernment of absolute /Being/.

4. The transformation to trans-categorial reason is not merely the recognition of objects of thought or being which are nondual, but rather the realization that there can be no such objects (for to be an object is precisely to be constituted in duality) and that consciousness itself must be transformed in meditation beyond categorial life.

5. The unity of divine being (oneness) is not a categorial "one" which stands in otherness to "two," not the one of monism or monotheism, but the trans-categorial /unity/ (absolute) beyond monism and dualism, which (as Upanishadic scripture reveals) is one without a second (Advaita). Only trans-categorial /unity/ can be a universal point of reference and sense for all possible and actual worlds.

6. Infinite Being cannot be relativized to any particular world; it must be trans-categorial. The God of any particular world is relativized, the "God" of trans-categorial /Being/ is absolute for all possible worlds.

7. Infinite Being cannot be objectified, cannot be an "object" of investigation for theology. Negative theology, understood as a critique of categorial theology, approaches trans-categorial theology. In this sense, negative theology is the recognition that no predicates may be affirmed or denied of infinite Being.

8. Categorial life, for any possible world, samsaric or non-samsaric, is inherently dual, /existential/, and the generic form of cate-

gorial life involves /becoming/, hence polarity and privation. Potentiality is the form of dual life and with this form of life comes privation, desire, action, morality and the possibility of salvation. /Sin/ is the generic condition of existence, the possibility of birth, death and salvation. The condition of /Sin/ (/morality/) is commensurate with the possiblity of being /good/. Morality applies to beings in /sin/, and the contrariety of good-and-evil, moral action and the virtuous life, categorially understood, cannot bring about salvation.

9. In samsaric worlds, existence is perpetual and one is condemned to immortality. In non-samsaric worlds one is condemned to existential death or mortality. True /Salvation/ must mean the possibility of transformation beyond the categorial opposition of mortality and immortality (/mortality/). Salvation is the transformation from categorial life to trans-categorial life, absolute /life/.

10. This does not mean that in salvation one "becomes God" in any categorial sense. This has caused much confusion. Being /One/ with God, living in the presence of infinite Being, requires a trans-categorial sense of /oneness/.

11. It is only in trans-categorial reason that /scripture/, the holy word, can make sense. The Logos can be flesh only in the nonduality of trans-categorial life. Only here can the Word be living, can all creation be the speaking forth of the infinite Word, where /speaking/ is /being/, the Word which is truth and life and the way. "In the beginning" cannot indicate the categorial sense of beginning, but the trans-categorial origin of creation.

12. The trans-categorial hermeneutic is not another language which one can understand and speak, but a radical transformation of life itself. It must be /lived/.

13. The generic form of religious life consists in the process of transformation (dialogue, dialectic) to trans-categorial life.

14. The universal Christ is the paradigm of religious being. Following the life of the Christ is not to follow certain moral teachings but to enter the path of trans-categorial life.

15. /Faith/ is not belief without evidence. That is the mistake of the categorial hermeneutic which requires that propositional belief be supported by independent evidence. Now we see that /Faith/ is what makes /belief/ and /truth/ possible. It is the trans-categorial posture of pure reason which makes categorial worlds possible. Rational /Faith/ is the light of Reason which Plato discerned in his recognition of nondual /Goodness/.

Notes

Chapter 2

1. This paper is a free and expanded version of my unpublished presentation at the Congress of the International Association for the History of Religions held at Lancaster, England in 1975, and of my paper "Pluralisme philosophique et pluralité des religions" presented at the 'Castelli' Colloquium at the University of Rome, 1977, published in the proceedings: *La philosophie de la religion: L'herméneutique de la philosophie de la religion* (Paris: Aubier, 1977), pp. 193–201. Cf. also my contribution to the fourth volume of *Contemporary Philosophy*, edited by R. Klibansky (Florence: La Nuova Italia, 1971), pp. 221–42: "Philosophy of Religion in the Contemporary Encounter of Cultures." It was originally presented at the 1978 session of the Working Group in Cross-Cultural Philosophy of Religion at the American Academy of Religion in New Orleans.

2. I insist that Man stands for *homo, anthropos, Mensch,* and not for males. I resist to be classified as a kind of 'human' (humankind) and to reify Man into an abstract humankind. The personal God is not 'Godkind'.

Chapter 3

1. Wilfred Cantwell Smith, an address presented to the Canadian Theological Society, Montreal, May 1961, and reprinted in *Religious Diversity*, ed. by W. Oxtoby (New York: Harper & Row, 1976), 9.

2. See John F. Kane, *Pluralism and Truth in Religion* (Chico, CA: Scholars Press, 1981).

3. John Hick, *Philosophy of Religion*, 4th ed. (Englewood Cliffs, NJ: Prentice Hall, 1990).

4. Wilfred Cantwell Smith, *Towards a World Theology* (Philadelphia: Westminster Press, 1981).

5. Charles Davis, "Religious Pluralism," a lecture read at the annual meeting of the Canadian Society for the Study of Religion, Montreal, May 1980.

6. Schleiermacher does say that scriptures are mainly for beginners in religion (*On Religion* [New York: Harper & Row, 1958], 34); and Paul Tillich does stress the self-transcending quality of scripture, that it participates in that to which it points (*Dynamics of Faith* [New York: Harper & Row, 1957]). But neither would allow the total transcendence of scripture found in Advaita Vedanta and Buddhism. It is also true that within Hinduism (e.g., Purva Mimamsa, Vaishishtadvaita Vedanta, *bhakti*, etc.), and in certain forms of Jodo Shinshu Buddhism, total transcendence of instrumental forms is not accepted.

7. Wilfred Cantwell Smith, "Traditions in Contact and Change: Towards a History of Religion in the Singular," in *Traditions in Contact and Change*, ed. by P. Slater, D. Wiebe, H. Coward and M. Boutin (Waterloo: Wilfrid Laurier University Press, 1983), 1–23.

8. Ibid.

9. Smith, *Towards a World Theology*, 137–39, 151–53, 183ff.

10. Ibid., 184.

11. Ibid., 185.

12. Ibid., 187.

13. Ibid., 186.

14. Karl Rahner, *Confrontations 1*, vol. 2 of *Theological Investigations*, trans. by David Bourke (London: Darton, Longman and Todd, 1974), 7.

15. Ibid.

16. Ibid., 139.

17. Nagarjuna, Mūlamadhyamakakārikā, trans. by K. K. Inada. (Tokyo: Hokuseido Press, 1970). Nagarjuna's dates are given as 150–250 C.E.

18. Immanuel Kant, *Religion within the Limits of Reason Alone*. (New York: Harper Torchbooks, 1960).

19. Calvin S. Hall, *A Primer of Freudian Psychology* (New York: Mentor, 1958), 89–91.

20. Hans Kung, *On Being a Christian* (New York: Doubleday, 1976), 123.

21. See Paul Knitter, "World Religions and the Finality of Christ: A Critique of Hans Kung's 'On Being a Christian' ," *Horizons* 5 (1978): 151–64.

22. Ibid., 156.

23. Smith, *Towards a World Theology*, 123, 145ff.

24. Jaspers' position paraphrased by Kane, *Pluralism and Truth in Religion*, 113.

25. In a recent article Heinrich Ott stresses the "openness" required for dialogue: "Dialogue between the religions has to be so open that it requires no common doctrinal presuppositions and expects no doctrinal results. Rather, this dialogue leads simply to a mutual respect in which the experience of one religion enlightens the other and allows itself to be enlightened by the other." Heinrich Ott, "Does the Notion of 'Mystery'—as Another Name for God—Provide a Basis for a Dialogical Encounter between the Religions?," in *God: The Contemporary Discussion*, ed. F. Sontag and M. D. Bryant. (New York: Rose of Sharon Press, 1982), 15.

26. Smith, *Towards a World Theology*, 180–91.

Chapter 5

1. Cf. George Mavrodes, "Real and More Real," *International Philosophical Quarterly*, 4 (December 1964): 554–61; and James Ross, *Philosophical Theology* (Indianapolis and New York, 1969), 254–78.

2. See his "Understanding a Primitive Society," *American Philosophical Quarterly*, 1 (October 1964): 307–24, and his *The Idea of a Social Science* (New York, 1958), 100–103.

3. "Winch and Rationality in Religion," *Sophia* 13 (July 1974): 19–29.

4. J. Pelikan points out (*The Christian Tradition*, vol. I [Chicago, 1971], 198f.) that Arians were accused of inconsistency because they continued to worship the Son while insisting that the Son was only a creature.

5. Cf. William Christian, *Oppositions of Religious Doctrines* (New York, 1972). One cannot usefully appeal to private revelations in these contexts, but one can appeal to numinous and mystical experience if both parties to the dispute accept its reality and/or validity.

6. Basil Mitchell, *The Justification of Religious Belief* (New York, 1974), 99.

7. By a "metaphysical system" I mean, roughly, a system of propositions which (*a*) when taken together articulate a more or less comprehensive worldview, which (*b*) can be evaluated as true or false, to which (*c*) reasons and arguments are relevant, and which (*d*) cannot be adequately evaluated by scientific criteria alone.

8. Eliot Deutsch, *Advaita Vedanta: A Philosophical Reconstruction*, (Honolulu, 1969).

9. Christian, *Oppositions of Religious Doctrines*, 89.

10. Keith Yandell, *Basic Issues in the Philosophy of Religion* (Boston, 1971), 221–26.

11. Keith Yandell, "Religious Experience and Rational Appraisal," *Religious Studies* 10 (June 1974): 186.

12. Ibid.

13. Stephen Pepper, "Metaphysical Method," *The Philosophical Review*, 52 (May 1943): 252–69.

14. Paul Tillich, *Systematic Theology*, vol. I (Chicago, 1951), 105.

15. Frederick Ferre and Kent Bendall, *Exploring the Logic of Faith* (New York, 1963), 171.

16. If self-stultification is regarded as a logical error, then the second criterion can be subsumed under the first. The fourth criterion can also be subsumed under others. If a system includes many ad hoc hypotheses it is less likely (*a*) to be coherent, (*b*) to be simple, and (*c*) to provide an illuminating explanation of the relevant facts. The sixth criterion can be subsumed under the seventh and eighth criteria. If a theory is contradicted by well-established data, then there are at least some facts which it cannot explain. It thus fails to provide an illuminating explanation of *all* the relevant facts. Fruitfulness can also be subsumed under the seventh and eighth criteria. Systems which are unable to assimilate new data and insights either fail in scope (because they ignore it) or (if they do not ignore it) fail to provide illuminating explanations.

17. Is "one and only one straight line can be drawn between any two points" one assumption or two (that is, that at least one straight line can be drawn between any two points and that no more than one can be drawn between any two points)? See Karl Hempel, *Philosophy of Natural Science* (Englewood Cliffs, NJ, 1966), 42.

18. Astrology produces this feeling in some very intelligent people. Ferre has suggested that a theory fails to illuminate or explain a range of experience if those whose experience is being considered continue to find it unilluminating or reductive. See his *Basic Modern Philosophy of Religion* (New York, 1967). Does this imply that we must, for example, rule out any theory of the occult which fails to credit the alleged occurrence of occult phenomena because those who value these phenomena will undoubtedly find such theories reductive?

19. Mitchell, *Justification of Religious Belief.*

Chapter 6

1. Ninian Smart, *Worldviews* (New York: Charles Scribner's Sons, 1983), 169.

2. Peter Berger, *The Heretical Imperative* (London: Collins, 1980).

3. Gordon Kaufman, *The Theological Imagination* (Philadelphia: Westminister Press, 1981).

4. John Hick, "Toward a Philosophy of Religious Pluralism," in *God Has Many Names* (Philadelphia: Westminster Press, 1980), 115.

5. Ibid.

6. John Hick, "On Grading Religions," *Religious Studies* 17 (1981): 467.

7. Wilfred Cantwell Smith, *Questions of Religious Truth* (London: Victor Gallancz, 1967), 67.

8. Ibid., 71, 81.

9. Ibid., 94–95.

10. Wilfred Cantwell Smith, *Towards a World Theology* (Philadelphia: Westminster Press, 1981), 60.

11. Hick, "On Grading Religions," 467.

12. Kaufman, *Theological Imagination,* 192.

13. Although Berger (*Heretical Imperative,* 155ff.) recognizes that the sociological plausibility of a religious viewpoint may vary with the historical situation, he also argues that the plausibility structure should have no bearing on evaluating truth-claims. Crisis situations or marginal situations (such as war, revolution, personal sorrow, death, etc.) can affect what people respond to as true, but that does not provide an epistemological basis for truth by itself in Berger's view.

14. Hick, "On Grading Religions," 467.

15. This is Kaufman's critique of several different approaches to religious pluralism, all of which implicitly presuppose that our present religious options are settled enough for us to determine what the proper interrelationships of religions are. He does not see the options as settled yet.

16. *Heretical Imperative,* 153.

17. *Theological Imagination,* 93–95.

18. *World Theology,* 173.

19. It is important to note that Smith's discussion of insider-outsider normative agreement relates to developing a world theology. Such a theology does not demand agreement on evaluating all specific religious phenomena.

20. With respect to Christianity, Kaufman argues (*Theological Imagination,* 203) that the emphasis on truth-claims will make the Christian

stance to others "basically argumentative and combative." In contrast, a Christian emphasis on reconciliation will help to build community.

21. See Mary Ann Stenger, "Paul Tillich's Theory of Theological Norms and the Problems of Relativism and Subjectivism", *Journal of Religion* 62 (1982): 368-69. The criteria suggested here are developed from Tillich's discussion of the characteristics of religious symbols in "The Religious Symbol," trans. James Luther Adams, *Journal of Liberal Religion* 2 (1940): 13-14. This discussion is paralleled in his analysis of the truth of faith in *Dynamics of Faith* (New York: Harper and Row, 1957), 96-98.

22. See Paul Tillich, "Kairos und Logos," *Gesammelte Werke* (Stuttgart: Evangelisches Verlagswerk, 1961), 75; "The Conquest of the Concept of Religion in the Philosophy of Religion," ibid., 122-23; *Christianity and the Encounter of the World Religions* (New York: Columbia University Press, 1963), 97.

23. Tillich, *Dynamics of Faith*, 97.

Chapter 7

1. There are some interesting essays on this topic in two volumes: *The Problem of the Two Truths in Buddhism and Vedanta*, Mervyn Sprung, Dordrecht: Reidel, 1973; and *The Cardinal Meaning: Essays in Comparative Hermeneutics: Buddhism and Christianity* (including an essay by Ninian Smart), edited by Michael Pye and Robert Morgan, Paris: Mouton, 1973.

Chapter 8

1. In developing this account of the logic of "schemes of doctrines," including "doctrines about other religions," I have been aided at many points by J. M. Bochenski, *The Logic of Religion* (New York: New York University Press, 1965); William A. Christian, *Meaning and Truth in Religion* (Princeton: Princeton University Press, 1964); idem, *Oppositions of Religious Doctrines* (New York: Seabury, 1972); idem, "Bochenski on the Structure of Schemes of Doctrines", *Religious Studies* 13 (1977): 203–19; and Ninian Smart, *Reasons and Faiths* (London: Routledge and Kegan Paul, 1958).

2. For the works of Justin and Clement referred to, see *The Ante-Nicene Fathers*, ed. Alexander Roberts and James Donaldson, and rev. A. Cleveland Coxe, 9 vols. (1884–6; rpt. Grand Rapids: Eerdmans, 1971), I, 162–93; II, 171–567. For Augustine, see *Concerning the City of God against the Pagans*, trans. Henry Bettenson and ed. David Knowles (Baltimore: Penguin Books, 1972).

3. See Jaroslav Pelikan, *The Christian Tradition*, vol. I: *The Emergence of the Catholic Tradition* (Chicago: University of Chicago Press, 1971), 55–67. The standard historical account of Christian doctrines about other religions is Louis Caperan, *Le Problème du salut des infidèles: Essai historique* (Toulouse: Grand Seminaire, 1934).

4. Norman Daniel, *Islam and the West* (Edinburgh: Edinburgh University Press, 1958), 184–94, 246–48.

5. I have in mind accounts of the doctrines about other religions in communities other than Christianity represented by works such as these: Muhammad Hamidullah, "Status of Non-Muslims in Islam," *Majallat al Azhar* 45 (1973): viii, 6–13; ix, 12–13; Yohanan Friedmann, "Medieval Muslim Views of Indian Religions," *Journal of the American Oriental Society* 95 (1975): 214–21; Sri K. Dhammananda, *Why Religious Tolerance?* (Kuala Lumpur: Buddhist Missionary Society, 1974); Phra Khantipalo, *Tolerance: A Study from Buddhist Sources* (London: Rider & Co., 1964); Jacob Katz, *Exclusiveness and Tolerance* (New York: Schocken, 1962); Steven S. Schwarzschild, "Do Noachites Have to Believe in Revelation?," *Jewish Quarterly Review* 52 (1962): 297–308; 53 (1962): 30–65; and Arvind Sharma, "All Religions are—Equal? One? True? Same?: A Critical Examination of Some Formulations of the Neo-Hindu Position," *Philosophy East and West* 29 (1979): 59–72.

Chapter 10

1. Hans-Georg Gadamer, *Truth and Method* (New York: Seabury Press, 1975).

2. Gadamer talks primarily about the past not being totally alien because one's present is formed in part by the past. But for some kinds of interpretation, such as dealing with diverse religious traditions, perhaps it is the openness to the future and a present connection which allows for what seems to be alien not to remain alien.

3. Gadamer calls "the conscious act of this fusion" the "task of the effective-historical consciousness" (ibid., pp. 273–74).

4. In discussing a comparable distinction between the historian and the critic, Gadamer suggests that the difference in point of view does not change the structure of understanding in which each is involved. Although at first Gadamer suggests the historical and critical tasks are quite different (ibid., p. 299), he concludes that each is involved in understanding the text as a unity of meaning, either the unity of the text (critic) or the unity of the historical tradition (historian), and each is involved in a task of application (p. 304).

5. Gadamer contrasts the experienced person, in terms of openness and awareness of the limits of one's knowledge, to the person "captivated by dogma" (p. 325).

6. Of course, this understanding of questioning concerns real questions, not rhetorical questions, pedagogical questions, distorted questions or false questions (p. 325).

7. Even if one determines that the question to which the text was related arose from presuppositions which we would no longer hold because of more recent investigation and knowledge, still one has asked the question to the point of recognizing its legitimacy at one time and has answered it by saying that it is no longer a question.

8. Gadamer says: "The horizon of understanding cannot be limited either by what the writer originally had in mind, or by the horizon of the person to whom the text was originally addressed" (p. 356).

9. Gadamer argues that this knowledge of a fundamental historical contingency for all human thought does not provide an absolute standpoint, even though acceptance of it pushes to be true absolutely. But it cannot be applied to itself without self-contradiction (p. 406). (This can be compared to Paul Tillich's use of the absolute paradox in "Kairo und Logos," *Gesammelte Werke* [Stuttgart: Evangelisches Verglagswerk, 1961].)

10. Gadamer says: "It is the center of language alone that, related to the totality of beings, mediates the finite, historical nature of man to himself and to the world" (*Truth and Method*, 415).

11. Paul Tillich's approach to the development of theological norms is similar to this process. Both are dialectical and both suggest the resolution of conflicts through the creation of a new norm (or, for Gadamer, a new horizon of understanding). See my discussion of Tillich on this point: Mary Ann Stenger, "Paul Tillich's Theory of Theological Norms and the Problems of Relativism and Subjectivism", *The Journal of Religion* 62: 4 (October 1982).

12. See my essay "Religious Pluralism and Cross-Cultural Criteria of Religious Truth," chapter 6 above.

Chapter 11

1. Carl Jung, *Psychology and Alchemy*, trans. R. F. C. Hull, in *The Collected Works of C.G. Jung*, eds. Herbert Read et al. (Princeton: Princeton University Press, 1977), 15.

2. Wilfred Cantwell Smith, *Faith and Belief* (Princeton: Princeton University Press, 1979).

3. Daisetz T. Suzuki, *Mysticism, Christian and Buddhist* (Westport, CT: Greenwood Press, 1975).

4. Frithjof Schuon, *Logic and Transcendence*, 2nd ed. (New York: Harper and Row, 1975).

5. For an analysis of the first ambiguity see my "Prometheus and Progress," *Theology Today* (October 1980). For a discussion of various contrasting aesthetics in Oriental Buddhist art, see my *The Laughing Buddha* (Longwood Academic, 1990), chs. 2–4. Chapter 3 may also be found in my essay, "The Comic Perspective in Zen Literature and Art," *The Eastern Buddhist* (May 1972).

6. Rudolph Otto, *The Idea of the Holy*, trans. John W. Harvey, enlarged ed. (London: Oxford University Press, 1936), 31.

7. Paul Tillich, *Theology of Culture* (New York: Oxford University Press, 1959), 10.

8. Otto, *Idea of the Holy*, 22.

9. Martin Buber, *I and Thou* (New York: Scribners, 1958), 79.

10. Johan Huizinga, *Erasmus and the Age of Reformation*, trans. F. Hopman (New York: Harper and Bros., 1957), 75.

11. Gerardus van der Leeuw, *Religion in Essence and Manifestation*, trans. J. E. Turner (New York: Harper and Row, 1963), II:680.

12. Otto, *Idea of the Holy,* 202.

Chapter 12

1. The argument presented here is simplified and composite to represent the logic underlying the relationship between ineffability and unanimity that appears implicitly or explicitly in the interpretations of religions and of mystical experience associated with *philosophia perennis*. Referring to the diversity of religious traditions Huston Smith stated: "Outwardly they differ, but inwardly it is as if 'invisible geometry' has everywhere been working to shape them to a single truth." Huston Smith, *Forgotten Truth: The Primordial Tradition* (New York: Harper and Row, 1976), 9. Similar assumptions about the "essence" of mystical experience appear in Margaret Smith, *The Way of the Mystics: The Early Christian Mystics and the Rise of the Sufis* (New York: Oxford University Press, 1978); Evelyn Underhill, *Mysticism: A Study in the Nature and Development of Man's Spiritual Consciousness*, 12th rev. ed., (London: Methuen, 1930); Frithjof Schuon, *The Transcendent Unity of Religions*, trans. Peter Townsend, (New York: Pantheon, 1953); Daniel Goleman, *The Varieties of the Meditative Experience*, (New York: E. P. Dutton, 1977); Aldous Huxley, *The Perennial Philosophy* (New York: Harper and Bros., 1945); and W. T. Stace, *Mysticism and Philosophy* (Philadelphia: J. B. Lippincott, 1960). Spokesmen for "Renaissance

Hinduism" such as Vivekananda, Aurobindo and Shivananda share this orientation.

2. Claudio Naranjo reduces the essence of meditation to a common attitude: "a practice in awareness, in centeredness and equanimity, in attunement to our nature, in the capacity of giving up ourselves and being available to our perceptions, in receptivity in freedom from pre-conceptions necessary to reception." Claudio Naranjo, "Meditation: Its Spirit and Techniques," in *On the Psychology of Meditation*, by Claudio Naranjo and Robert E. Ornstein (New York: Viking Press, 1971), 32.

3. John Blofeld makes the argument quite explicit: "Descriptions by people widely separated in time and place are strikingly similar, especially if allowance is made for four divisive factors: the impossibility of accurately describing an experience that transcends all concepts for which words exist; the pious tendency to reconcile all religious experience with cherished doctrines; the prohibition in some societies against expressing views not in accord with the prevailing doctrines; and the need to make descriptions intelligible and acceptable to others." John Blofeld, *The Tantric Mysticism of Tibet: A Practical Guide*, (New York: E. P. Dutton, 1970).

4. See Agehananda Bharati, "The Hindu Renaissance and Its Apologetic Patterns," *Journal of Asian Studies* 29:267–87; and Gita Mehta, "Neon India," *Harper's* 259:1551 (August 1979): 41–60.

5. See Wayne Proudfoot, "Religious Experience, Emotion and Belief," *Harvard Theological Review* 70: 361–64.

6. Sacredness is naturally associated with the *arche* character of mystical experience. As the opening lines of the *Tao Te Ching* have it: "The Tao that can be told of is not the eternal Tao." Thus, it is ineffable. "Nameless, it is the origin of Heaven and earth"; nevertheless, "Nameable, it is the mother of all things." Tao is both source and course of things. Here in essence is the problem of reification of the a-structural into human structures. Somehow the nameless origin becomes the nameable mother of all things. "That they are the same is the mystery." The ineffability in question is weak rather than strong. *Tao Te Ching*, in William T. deBary et al., *Sources of Chinese Tradition*, vol. 1: *Introduction to Oriental Civilizations* (New York: Columbia University Press, 1960), 51.

7. Shankara, *The Vedanta Sutras of Badarayana with the Commentary by Shankara*, trans. George Thibaut, *Sacred Books of the East* (New York: Dover, 1962), vol. 34, part I, pp. 16–37.

8. Ibid., part I, pp. 14, 150, 424; part II, p. 14.

9. Nyanaponika Thera, *The Heart of Buddhist Meditation: A Handbook of Mental Training Based on the Buddha's Way of Mindfulness* (New York: Samuel Weiser, 1970), 30–45.

10. According to Bugault, *prajna* (wisdom) is in the middle between the extremes of transcendental truth and conventional truth for the Mahayana tradition also. Wisdom and ordinary knowledge are both continuous and discontinuous. Guy Bugault, *La Notion de "Prajñā" ou de Sapience sélon les Perspectives du "Mahāyāna": Part de la Connaissance et de L'Inconnaissance dans L'Anagogie Bouddhique*, Publications de l'Institute de Civilisation Indienne, no. 32 (Paris: Éditions E. De Boccard, 1968), 75–76, 229.

11. See Clifford Geertz, "Religion as a Cultural System," in *Anthropological Approaches to the Study of Religion*, ed. M. Banton, Association of Social Anthropologists monographs no. 3 (London: Tavistock Publications, 1963), 1–46.

12. Bugault, La Notion de "Prajñā",211, says that the dialectic of Nagarjuna, Buddhapalita and Chandrakirti is not dogmatic or didactic like that of Hegel. Dialectic's unique function here is to destroy all points of view (*drishti*), using one against the others, to make an opening for an eventual liberating intuition that issues into emptiness abruptly and instantaneously. The truth is unveiled by separating it from the untrue. This manner of revelation probably reinforces the *arche* character of the wisdom attained because attainment is not directly produced by any of the techniques employed to approach it. Resolution must not appear to be the product of the process by which it is reached.

13. The induction of the "doubt mass" or "great doubt" by techniques of negative reinforcement in Ch'an and Zen is a parallel variation on this *via negativa*. See the discussion in Chung-Yuan Chang especially, *Original Teachings of Ch'an Buddhism: Selected from the Transmission of the Lamp*, (New York: Vintage, 1969); also Ernest Becker, *Zen: A Rational Critique* (New York: Norton, 1961), 44–48, 57-58; Garma Chen-Chi Chang, *The Practice of Zen* (New York: Harper and Row, 1959), 79, 91, 94–96, 103–11, 143–44, 150–55, 225 n9; Richard DeMartino, "The Human Situation and Zen Buddhism," in *Zen Buddhism and Psychoanalysis*, D. T. Suzuki et al. (New York: Grove Press, 1963), 163-68; Philipp Kapleau, ed., *The Three Pillars of Zen: Teaching, Practice, Enlightenment* (Boston: Beacon Press, 1967), 71–82; D. T. Suzuki, *Zen Buddhism: Selected Writings of D. T. Suzuki*, ed. W. Barrett, (Garden City, NY: Doubleday, 1956), 102–3, 135–38.

14. See Conrad Hyers, *Zen and the Comic Spirit* (Philadelphia: Westminster Press, 1973), 54–59.

15. See Robert A. Paul, "A Mantra and its Meaning," in *The Psychoanalytic Study of Society*, ed. Werner Muensterberger, vol. 9 (New York: The Psychohistory Press, 1979).

16. The assumption of the unity of mystical texts is comparable to the traditional Vedanta theological assumption of the unity of the Vedas or to the traditional Christian theological assumption of the unity of biblical revelation.

17. Shankara, *Vedantas Sutras*, part I, pp. 298, 312; part II, p. 375.

18. Ibid., part I, p. 298.

19. Ibid., pp. 400–34.

20. Ibid., pp. 440–43.

21. Ibid., part II, pp. 168–69. See also Frederick J. Streng, "Language and Mystical Awareness," in *Mysticism and Philosophical Analysis*, ed. Steven T. Katz (New York: Oxford University Press, 1978), 164.

22. Ramanuja, *The Vedanta Sutras with the Commentary by Ramanuja*, part III, trans. George Thibaut, *Sacred Books of the East*, vol. 48 (Delhi: Motilal Banarsidass, 1966), 52–54.

23. Ramanuja, *Ramanuja's Vedarthasamgraha: Introduction, Critical Edition and Annotated Translation*, ed. and trans. J. B. Van Buitenen, Deccan College Monograph Series, no. 16 (Poona: Deccan College Postgraduate and Research Institute, 1956), 296–99; and Ramanuja, *Vedanta Sutras*, 14–6.

24. "Heart Sutra," in Edward Conze et al., *Buddhist Texts through the Ages Translated from Pali, Sanskrit, Chinese, Tibetan, Japanese and Apabhramsa* (New York: Harper and Row, 1964), 152.

25. This argument based on evidence from the Zen tradition could be expanded to the whole Mahayana tradition. Katz, Gimello and Streng, in *Mysticism and Philosophical Analysis*, ed. Steven T. Katz, argue from evidence in a variety of Mahayana sources that Buddhist insight or emptiness is not the same as the oneness of Being. Gimello notes that the "Ten Ox-herding Pictures" of Zen Buddhism do not end the series at the blank circle, but go beyond it to return to the marketplace (Robert Gimello, "Mysticism and Meditation," in ibid., 192). The blank circle corresponds to the Vedanta non-dual experience.

26. See Steven B. Beyer, "The Doctrine of Meditation in the Hinayana," in *Buddhism: A Modern Perspective*, ed. Charles S. Prebish (London and University Park, PA: Pennsylvania State University Press, 1975), 137; Bugault, *La Notion de "Prajñā"*, 73–75; L. S. Cousins, "Buddhist Jnana: Its Nature and Attainment According to the Pali Sources," *Religion: A Journal of Religion and Religions* 3 (1973): 115–31; Gimello, "Mysticism and Mediation," 185–86; Paravahera Mahathera Vajirnana, *Buddhist Meditation in Theory and Practice: A General Exposition According to the Pali Canon of the Theravada School*, (Colombo: Gunasena & Co., 1962), 417.

27. Hui-Neng, *The Platform Sutra of the Sixth Patriarch: The Text of the Tun-Huang Manuscript*, trans. Philip B. Yampolsky (New York: Columbia University Press, 1967), 136.

28. See Hakuin, in William T. de Bary, ed., *The Buddhist Tradition in India, China, and Japan*, (New York: Modern Library, 1969), 391.

29. For other discussions of the differences between Mahayana and Hinayana or Theravada *nirvana* experiences, see Bugault, *Le Notion de "Prajñā,* 47–48; and Winston L. King, "Zen as a Vipassana-Type Discipline," in *Asian Religions: History of Religion (1974 Proceedings)*, comp. Harry Partin (Tallahassee, FL: American Academy of Religion, 1974), 62–79.

30. See Walter Principe, "Mysticism: Its Meaning and Varieties," in *Mystics and Scholars: The Calgary Conference on Mysticism, 1976*, eds. Harold Coward and Terence Penelhum, SR Supplements, no. 3 (Waterloo, Ontario: Corporation Canadienne des Sciences Religieuses, 1977), 7; and Frits Staal, *Exploring Mysticism: A Methodological Essay* (Berkeley: University of California Press, 1975), 108.

31. See B. K. Anand, G. S. Chhina and Baldev Singh, "Some Aspects of Electroencephalographic Studies in Yogis," in *Altered States of Consciousness: A Book of Readings*, ed. Charles T. Tart (New York: John Wiley & Sons, 1969), 503–6; Victor F. Emerson, "Research on Meditation," in *What is Meditation?*, ed. John White (Garden City, NY: Doubleday, 1974), 225–43; Ernest Gellhorn and William F. Kiely, "Mystical States of Consciousness: Neurophysiological and Clinical Aspects," *Journal of Nervous and Mental Disease* 154:399–405; Akira Kasamatsu and Tomio Hirai, "An Electroencephalographic Study of the Zen Meditation (Zazen)," in Tart, *Altered States,* 489–502.

32. See Agehananda Bharati, *The Light at the Center: Context and Pretext of Modern Mysticism* (Santa Barbara, CA: Ross-Erikson, 1976).

Chapter 13

1. This essay was originally presented to the Working Group in Cross-Cultural Philosophy of Religion at the American Academy of Religion in New Orleans in 1978. Subsequently some portions of the sections on Tillich and Nishitani appeared in "Three approaches to authentic existence: Christian, Confucian and Buddhist," *Philosophy East and West* 32:4 (October 1982): 371–91; and in "Three Religious Ontological Claims: 'Being-Itself,' 'Nothingness within Somethingness,' and 'The Field of Emptiness' ", in *Traditions in Contact and Change*, ed. Peter Slater and Donald Wiebe, Selected Proceedings of the XIVth Congress of the International Association for the History of Religions (Waterloo, Ontario: Wilfred Laurier University Press, 1983), 249–266.

2. Paul Tillich, *Systematic Theology*, vol. 1 (Chicago: University of Chicago Press, 1952).

3. Hellmut Wilhelm, *Heaven, Earth, and Man in the Book of Changes* (Seattle: University of Washington Press, 1977).

4. Keiji Nishitani, "The Standpoint of Sunyata", trans. Jan van Bragt, *Eastern Buddhist*, n.s., 6:2 (October 1973).

5. For further elaboration of these ideal types, or "structures," of religious life see my *Understanding Religious Life*, 3rd ed. (Belmont, CA: Wadsworth, 1985), chs. 3–5.

6. The quotations and discussion of Tillich in this section are from or based on passages from the following pages of *Systematic Theology*, vol. 1: 163–64, 169, 171, 174, 179, 188–91, 196, 202, 238.

7. The quotations and discussion of the *Book of Changes* in this section are, unless otherwise noted, taken from the following pages of Wilhelm, *Heaven, Earth, and Man:* 14, 37–41, 44–50, 53, 72, 140, 152–53, 191, 194, 197.

8. See also Hellmut Wilhelm, *Changes: Eight Lectures on the I Ching*, trans. C. F. Baynes (New York: Harper & Row, 1954), 18–19.

9. Ibid., 33–34.

10. Ibid., 20.

11. The quotations and discussion in this section, unless otherwise noted, are taken from the following pages in Nishitani, "The Standpoint of Sunyata": 64, 66–68, 70, 77. See also Keiji Nishitani, *Religion and Nothingness*, trans. Jan van Bragt (Berkeley: University of California Press, 1982).

12. See Keiji Nishitani, "Nihilism and Sunyata," trans. Yamamoto Seisaku, *Eastern Buddhist*, n.s. 4:2 (October 1971): 30–49; 5:1 (May 1972): 55–69; and 5:2 (October 1972): 95–106. For another useful examination of negativity in certain Buddhist and Western formulations, see Masao Abe, "Non-being and *Mu*: The Metaphysical Nature of Negativity in the East and West," *Religious Studies*, 11:2 (June 1975): 181–92.

13. Keiji Nishitani, "Standpoint of Emptiness," *Eastern Buddhist*, n.s. 6:1 (May 1973): 70.

Chapter 14

1. In the context of comparative ontology a possible world is a coherent and intelligible world system and language form, and if a world is possible then it is actual. If, for example, we speak of the Hindu or Christian worlds as possible, then this is the same as saying that they are actual, for to be intelligible is to be actual. And it is not here assumed that there can be only one intelligible or actual world.

2. From a logical point of view any general term—"justice," "piety," "triangularity," etc.—specifies a categorial universal. A categorial universal has determinate content and specifies a class of possible instances.

3. For a more developed and systematic discussion of these and the immediately following points concerning the two types of opposition, cate-

gories and ontological structures, see the following papers of this author: "Formal Ontology and Movement Between Worlds," *Philosophy East and West* 26:2 (April 1976); "Formal Ontology and the Dialectical Transformation of Consciousness," *Philosophy East and West* 29:1 (January 1979); "Nagarjuna, Aristotle and Frege on the Nature of Thought," *Buddhist and Western Philosophy*, ed. Nathan Katz (New Delhi: Sterling Publishers, 1980); "Comparative Ontology and the Interpretation of Karma," *Indian Philosophical Quarterly* 6:2 (January 1979); "Comparative Ontology: Relative and Absolute Truth," *Philosophy East and West, 31:1* (January 1981).

4. For a more detailed development of these points, see the works cited in the previous note.

5. Of course, the opposition between distinct language systems or ontologies is not the same as contrary or polar opposition. Contrary opposition is intra-categorial only. Polar terms (categories) are never opposed in contrary opposition, only in complementary (external) negation. Similarly, different worlds or language systems are not opposed as logical contraries.

6. In this play on the spatial metaphor (logical space) it would be helpful to think of Einstein's relativistic space. For a discussion of this see my "Ontological Relativity: A Metaphysical Critique of Einstein's Thought," in *Albert Einstein as an Inter-Cultural and Inter-Disciplinary Phenomenon*, Proceedings of the Hofstra University Centenary Conference on Einstein (Greenwood Press, San Francisco 1981).

7. Metaphors appear to be creative "category mistakes" to categorial thought. They may be permitted in poetic discourse (e.g, "Love is blue"), but not in propositional discourse.

Contributors

WILLIAM A. CHRISTIAN SR. is Professor Emeritus of Religious Studies at Yale University. He is the author of *Meaning and Truth in Religion, Oppositions of Religious Doctrines,* and most recently, *Doctrines of Religious Communities* (Yale University Press, 1987). His area of research is philosophy of religion.

HAROLD COWARD is Professor of History and Director of the Centre for Studies in Religion and Society at the University of Victoria in British Columbia. His recent publications include *The Philosophy of the Grammarians,* with K. Kunjunni Raja (Princeton University Press, 1990), *Mantra: Hearing the Divine in India,* with David Goa (Anima Books, 1991), and *Derrida and Negative Theology,* with Toby Foshay (SUNY Press, 1992). His current areas of research are environmental ethics, and human nature, East and West.

THOMAS DEAN is Associate Professor of Religion at Temple University and Temple University Japan. His recent publications include "Universal Theology and Dialogical Dialogue" in *Toward a Universal Theology of Religions,* ed. Leonard Swidler (Orbis, 1987) and "Masao Abe on Zen and Western Thought" in *Eastern Buddhist* (Autumn 1989; Spring 1990). His research is on cross-cultural philosophy of religion, and Heidegger and the Kyoto School.

JOSEPH A. DINOIA is Professor of Theology at the Dominican House of Studies in Washington D.C. His most recent publication is *The Diversity of Religions: A Christian Perspective* (Catholic University of America Press, 1992). His areas of research include theology of religions, nature and method of theology, and philosophical theology.

JOHN Y. FENTON is Associate Professor of Religion in the Department of Religion at Emory University. His publications include *Transplanting Religious Traditions: Asian Indians in America* (Praeger, 1988), and *South Asian Religions in the Americas: An Annotated Bibliography of Immigrant Religious Traditions* (Greenwood, forthcoming). His areas of research include religion and intermarriage among South Asian immigrants in America, and a textbook on Asian religions today.

ASHOK K. GANGADEAN is Professor of Philosophy in the Department of Philosophy at Haverford College. His publications include *Meditative Reason: Towards Universal Grammar* (Peter Lang, 1993), *Time, Truth and Logic* (forthcoming), and *Between Worlds: Alterity, Meaning and Truth* (forthcoming). His areas of research include logic, philosophy of language, ontology, comparative philosophy and religion, and East-West philosophy.

CONRAD HYERS is Professor of Religion in the Department of Religion at Gustavus Adolphus College in St. Peter, Minnesota. His publications include *The Meaning of Creation: Genesis and Modern Science* (Westminster, 1984), *Once-Born, Twice-Born Zen: The Rinzai and Soto Schools of Japan* (Longwood, 1989), and *The Laughing Buddha: Zen and the Comic Spirit* (Longwood, 1990). He is completing work on *The Tragic Spirit and Comic Reconciliation*.

RAIMUNDO PANIKKAR is Professor Emeritus in the Department of Religious Studies at the University of California, Santa Barbara. His recent books are *The Silence of God: The Answer of the Buddha* (Orbis, 1989), *La Torre di Babele: Pace e Pluralismo* (1990), *Der Weisheit eine Wohnung bereiten* (1991; English translation forthcoming), and *La Nueva Inocencia* (1992). His areas of research include metaphysics, comparative religion, and Indology.

NORBERT M. SAMUELSON is Professor of Religion in the Department of Religion at Temple University in Philadelphia. His recent publications include *The Exalted Faith of Abraham Ibn Daud*

(1986), *An Introduction of Modern Jewish Philosophy* (1989), and *The First Seven Days: A Philosophical Commentary on Genesis 1* (1992). His areas of research include religion and physics, the philosophy of Franz Rosenzweig, and medieval Jewish philosophy.

NINIAN SMART is J. F. Rowny Professor of Comparative Religions in the Department of Religious Studies at the University of California, Santa Barbara. Some of his recent publications include *The World's Religions* (1989), *Doctrine and Argument in Indian Philosophy*, 2nd edition (1992), and *Buddhism and Christianity: Rivals and Allies* (1992). His current area of research and writing is on phenomenology of religion.

MARY ANN STENGER is a Professor of Religious Studies at the University of Louisville. Her recent publications include "The Limits and Possibilities of Tillich's Ontology for Cross-Cultural and Feminist Theology" in *God and Being/Gott und Sein*, edited by Gert Hummel (Berlin: Walter de Gruyter, 1989), and "Feminism and Pluralism in Contemporary Theology" in *Laval theologique et philosophique* (October 1990). Her current area of research is religious pluralism and feminism.

FREDERICK J. STRENG was Professor of Religious Studies in the Department of Religious Studies at Southern Methodist University. Among his publications were *Emptiness: A Study in Religious Meaning* (1967), *Understanding Religious Life*, 3rd edition (1985), and "The Transcendental in a Comparative Context" in *Culture and Modernity: East-West Philosophic Perspectives*, ed. Eliot Deutsch (1991). His areas of research included the plurality of religious life, and interreligious dialogue.

WILLIAM J. WAINWRIGHT is Professor of Philosophy in the Department of Philosophy at the University of Wisconsin, Milwaukee. His major publications include *Mysticism* (University of Wisconsin Press, 1981), *Rationality, Religious Belief and Moral Commitment*, edited with Robert Audi (1986), and *Philosophy of Religion* (Wadsworth, 1988). His major area of research is religious epistemology.

Index

absolute reality. *See* worldviews
absolute truth. *See* truth, types of
ambiguity. *See* religious experience
American Academy of Religion: Hart report on religious studies, ix–x; proceedings, ix, 2
Arberry, A. J., 177

Barth, Karl, 183
being/nonbeing, 207, 209–15, 220, 222
Berger, Peter: comparative analysis of views, 94–107; on cross-cultural truth criteria, 90–91; *The Heretical Imperative,* 90, 251n. 13
Blofeld, John, 256n. 2
Bochenski, J. M., 78, 252n. 1
Buber, Martin, 134, 186
Bugault, Guy, 257nn. 10, 12, 259n. 29
Bultmann, Rudolf, 69

Campbell, Joseph, 175
Castelli, Enrico, 40
Chicago school of comparative religions, 22
Christian, William: on cross-cultural philosophy of religion, 78; *Meaning and Truth in Religion,* 2, 21, 249n. 5, 252n. 1; *Oppositions of Religious Doctrines,* 252n. 1
Christianity and the Encounter of the World Religions (Tillich), 252n. 22
comparative philosophy Asian-Western. *See* cross-cultural philosophy of religion
comparative religions. *See* cross-cultural philosophy of religion

Cook, Cardinal, 171
criteria of truth. *See* truth, criteria of
cross-cultural philosophy of religion: and comparative philosophy, Asian-Western, 3–5; and future theology, 29; using Gadamer's thought, 162–68; history of, 1–3; and history of religions, 2–5, 18, 20–21; impetus for, ix–x; inclusion of worldviews, 19, 21, 23, 29–31, 205–207; inherent limits of, 41–42; and mysticism, 190–91, 204; and phenomenology of religions, 2–6, 207; and Western philosophy of religion, 3–5; scope of, 3–5, 13–14, 87, 132, 233, 242–45; types of, 35–39. *See also* Christian, William; Smart, Ninian

Dalai Lama, 171–72
Das Gebet (Heiler), 177
Davis, Charles, 47
dialectics. *See* Gadamer, Hans-Georg; inter-religious dialogue
doctrinal schemes. *See* logic; worldviews
doctrines. *See* religious doctrines
duality (dualism)/nonduality (nondualism): and experience, 184–85; as logic systems, 227, 233–43; as types of truth, 75, 230–33, 244–45; as worldviews, 174, 178, 186–87. *See also* subject-object consciousness
Dynamics of Faith (Tillich), 252n. 21
Dyson, Freeman, 184

Einstein, Albert, 261n. 6

Eliade, Mircea, 175
emptiness (*sunyata*), 177, 181, 196, 199–201, 217–23. *See also* nothingness
Emptiness: A Study in Religious Meaning (Streng), 2
epistemology. *See* truth, criteria of
equality, religious, 52–53, 96
ethics. *See* truth, criteria of
exoteric/esoteric, 175
experience. *See* religious experience

faith, 69–70, 173, 178–89, 245
Ferre, Frederick, 81, 250n. 18
fideism, 67
Freud, Sigmund, 56–57

Gadamer, Hans-Georg: on conflicting truth claims, 162–68; on dialectics, 155–56, 161, 253nn. 2–4, 254nn. 5–10; and dialogue, 156, 158, 161–62, 167; on experience, 154–55; "horizon" concept, 152–54; on language, 156–62; *Truth and Method,* 151
Gangadean, Ashok, 260n. 3
Gimello, Robert, 258n. 25
God, personal (theism), 17, 50–52, 247n. 2
Goleman, Daniel, 255n. 1

Hakuin, 200–201
Hebrew prophets, 48
Heiler, Friedrich, 177
The Heretical Imperative (Berger), 90, 251n. 13
hermeneutics, types of, 34–35, 39–43, 151–68, 205–208, 225–45. *See also* religious pluralism; Gadamer, Hans-Georg
Herméneutique de la philosophie de la religion (Castelli), 40
Hick, John: comparative analysis of views, 94–107; on cross-cultural truth criteria, 92–93; on God in non-theistic religions, 51; *An Interpretation of Religion*, 2; *Philosophy of Religion,* 2; "On Grading Religions", 92; *Problems of Religious Pluralism,* 2; on religious pluralism, 47; *Truth and Dialogue in World Religions: Conflicting Truth-Claims,* 2
history of religions. *See* cross-cultural philosophy of religion
holy/sacred. *See* Otto, Rudolf; religious experience
Hui-Neng, 200
Huizinga, Johan, 187
humanization. *See* Kaufman, Gordon; truth, criteria of
Huxley, Aldous, 255n. 1

I Ching, 212–17
ideologies. *See* worldviews
inclusivism, 172–74
incommensurability. *See* worldviews
identity: and difference, 47, 227, 233–34, 237–40; principle of, 115, 191, 233–39
ineffability. *See* religious experience
An Interpretation of Religion (Hick), 2
inter-religious dialogue: and dialectics, 40–41; 134–48, 155–57; "dialogical dialogue", 41; future presuppositions of, 59–63; and language, 135–36, 138–40, 156–62, 168, 225–45; logic of, 133–49; possible positions, 67–69, 133–34, 172–76
The Intrareligious Dialogue (Panikkar), 2
Irenaeus of Lyons, 111–13

Jaspers, Karl, 47, 61
Jung, C. G., 171

Kant, Immanuel, 56
Kaufman, Gordon: comparative analysis of views, 94–107; on cross-cultural truth criteria, 91–92, 251n. 15; humanization criterion, 92, 94–95, 97–101, 103, 105–107; *The Theological Imagination,* 91, 251n. 20
Klee, Paul, 185
Knitter, Paul, 57
Kung, Hans, 57–58

language. *See* inter-religious dialogue; religious doctrine; religious experi-

ence; religious pluralism; symbolism, religious
Leeuw, Gerardus van der, 187
logic: categorial/transcategorial, 227–28, 231–45; of doctrinal schemes, 73–85, 111–32; of dialogue, 133–49; Indian, 231–32, 239–43 (*see also* Ramanuja; Shankara); Western, 228–31, 233–39 (*see also* philosophy of religion). *See also* duality/nonduality; religious doctrine
The Logic of Religion (Bochenski) 252n. 1
Logos / logos 33–34, 41, 47, 58, 211, 226–28, 242–43, 245

Mahāparinibbāṇasutta 112
Masao Abe, 260n. 12
The Meaning and End of Religion (Smith), 2
Meaning and Truth in Religion (Christian), 252n. 1
meditation, 181, 183, 192, 194, 196, 199–201. *See also* truth, types of
metaphysical systems. *See* worldviews
Mitchell, Basil, 79, 82
Muhammad, 46, 48
mysticism. *See* cross-cultural philosophy of religion; religious experience
myth/*mythos,* 20–22, 30, 33–34, 185, 208

Nagarjuna, 48, 56, 195–96
Naranjo, Claudio, 256n. 2
Nishitani Keiji, 217–22
nothingness, 215, 219. *See also* emptiness

ontology. *See* worldviews
Oppositions of Religious Doctrines (Christian), 2, 21, 249n. 5, 252n. 1
Ott, Heinrich, 249n. 25
Otto, Rudolf, 180–84, 187–88

Panikkar, Raimundo: *The Intrareligious Dialogue,* 2; the "Unknown Christ", 49
paradox. *See* religious experience; universal truth

Pelikan, Jaroslav, 249n. 4
Pepper, Stephen, 80
phenomenology of religions. *See* cross-cultural philosophy of religions
philosophy of religion (Western): inherent dualism of, 230–31, 233–39; limits of, 17–19, 36–39, 230. *See also* cross-cultural philosophy of religion
Philosophy of Religion (Hick), 2
pluralism. *See* religious pluralism
Problems of Religious Pluralism (Hick), 2

Rahner, Karl, 48–49, 54–55, 94–95
Ramanuja, 199, 201
reason. *See* truth, criteria of; truth, types of
Reasons and Faiths (Smart), 1, 68, 252n. 1
reductionism. *See* worldviews
relativism: avoidance of, 29, 102, 165; naiveté of, 78–79, 88; and worldviews/metaphysical systems, 225–26, 229, 240–41; of universalist theories, 175–76. *See also* truth, types of
religious doctrines: comparative logic of, 114–32, 250n. 16, 253n. 5; hermeneutics of, 112; internal/external evaluation, 127, 137–40, 144–45; oppositions of, 30, 73–75, 114–16, 172–73; about other religions, 117–32; structure of, 111–14, 118, 127, 131
religious experience: ambiguity of, 171–72, 179–88; differing traditions, 26, 198–203, 225; of holy/sacred, 177, 179–88; ineffability of, 184, 189–204; instrumentality of, 48–49; mystical language, 189–204, 206, 222, 255n. 1, 256n. 6; as non-rational, 183–84; as paradoxical, 179–82; prophetic/mystical polarity, 174, 177–88; universality of, 41, 53, 69–70, 189–91. *See also* duality/nonduality
religious pluralism: acceptance of, 42–43, 175; as catalyst for religious development, 45–46; common approaches to, 46–50; conversion problem, 50; and dialectics, 230; and freedom, 47; and future theology,

54–59; hermeneutics of, 34–35, 39–43, 151–68, 206, 208, 225–45; language, 33, 128, 140–49; and philosophy of religion, 2; present day difficulties, 50–53, 100; and theology, 45, 94–95; and truth, ix–x, 2, 18, 21, 80–84, 88–89, 134–36, 140, 151, 178; understanding within, 2, 35, 41, 90, 107, 143, 151, 153, 155–56
ritual, 23, 28, 208, 242
Ryobu Shinto, 49

salvation (transformation). *See* truth, criteria of; worldviews
san chiao, 49
Schleiermacher, Fredrich, 53, 94–95, 181, 248n. 6
Schuon, Frithjof, 175, 255n. 1
selfhood, 206, 209–12, 219–23
Shankara, 48, 193–96, 199, 201
silence, 59, 185, 231
Smart, Ninian: on cross-cultural philosophy of religion, 4, 78, 83, 88; on prophetic/mystical polarity, 177; *Reasons and Faiths,* 1, 68, 252n. 1; *Worldviews: Cross-Cultural Explorations of Human Beliefs,* 2; *The Yogi and the Devotee,* 69
Smith, Huston, 255n. 1
Smith, Wilfred Cantwell: comparative analysis of views, 94–107; on cross-cultural truth criteria, 93–94; on humanists, 60; insider-outsider criterion, 93–94, 98–100, 102–103, 105, 107, 251n. 19; *The Meaning and End of Religion,* 2; on religious pluralism, 47; on the structure of faith, 173; on the study of religion, 45, 49; on theistic/non-theistic divergence, 51–52; *Towards a World Theology,* 2, 62–63, 93; on universal truth, 69, 175
speech acts. *See* truth, types of
Stace, W. T., 75, 255n. 1
Stenger, Mary Ann, 252n. 21
Streng, Frederick: *Emptiness: A Study in Religious Meaning,* 2; on prophetic/mystical polarity, 177; *Understanding Religious Life,* 260n. 5
subject-object consciousness, 184–85, 193, 199, 201, 211–12, 219, 221, 230–31, 233–34, 244. *See also* duality/nonduality
Suzuki, D. T., 174
symbolism, religious: and anthropology 22; criteria for 30–31, 105–106; in definition of religion, 34; of God, 51, 89, 103, 212; and history of religions, 23; and language, 22–23, 28; universality of, 18, 208, 241. *See also* Tillich, Paul
Systematic Theology (Tillich), 209–12

theology, comparative. *See* worldviews
theism. *See* God, personal
The Theological Imagination (Kaufman), 90, 251n. 20
Tillich, Paul: on being/nonbeing, 207, 209–12, 220; *Christianity and the Encounter of the World Religions,* 252n. 22; *Dynamics of Faith,* 252n. 21; on philosophical theories, 81; on prophetic/mystical polarity, 177, 181; on scripture, 248n. 6; on symbol, 105–106, 209–12; *Systematic Theology,* 209–12; on transcendence, 61; on theological truth, 105–106, 254n. 11; on "ultimate concern", 23, 173
Toulmin, Stephen, 83
Towards a World Theology (Smith), 2, 62–63, 93
transcendence. *See* worldviews
transformation, structures of. *See* truth, criteria of; worldviews
translation. *See* worldviews
Troeltsch, Ernst, 49, 53, 94–95
Truth and Dialogue in World Religions: Conflicting Truth-Claims (Hick), 2
Truth and Method (Gadamer), 151
truth, criteria of: ethical/moral, 26, 29–30, 70, 90, 92, 103–105; experience as, 25–26, 105–107; history as, 25, 52, 70; humanization, 92, 94–95, 97–101, 103, 105–107; imposition of, 43, 49–50, 58; insider/outsider, 93–94, 98–100, 102–103, 105, 107; and language, 158–62, 225–45; possible positions, 67–71, 77–79, 90–104; problem areas, 89, 96–104; psychological, 27–28, 56–58, 70, 188; rationality/reason as, 38, 43, 73–85, 97–98, 103–105,

112, 136, 159, 195; across religions, 3–5, 88–107, 163–68; and religious authority, 27, 70, 77, 96, 136, 143; and religious doctrines, 73–85, 89, 103–104, 118, 121–23, 133, 136–40; religious experience as, 69–70, 89–91, 96–98, 151, 154–55, 168, 188, 190, 193–94, 206; and transformation, 99, 195–96, 205–23, 225–30, 236, 239, 243–45; tradition as, 136; among worldviews, 24–29, 205–23, 228–33

truth, types of: absolute vs. relative, 79, 91–92, 98–102, 106, 165–66, 173, 188, 220; and authenticity/genuineness, 75–77, 92, 184, 190–202; common, 112, 176; existential truth, 23, 25–26, 93, 105–107; "meditative" (non-dual) truth, 227, 231–33, 239–44; propositional truth, 55, 73–85, 104–106, 134–36, 143, 227–28, 232–39, 261n. 7; speech acts, 135–36, 140, 143. *See also* duality/nonduality; universal truth

truth-claims: absolute, 48–49, 56–61, 89, 94–107, 112, 135, 161–62, 166, 172–73, 175–76, 186, 188, 193, 204–23, 225–33, 243–44; conflicting, 4–5, 13, 74–75, 79–84, 89, 96–98, 103–104, 106, 141–42, 147–49, 162, 164–65, 167, 172, 178–79, 188; and cross-cultural philosophy of religion, ix–x; internal/external evaluations of, 24–25, 127, 137–40, 144–45; oppositions of, 29–30, 111–16. *See also* religious pluralism

ultimate (absolute). *See* truth, types of; truth-claims
Underhill, Evelyn, 255n. 1

Understanding Religious Life (Streng), 260n. 5
understanding. *See* religious pluralism
universal truth: balanced with particularity, 74–75, 78, 94–95, 98–102, 153–54, 162–63, 179, 226–33, 240; as coercion, 47; imposition of, 49–50, 172–76; insider-outsider criterion, 93–94, 98–100, 102–103, 105, 107; instrumentality of all religions, 47–49; and language, 158–62, 260n. 2; "the One and the many", 47–48, 166; through paradox, 176–88; pretensions of, 35–36; theories of 172–76. *See also* symbolism, religious

Watt, John, 77
Western philosophy of religion. *See* logic; philosophy of religion (Western)
Wilhelm, Helmut 212–17
Winch, Peter, 77
worldviews: and anthropology, 27–28; doctrinal schemes as, 79–80, 84; incommensurability of, 54, 226, 229; and language, 262n. 5; properties of, 19, 80–84, 159–60, 228–29, 260n. 1, 249n. 7; and reductionism, 39, 41–42, 56–58, 227–28; and secular ideologies, 18–19, 22, 28; as structures of transformation, 205–23, 228–33; and transcendence, 13, 26, 51–52, 58, 60, 62, 183–84, 231; translation of, 36, 62, 140, 146, 157–58, 227. *See also* duality/nonduality
Worldviews: Cross-Cultural Explorations of Human Beliefs (Smart), 2

Yandell, Keith, 81
yin and *yang,* 212–17
The Yogi and the Devotee (Smart), 69